Men After #MeToo

Kenneth Reinicke

Men After #MeToo

Being an Ally in the Fight Against Sexual Harassment

Kenneth Reinicke
Department of Social Sciences
and Business
Roskilde University
Roskilde, Denmark

ISBN 978-3-030-96910-3   ISBN 978-3-030-96911-0 (eBook)
https://doi.org/10.1007/978-3-030-96911-0

© The Editor(s) (if applicable) and The Author(s), under exclusive license to Springer Nature Switzerland AG 2022
This work is subject to copyright. All rights are solely and exclusively licensed by the Publisher, whether the whole or part of the material is concerned, specifically the rights of translation, reprinting, reuse of illustrations, recitation, broadcasting, reproduction on microfilms or in any other physical way, and transmission or information storage and retrieval, electronic adaptation, computer software, or by similar or dissimilar methodology now known or hereafter developed.
The use of general descriptive names, registered names, trademarks, service marks, etc. in this publication does not imply, even in the absence of a specific statement, that such names are exempt from the relevant protective laws and regulations and therefore free for general use.
The publisher, the authors and the editors are safe to assume that the advice and information in this book are believed to be true and accurate at the date of publication. Neither the publisher nor the authors or the editors give a warranty, expressed or implied, with respect to the material contained herein or for any errors or omissions that may have been made. The publisher remains neutral with regard to jurisdictional claims in published maps and institutional affiliations.

This Palgrave Macmillan imprint is published by the registered company Springer Nature Switzerland AG
The registered company address is: Gewerbestrasse 11, 6330 Cham, Switzerland

Contents

1 **Introduction** 1
   1.1   The Point of Departure 4
   1.2   Why Focus on Men? 7
   1.3   Bad Men or Mad Men? 8
   1.4   Men as Allies 10
   1.5   The Interview Material 14
   1.6   Data Analysis 16
   1.7   Overview of the Book 16
   References 20

2 **The Concept of Sexual Harassment** 25
   2.1   Basic Definitions 29
   2.2   Who Is Violated by Sexual Harassment? 30
   2.3   The Consequences of Sexual Harassment 31
   2.4   Societal Explanations of Sexual Harassment 32
   2.5   Reading About Women's Experiences 37
   2.6   The Crime Paradox 38
   2.7   Women's Reactions 40
   2.8   Sexual Harassment Versus Being Flattered 46

	2.9	Summary	47
		References	49
3	**The Danish #MeToo Context**		55
	3.1	The Nordic Countries	55
	3.2	Politics of Masculinities in Denmark	57
	3.3	The First #MeToo Wave: 2017–2018	60
	3.4	The Second #MeToo Wave: 2020	66
	3.5	The Debate About the Sexual Assault Law	68
	3.6	Summary	72
		References	73
4	**Why Have Men Not Been Held Responsible?**		77
	4.1	Hegemonic Masculinity	79
	4.2	Men and Gender Equality	81
	4.3	Men and Feminism	84
	4.4	Men's Negative Health Outcomes	86
	4.5	The Invisibility of Men's Destructive Behaviour	88
	4.6	The Gender-Neutral Approach	90
	4.7	Stories from Popular Culture That Defend Sexual Harassment	93
	4.8	The Man Box	95
	4.9	Non-Hegemonic Masculinities	97
	4.10	Ethnicity and Violence	99
	4.11	Summary	100
		References	101
5	**Who Perpetrates Sexual Harassment and Why**		107
	5.1	Socio-demography	109
	5.2	The Social-Psychological Model	109
	5.3	Typological Descriptions	111
	5.4	Social Bonding	113
	5.5	Peer Pressure and Lad Culture	117
	5.6	Youth and Rape Culture	119
	5.7	The Penetration Norm	125
	5.8	Do Men Know When They Violate Someone's Boundaries?	128

5.9	When Sexual Harassment Is 'Allowed'	130
5.10	When Men Are Exposed to Inappropriate Sexual Behaviour	133
5.11	Summary	135
References		138

6 Men's Responses to #MeToo — 145
6.1	Positive Reactions	149
6.2	Defensive Reactions	152
6.3	Men's Overall Responses in Denmark	157
6.4	The Attitude of the Interviewed Men Towards #MeToo	159
6.5	The Debate Is Important, but…	162
6.6	Has #MeToo Changed Their Views on Sexual Harassment?	165
6.7	Summary	166
References		167

7 Flirting After #MeToo — 171
7.1	Does No Always Mean No?	174
7.2	The Missing Language	176
7.3	The Consent Law	179
7.4	Does Sexual Harassment Have a Statute of Limitations?	182
7.5	Naming the Perpetrator	183
7.6	Summary	185
References		186

8 Will Men Take a Stand? — 189
8.1	The Bystander Approach	191
8.2	Why Do Men Not Challenge Other Men's Sexist Attitudes?	193
8.3	Talking to Male Friends About #MeToo	194
8.4	The Challenge of Having to Intervene When Other Men Sexually Harass Someone	196
8.5	Speaking Publicly About #MeToo and Feminism	201
8.6	How to Walk into 'New Man's Land'?	203

	8.7	Educational Initiatives	204
	8.8	Engaging Boys	205
	8.9	It Is Not Just 'the Bad Boys' Who Sexually Harass	207
	8.10	An Eye Opener	209
	8.11	Summary	210
		References	213
9	**Conclusion**		217
		References	229

References 233

Index 257

1

Introduction

One summer day five years ago, my wife and I were waiting at a pedestrian crossing in Copenhagen. On one side stood an elderly woman in her mid-70s and on the other a younger woman in her mid-20s with a stroller. While we were waiting for the green light, a van drove up and kept close to us. The driver of the car, who was in his mid/late thirties, looked at us and then said to the young woman with the stroller, 'Cool that you look so good when you have just given birth.' The young woman did not react and could not even be bothered to look at the driver in the car. The elderly woman, on the other hand, who may have been hard of hearing, leant forward and said, 'I beg your pardon?', at which the man in the car loudly and irritably replied, 'It's not you I'm talking to, old lady.'

This rather insignificant episode is not particularly crude compared to the many other examples of sexual harassment I shall discuss in this book. It is nonetheless interesting because it demonstrates a typical reason why men engage in sexual harassment and how men relate to the reactions of victims when they do not reciprocate their comments.[1] First, it is interesting to note the man's sense of *entitlement* to even imagine that it would be all right to comment on the young woman's body and appearance, as there had been no prior 'invitation' or contact between them. Most likely, he may think that he 'just' asserts his right to comment on her body, defining her as a sexual object (Tuerkheimer, 1997). Second, it is symptomatic of sexual harassment that if women do not respond to unwelcome harassment and comments, men tend to become offended, angry or—as we shall see later—make threats of violence and rape. In addition, it has been interesting to note people's reactions when I have told them about the episode. The reactions have varied from comments like 'completely inappropriate and rude' to 'it was nice of him to give her a compliment.'

The example shows that there are ongoing discursive struggles over the meaning of sexual harassment. The perception of what constitutes sexual harassment is context dependent, and in many respects, there is no common understanding of this phenomenon, just as there are no simple diagnoses. What is sexual harassment to one person may be seen as funny by another and inconsequential by a third (Fairchild, 2010: 194). Therefore, the story of sexual harassment is complicated. Sexual harassment is both reason for and the consequence of women's inequality. It is not always easy to specify where commonly accepted behaviour has its limits and where harassment begins. Power and definitions are linked to each other in intricate ways.

It is crucial to ask when sexual harassment can be seen as a *culturally acceptable* practice related to 'ordinary' masculinity, and when it is culturally defined as harassment and therefore constitutes *deviant* behaviour. The boundary between the two is fluid and varies from case to case and between cultures. If we situate sexual harassment within the broader context of interpersonal violence, it is important to note that whereas domestic violence can represent both a form of power and a source of shame (Hearn, 1998), sexual harassment can be a form of

---

[1] When talking about gender in this book, the focus is mainly on cisgender, which means a person whose gender identity aligns with the sex assigned at birth. When talking about men and women, the focus is typically on heterosexual men and heterosexual women.

power and a source of humour. In this respect, it is caught up in prejudices, myths and jokes. Sexist and disparaging humour initiated by men towards women are widespread and may serve to derogate and belittle women as a group (Ferguson & Ford, 2008; Thomae & Pina, 2015). The difficulties in categorizing and explaining sexual harassment have made it *acceptable* for men to perpetrate it and a *taboo* for women to challenge it (MacKinnon, 1979). According to Bates (2014: 29),

> Sexism seems to occupy a ludicrously acceptable position when it comes to public discourse, with general willingness to laugh and ignore it rather than define it as the prejudice it is. And this makes it particularly difficult to fight, allowing objectors to be ridiculed as 'overreacting' while perpetrators can take up cowardly defences behind the poor shield of 'humour' or 'irony'.

As a result, sexual harassment seldom has any consequences for the perpetrator, due to institutional complicity or unwillingness to investigate it (Salter, 2019). Despite the fact that sexual harassment arises out of disrespect for women and can cause major harms for the victim, in most cases it is not characterized as a criminal act. Therefore, sexual harassment tends not to be considered a social problem in the same way as violence and rape. Women have been stigmatized, silenced and disbelieved, with the implication, typically, that talking and complaining about sexism are signs of overreaction. Three powerful silencing factors in particular have made sexual harassment difficult to combat: the invisibility of the problem, that it is by default socially acceptable and the tendency to project guilt and blame onto the victim (Bates, 2014).

Most societies tolerate a certain degree of bad behaviour from men without defining it as deviant. Moreover, much of this behaviour would be framed as completely 'normal', if not expected of men. What may be an accepted sociocultural norm in one culture may in another one be perceived as a violation of the individual (Luthar & Luthar, 2008). A Spanish study showed that many victims of sexual harassment did not perceive unwanted sexual advances as attacks against their sexual freedom, nor as episodes of gender discrimination, but rather as something unpleasant and unavoidable (McDonald, 2012; Valiente, 1998).

Sexually harassing behaviour does not include culturally deviant behaviour only and is not simply a matter of explicit sexist attitudes and inappropriate sexual desires. Some forms of sexual harassment, such as when men in groups evaluate and comment on women's bodies, are behaviours that help produce and reproduce shared masculine identities and social relations. Therefore, we need theoretical explanations that take into account the complexity and diversity of sexually harassing behaviours and their potentially multifaceted social meanings. Sexual harassment is as much about relations between men as it is about relations between men and women (Benard & Schlaffer, 1984; Quinn, 2002).

1.1 The Point of Departure

The point of departure for *Men after #MeToo* is the emergence of the #MeToo movement in 2017, which was a momentous event that triggered major changes as the exposure of sexual harassment gained momentum on an unprecedented scale (Mendes et al., 2018). Heiner (2012) states that societal issues become a social problem when they are recognized as bad or undesirable by a significant number of people or a number of significant people who mobilize to eliminate it. *Men after #MeToo* is mostly concerned with public harassment. Nevertheless, when needed the book also draws on examples from workplace harassment to illustrate the omnipresent nature of the phenomenon.

Millions of people around the world shared their stories. Broadly speaking there are two types of reactions to this movement. The first sees #MeToo as 'rewriting history' and as a breakthrough for the feminist movement, with several commentators declaring that it is the most meaningful gender equality initiative since women got the vote. The second depicts #MeToo as an unjustified pillorying, smear campaign and witch-hunt against men, which risks demonizing all men and jeopardizing their legal rights.

The #MeToo movement's messages have been received differently in different parts of the world. The reactions to and consequences of the #MeToo revelations have been far stronger and more severe in some countries than in others. Kunst et al. (2018) describe how different cultural contexts have differing levels of gender equality, which shape culturally contingent reactions to #MeToo. See, for example, studies on the different impact of #MeToo in the UK (De Benedictis et al., 2019), in India (Guha, 2021; Naik, 2020), in Germany (Eilermann, 2018), and in Spain and France (Arriaza Ibarra & Berumen, 2019). In countries like Sweden and the USA, the #MeToo movement has had major repercussions with high-profile resignations and the introduction of tough legislative measures (Askanius & Hartley, 2019). In other countries, for example, Denmark—the focal point of the present study—we have seen a more defensive reaction to #MeToo, with leading forces in society quick to redirect the discussion to the issue of men's legal rights, rather than focusing on the reasons why some people feel they have the right to harass others.

Typically, sexual harassment has been 'unspeakable'. In some contexts, because gender equality is generally taken for granted. In other contexts, 'through the invalidation and annihilation of any language for talking about structural inequalities' (Gill, 2011: 63). This has meant that it is not easy to challenge sexism, because attention has been centred on individual free choice and responsibility rather than on the structural and cultural reasons for women's exposure to sexual harassment.

Sexual harassment was described by Davis (1994) as 'the harm that has no name', and there are many subtle and effective 'silencing manoeuvres' which prevent it from being regarded as a serious societal problem ('not a big deal'), with serious consequences for its victims. There is a great lack of recognition around the fact that everyday sexism is a problem and a lack of understanding of these everyday experiences that women in particular have. Although the core focus of the book is not intersectionality it seems crucial to acknowledge that Davis (1994) was focusing specifically on the experiences of African-American women. While there are undoubtedly similarities across women's experiences, there are also important differences. However, when women are conceived as an undifferentiated whole, the importance of how intersectionality might shape women's experiences of harassment disappears.

If we look at the role of social media in creating the #MeToo movement, it seems clear that as a driving force, the international #MeToo movement represents a new form of feminism that publicly exposes everyday forms of sexism and urges men to scrutinize how they view and approach women. The movement has, to a large extent, given women the courage to speak up about sexual harassment and has unleashed both heated feelings and debates. Despite the fact that online activist movements like *Hollaback* (2005), *Stop Street Harassment* (2008) and *The Everyday Sexism Project* (2012) were in operation several years before #MeToo they did not gain the same traction.

Thus, for years, feminist scholars and activists had tried to theorize about and define sexual harassment as a collective societal problem, and for decades, victims and survivors had spoken out about their experiences of harassment and abuse (Gavey, 2005; Serisier, 2020). As such, we shall not overstate the novelty of #MeToo. What is unique about #MeToo is the number of testimonies that have come forth and the way in which these testimonies have been given mainstream media exposure, as well as how sexual harassment has been more exposed as a general collective and mainstream social problem.

However, looking more deeply at the effectiveness of social media activism, one can ask whether it increases motivation for activism or only encourages people to post and like other people's thoughts. Social media platforms offer unique opportunities for victims to share personal stories and receive emotional and social support to which they might not have access in person (Schneider & Carpenter, 2019). Nevertheless, it seems clear that there are both optimistic and pessimistic approaches to the role that social media can play in social movements (Kidd & Mcintosh, 2016). Shirky (2008) emphasizes the power of new technology to foster speedy assembly, whereas Gladwell (2010) adopts a more sceptical position, saying that social media platforms are built around weak ties, which will not make people go out on the streets.

1.2 Why Focus on Men?

Men after #MeToo discusses how the voices of victims of sexual violence and harassment are now changing our societies and influencing men. Based on an explicit focus on men and sexual harassment, the book sets out to create a deeper understanding of why sexual harassment occurs and how we, as a society, can confront the phenomenon. The book intends to fill a gap in understanding men's conduct of sexual harassment through the voices of twenty-five men aged 21–30 from Denmark.

Men after #MeToo differs from other writings on sexual harassment by focusing on manhood and on men's responsibilities and opportunities for change. The book offers reflections on male gender roles in the wake of the #MeToo debates. It discusses why men engage in sexual harassment, explains why sexual harassment is so difficult to handle and gives ideas for confronting it. The book aims to fill a gap in the literature, as previous books have mostly looked at women's accounts of being subjected to sexual harassment and at its repercussions (Bates, 2014; Gardner, 1995; Larkin, 1997; MacKinnon, 1979; Smith, 1988; Stanko, 1995).

Most research on sexual harassment has focused on how to define it, on what the incidence rates are and on the experiences of self-reported victims (O'Donohue et al., 1998; Pina et al., 2009). It is understandable that these studies have explored the phenomenon from the perspective of those who have been harassed. If, however, we want to tackle the cultural acceptance of this phenomenon and the victim-blaming of women, then we need to shift perspective, that is, to conceptualize sexual harassment differently. To combat sexual harassment, it is all important to understand its causes. Society must encourage critical reflection around rigid norms surrounding what manhood means and we must ask ourselves what prevents and what facilitates sexual harassment.

A typical feature of power and privilege is the ability of dominant groups to behave in ways that do not draw attention and therefore go unchallenged (Katz, 2006). Moreover, the critical focus on men must be stated openly, because it is difficult to address a problem effectively if we are not willing to talk about it directly. There has been an overwhelming silence when it comes to male gender roles and masculinity, which are seldom problematized. It is rare to find any in-depth discussion about what types of culture produce violent and harassing men. Yet, in confronting men, we also need to be careful. Despite the fact that it is men who commit the overwhelming proportion of sexual harassment, it is not all men who do so. Hence, we need to establish a balance between generalizing and being specific, and to avoid trivializing the analysis.

1.3 Bad Men or Mad Men?

What kind of analysis should we advance? Should one tackle the issue structurally, or is the problem more simply that the behaviour of individual men needs correction? Many people mistakenly see sexual harassment as perpetrated by only a tiny minority of deviant men. The idea of a few men 'behaving badly' (Loney-Howes, 2019: 23) has been widespread. I will argue that we need a multifaceted approach to study the issue of sexual harassment, because no single explanation can clarify how and why it occurs, and why it occurs in so many different contexts. It is often the case that for young men, sexual harassment is a way to earn respect within their peer group (Phipps, 2017). We must understand the pressure among boys to behave in sexually aggressive ways (Flood & Pease, 2006). Seen in this light, it is important to point out that men who engage in sexual harassment are not predominantly men with mental or personality disorders. Instead, there is often a *link between traditional attitudes of masculinity and the practice of sexual harassment*, making it difficult to separate sexual harassment from the construction of masculinities. This is because sexual harassment is often done by men in groups (Gardner, 1995), which means that, in many ways, other men are the intended audience (Grazian, 2007; Pascoe, 2005). Furthermore, men are not always aware that their harassing behaviour is a misuse of power because it might be seen as an innocent play and homosocial activity, which creates social bonding and intimacy among men (Quinn, 2002; Thomae & Pina, 2015). Therefore, we have to associate sexual harassment with the way men are socialized. This means looking at attitudes that feed into sexual harassment.

During a lecture I gave in early 2018 on men and masculinity, a middle-aged man raised his hand and said—with reference to Harvey Weinstein—that we must not forget that sexual harassment 'is primarily about psychopaths' abuse of power'. This is a tempting but simplistic and erroneous notion of sexual harassment. There is nothing profoundly distinctive about men who engage in sexual harassment. We have to bring a broader community perspective to sexual harassment prevention. It is crucial to emphasize that even men who are perceived as 'good' and 'normal' also conduct sexual harassment.

However, it is not easy to find acceptance for the idea that men's sexual harassment is a product of social forces, since we often prefer to focus on individual destinies. It is therefore important to look at the significance of culturally conditioned notions of masculinity if we are to get at the various motives for men sexually harassing women. Underlying sexual harassment there are often stories of 'ordinary' men's power and privileges over women.

Therefore, *Men after #MeToo* looks deeper into the socialization processes of men, raising the question of why so many men feel entitled to harass women sexually. What makes them choose such a path? What conditions make such people and their actions possible? In particular, the book looks deeper into the reasons why particular types of men commit particular types of sexual harassment, in what contexts and for what reasons they do it.

It is both fruitful to try to figure out how the men committing sexual harassment differ from those who do not, and interesting to focus on the commonalities between them. The point is that men committing sexual harassment are not monstrously different persons. This is why I will look at the culture most men grow up with and how it produces sexually harassing men. We need to examine the whole range of behaviours, attitudes and beliefs which together form the basis for men's harassing behaviour.

The book argues that we must understand the construction of masculine identities and the role that sexually harassing behaviours play in bringing them about. Scholars have argued that power and gender are central issues in understanding sexual harassment (Fitzgerald et al., 1995). We therefore need gendered analysis to identify the social drivers of sexual harassment. The theoretical approach used in the book is located within critical studies on men and masculinities (Connell, 1995; Flood, 2011; Hearn, 1998; Messner, 1997; Pease et al., 2001; Salter, 2016), which have emphasized the importance of patriarchy, hegemonic masculinity, cultural domination and differences between men. I see men and masculinities as socially constructed, variable and changing over time and space, and as intersecting with other social divisions such as age, race, ethnicity, class and sexual orientation.

Men are not born as sexual harassers. Men do not make it up on their own. They are brought up to assert a tough and dominant masculinity. Sexual harassment takes place in a culture which encourages and permits men to engage in this behaviour. This means that we will have to examine the ways in which we pass down social norms concerning masculinity from one generation to the next. We must also look at bonding experiences between men, which can explain a lot about sexual assault and sexual harassment, especially among adolescents. More generally, we must challenge the cultural belief systems that support sexual harassment and the various institutions that shape what we expect from boys. If we hope to see a radical reduction of sexism, we need to reach the level where men who behave in a sexist way lose status and get into trouble when they engage in sexual harassment—not only with the authorities but also with their friends and peers.

1.4 Men as Allies

Sexual harassment is a men's issue, because women do not harass themselves. Nevertheless, we often assume that the burden of preventing rape, domestic violence and sexual harassment fundamentally falls on the shoulders of women and girls. Men often do not know how they can play a positive part in stopping sexual violence. It is a huge problem that we tend to think that gender issues are synonymous with women's issues. Men's central role is either overlooked or rendered invisible (Katz, 2006). Part of the problem concerning sexual harassment is that we call it a women's issue. With regard to sexual harassment, society often blames someone or something else rather than men, which renders men invisible in discourses about sexual harassment, even though it is men who are primarily concerned. PettyJohn et al. (2019) state that it creates a paradoxical issue when society 'relies solely on women to convince men to change this dynamic in which those who suffer the most from the oppression of sexual harassment (women) are expected to somehow have influence over those who are privileged in this dynamic (men)' (PettyJohn et al., 2019: 2).

It is not sufficient to work with women to improve the conditions of life for women. Ted Bunch, the co-founder of A Call to Men, has said in relation to violence, 'only men can end men's violence against women'. The same goes for sexual harassment, and the transformation must start with men becoming more aware and realizing that they are an important part of the solution. The solution is not primarily to empower our young daughters but to teach our sons differently. We shall not ask all these questions about women, e.g., why did she do this, why did she do that? Instead, we shall turn the focus onto the man.

Research shows that men have a high level of influence on other men's behaviour, and that it may improve outcomes if men take a larger role in prevention (Fabiano et al., 2003). It is, of course, worth acknowledging that while men can be more effective in talking to other men, this can also risk reinforcing gendered norms that suggest that women are less authoritative and not worth listening to compared to men. As such, it is important to strike a balance; ultimately, however, my assumption is that we have to listen to what men have to say about their gender, and that any effective attempt to improve the situation of women must involve men—if it does not, it is doomed to fail.

Some people may think it odd to invite men to come forward and speak, if they are the problem. I will argue that instead of seeing men as perpetrators and women as victims, men can and must contribute to a cultural shift that will bring about change. It is important to see men not only as perpetrators or potential perpetrators but also as empowered bystanders (Foubert & Newberry, 2006; Katz, 2006; McMahon & Dick, 2011). Although some men embody root causes of sexual harassment, men can also be part of the solution and be allies in the process of change (Flood, 2011). Furthermore, there are pragmatic reasons to involve men in change and gender equality work, both at a general societal level and at a more individual level within the context of organizations and companies. Any reform requires resources, and it is often men who control the resources that can change the life situations of both men and women (Connell, 2003; Kaufman & Kimmel, 2011).

If we want to bring about change, we need to change our institutions. I shall argue that it is only possible to fight the pervasive and deeply rooted phenomenon of sexual harassment if a combination of law enforcement measures, social change efforts and targeted prevention initiatives are introduced. Law and policy are crucial tools of prevention. They have a far-reaching effect and can shift cultural norms, help establish prevention strategies and enable violence prevention work. In addition, these tools might have an impact on what can be taught in school on sexuality and intimacy.

What part can men play in combating sexual harassment? How are we going to bring more men into the conversation about sexual harassment? As a society, we need to break the silence, and men need to hold other men accountable—which is, needless to say, easier said than done. This book discusses how to embark upon this journey in such a way as to help men think critically without becoming defensive. Few men dare or feel tempted to talk publicly about such matters. Convincing other men to make sexual harassment a priority is not an easy sell. The reasons why men prefer to be silent have to do with masculine thinking of 'what is it in for me?' Furthermore, it is worth mentioning the risk of social embarrassment, the belief that others are more supportive of harassment than they actually are, and the risk of loss of social and cultural capital if they speak out. Katz (2006: 8) posits that we need men to do something about the problem by educating and organizing other men in numbers great enough to prompt a real cultural shift. Men are often quite effective when it comes to changing men's attitudes because men are more likely to listen to what other men have to say.

Flood (2019) posits that when men are asked to address their own potential perpetration of violence against women or their complicity in this, many are uninterested or reluctant, and some react with hostility. A crucial question, then, is how we can include men in the dynamic changes in society. How do we get men to stand up as partners and allies of women in the struggle for justice in a society marked by increasing ethnic diversity and where women and LGBT people are advancing and challenging (heterosexual) men? Banyard et al. (2004) suggest that engaging men as allies to promote pro-social behaviour can reduce their resistance by reframing their involvement as helpful rather than placing them in a position of blame. The book will argue that the #MeToo movement constitutes a potential learning moment, which gives men the chance to reflect on things that they did not have to think about previously. For some men this moment represents an opportunity for change (Flood, 2019; PettyJohn et al., 2019). What has long been common knowledge among women has now potentially become common knowledge for men too.

What are the obstacles that prevent men from engaging fully in a conversation about gender equality? We must realize that men do not know that gender matters for them in the same way that women know that gender matters for them. For most men, gender is invisible—they do not see it. It is crucial to acknowledge the complexity of efforts to involve males as allies in gender equality policies. Maybe #MeToo can prompt men to reflect on the ways they treat women. Men lack a vocabulary that will enable them to talk about abuse. They may be able to help minimize abuse and harassment by overtly refusing to tolerate any sexually inappropriate behaviour that they encounter. However, the burning issue remains how to motivate men to engage themselves in debates on sexual harassment when many men perceive the very arena for those debates as dangerous and inaccessible.

Furthermore, it is urgent and crucial to raise questions about men's awareness and understanding of their actions. Some men may not even be aware that they indulge in sexual harassment. Therefore, combating sexual harassment also means refraining from accusing all men of being sexist and in general being careful not to paint a negative picture of all men. It is not about vilifying men. To a certain extent, we must not demonize men for being structurally determined by culture. Therefore, the way we approach men must not be an indictment of manhood. Instead, it must be an invitation to do things differently.

1.5 The Interview Material

Men after #MeToo is based on qualitative interviews with twenty-five men, aged from 21 to 30. The average age of the men was 24 years. Among the men interviewed, twenty-two were from an ethnic majority background and three from an ethnic minority background. The interviews were carried out during summer and autumn in 2020. Most of the interviews (19) were face-to-face interviews and took place either in the home of the interview participant or at a university campus outside Copenhagen. Some (6) of the interviews were recorded on the telephone. The interviews lasted 43–71 minutes each. The average length of the interviews was 57 minutes. A semi-structured interview guide was used, which allowed the questions to be prepared ahead of time and simultaneously allowed the informants to express their views in their own terms.

The interviews delve into men's perception of sexual harassment, in particular whether they are willing to take responsibility for change. The focus was on men's thoughts about changing discourses on sexual harassment in the aftermath of #MeToo. On a personal level, to what degree, if any, has #MeToo brought about new reflections and a change in behaviour towards women and other men? Have they themselves engaged in types of sexually aggressive behaviour? Particular attention will be paid to whether the men talk with their peers about the issue of sexual harassment and whether they find it difficult to intervene when witnessing other men's inappropriate comments and behaviour. A further focus will be on whether men are willing to try to create social change by taking an advocacy role and speaking out about sexual harassment in public. The reason why I will examine these aspects more closely is that I am particularly interested in what men are willing to do to stop sexual harassment and what holds men back from participating in this effort.

I originally planned to recruit most of the sample from secondary and higher education and vocational education institutions. I wished to recruit respondents from various education types and levels. Due to the circumstances of COVID-19 and limited access to such education institutions, I had to adapt the recruitment strategy so that participants were recruited mostly from a university outside Copenhagen.

This choice meant that the men interviewed, given their higher level of education than the average young man of the same age, had more open gender-equitable ideas about masculinity and were able to understand and empathize with the perspectives and experiences of women. Therefore, the sample is biased and not representative as regards the breadth of young men's attitudes towards #MeToo.

However, with regard to understanding the deeper causes behind a given problem and its consequences, it might be an advantage to operate with a more extreme and critical case because it often reveals more information. Unlike a more representative sample, the chosen sample of men constitutes a 'most likely' scenario (Flyvbjerg, 2006). This means that if the men interviewed, all things considered (e.g., age and education level), are not likely to speak out about sexual harassment and challenge other men, in all probability the majority of men anywhere, at least in Denmark, will also not exhibit such behaviour.

Most of the men were recruited through written invitations distributed to lists of students. The invitation described the purpose of the interview and the measures taken to ensure confidentiality and anonymity. A few of the men were recruited through snowball recruitment methods (Noy, 2008). When the participants showed up on the scheduled day for the interviews, or when the day for the telephone interview came, the conditions were repeated verbally with a specific emphasis on the measures taken to ensure confidentiality and anonymity in the study (see also Reinicke et al., 2019).

The book's empirical data also consists of an analysis of autobiographical narratives from the Danish edition of the Everyday Sexism Project website, which points to the need for a new language to capture the social realities of sexual harassment. The reason I have chosen to analyze the narratives from the Everyday Sexism Project is to illustrate the theoretical point about the existence of a striking discrepancy between the dominant discourses on sexual harassment and how the victims experience sexual harassment. The selection of stories from the Everyday Sexism Project is made with the intention of avoiding any focus on 'extreme' and non-representative stories. Instead, I have tried to capture narratives that illustrate the deeper cultural processes and mechanisms underlying the practice of sexual harassment and how its victims react.

1.6 Data Analysis

The author conducted the data analysis. The first specific step in processing the empirical data was that each interview was audiotaped and listened to by the interviewer two to three times to maintain close connection to the oral discourse and to identify possible focal points prior to the next interview (Kvale & Brinkmann, 2009; Reinicke, 2020). This was done because new data might alter the questions that are asked. Inspired by grounded theory (Strauss & Corbin, 1990) and as the second step in the analysis of the data, a coding of the material was made inductively based on key issues raised by participants. Grounded theory has paved the way for analysis to develop and unfold in a reflexive, interpretive way throughout the research process. It has been the aim to adhere closely to the raw information to better understand all types of reasoning and experiences (Kvale & Brinkmann, 2009). Grounded theory was used in the coding process for the interviews with the men to review and refine the material, and to discover new themes in the narratives that had not been searched for explicitly (Charmaz, 2006). The data was initially coded with reference to various concepts or words describing what was being talked about. This made it easier to create an overall impression of the collected material.

The theoretical framework on sexual harassment has also inspired the coding process and the identifying and labelling of concepts and phrases. The data analysis has been a combination of a bottom-up analysis and top-down theory-led reading where the intake of information emerged from the analyses, and some developed a priori. The bottom-up approach did allow a wide pool of specific characteristics to be considered in the analysis, whereas the top-down theory approach focused its analysis on systematic and comprehensive factors (Reinicke, 2020).

1.7 Overview of the Book

Chapter 2 of *Men after #MeToo* focuses on the challenge of having to define sexual harassment in a clear and understandable way. It explores why it has been difficult to agree on definitions of sexual harassment.

Who is violated by sexual harassment and what are the consequences of sexual harassment? It points out that the lack of agreement is a problem because it can be difficult to clarify what sexual harassment is and what sexual harassment is not. In addition, it argues that sexual harassment is a matter of individual perception because there are a great number of potential individual and situational variables that can influence the perception of harassment. The chapter also examines different societal models which are frequently used to explain sexual harassment. Furthermore, the chapter discusses the nature of sexual harassment and women's experiences of it through narratives from the Everyday Sexism Project (a website that exists to catalogue instances of sexism experienced on a day-to-day basis).

To better understand the societal and cultural setting in which the interviewed men are situated, Chapter 3 gives a brief outline of the major events and reactions which the #MeToo movement has set in motion in Denmark. It gives an indication of where the movement has taken us and how it has influenced political agendas and conversations. It discusses whether dominant notions of masculinity have been challenged in the Danish #MeToo debate. Beyond that, from an institutional perspective it looks at what kind of attention has been paid within the last 20–30 years to the issue of men and masculinities. When the first wave of #MeToo gained global momentum in 2017, it did not really hit Denmark. It was in 2020 that #MeToo first became a real national conversation in Denmark when shockwaves were sent through society.

Chapter 4 examines some of the societal conditions that make it difficult and sometimes culturally sensitive to focus on men as socially gendered, especially when it comes to the more controversial aspects of men's everyday lives. Men, masculinity and men's powers and practices have typically been taken for granted (Hearn & Pringle, 2006). In particular, topics such as violence, prostitution, sexual harassment and rape have been systematically trivialized when it comes to linking these problems with men's socialization. One rarely comes across discussions addressing how culture and upbringing form men's lives and are somehow responsible for the fact that it is typically men who buy sex and commit violence, sexual offences, and rape. Rather, the focus has been on the social and *gender-neutral* aspects of these problems, which has meant that not enough attention has been paid to the socialization processes that are (also) at the root of men's problems and aggressive behaviour.

In Chapter 5, we start to hear the voices of the interviewed men. The chapter explores why it is so appealing to men and boys to engage in sexual harassment. What are the factors that cause men, individually as well as collectively, to commit sexual harassment? What are the strategies men employ to naturalize and justify their actions? It is not easy to pin down who those men are who harass women sexually. For the same reason, there is not much knowledge about the *motives, characteristics* and *behaviour* of male perpetrators of sexual harassment. Sexual harassers make up a heterogeneous population and their motivations, characteristics, cognitions, and behaviours differ a great deal (Page & Pina, 2015). There is a degree of consensus that the explanation for sexual harassment by men is rooted in a combination of cultural, social and personal factors, but little agreement about which factors are the most important (DeGue et al., 2010; Pina et al., 2009).

Chapter 6 discusses why some men are able to change their behaviour and be ready to oppose the culture of assault, while other men hesitate and prefer not to see the #MeToo movement as an opportunity for change. It is difficult to determine how men really feel about the #MeToo movement and how they are dealing with society's growing rejection of men who harass. Do they look at some of the relationships among their friends differently, recognizing some abusive or potentially abusive situations? It is not possible to get all men to support #MeToo. Some men feel that #MeToo offers them new possibilities and others will feel that they lose privileges. At the same time, there is profound resistance among men to #MeToo's call for critically addressing their own behaviour and interactions.

Chapter 7 asks whether dating and flirting require more attention in the era of #MeToo. Do men feel that they can approach women without being afraid of violating their boundaries? What do men think about the importance of creating a language about flirting and sex, awkward situations, vulnerability, the fear of rejecting and being rejected? Do they perceive boundaries to be fluid and difficult to identify, both in themselves and in others? What about the problematic relation between being a 'conqueror' who is expected to take the initiative without being someone who violates other people's boundaries? How does it feel to carry that responsibility, and how does it feel when they fail to live up to it?

A question that is often asked is how men can play a positive role in changing some of the norms in male-dominated culture that support sexist abuse. #MeToo allows men to recall instances in their own lives when they did not step in and remind themselves that there are certain instances when they can intervene when, for instance, a friend is making a sexist comment. Therefore, Chapter 8 explores whether #MeToo has helped men frame how to talk to their friends and whether #MeToo has positively influenced men's attitudes about intervening as a bystander. Do men perceive themselves to have a primary role to play? Do they feel they have an obligation to intervene when witnessing other men's abusive behaviour? Furthermore, the chapter examines how we can provide tools for men to stop sexual harassment. Without confronting men's sense of entitlement, we will never be able to convince men that sexual harassment is not fair. However, how do we overcome the obstacles and make gender visible for men? It seems crucial to help men understand the structure of patriarchy. Men and boys often lack a vocabulary to discuss sexuality and intimate life in a non-misogynist way. Given this, how can we facilitate self-reflection and discussion?

Chapter 9 (Conclusion) provides a summary of the findings and asks whether we are only scratching the surface or if society has reached a new state of willingness to change that might herald a genuine paradigm shift. The #MeToo movement has revealed the considerable power present in feminism on social media, but the resistance to these powers also highlights the deeply rooted nature of male privilege and how far we have yet to go. It has become possible to talk about the problematic behaviour of men in new ways, but this still raises the question of whether we have already witnessed the most prominent changes resulting from the #MeToo movement—or whether big transformations are yet to come.

References

Arriaza Ibarra, K., & Berumen, R. (2019). #MeToo in Spain and France: Stopping the abuse towards ordinary women. *Interactions: Studies in Communication & Culture, 10*(3), 169–184.

Askanius, T., & Hartley, J. M. (2019). Framing gender justice: A comparative analysis of the media coverage of #Metoo in Denmark and Sweden. *Nordicom Review, 40*(2), 19–36.

Banyard, V. L., Plante, E. G., & Moynihan, M. M. (2004). Bystander education: Bringing a broader community perspective to sexual violence prevention. *Journal of Community Psychology, 32*, 61–79. https://doi.org/10.1002/jcop.10078

Bates, L. (2014). *Everyday sexism*. Simon & Schuster.

Benard, C., & Schlaffer, E. (1984). The man in the street: Why he harasses. In A. M. Jagger & P. S. Rothenberg (Eds.), *Feminist frameworks: Alternative theoretical accounts of the relations between women and men* (3rd ed., pp. 70–72). McGraw Hill.

Charmaz, K. (2006). *Constructing grounded theory: A practical guide through qualitative analysis*. Sage.

Connell. R. W. (1995). *Masculinities*. Polity.

Connell, R. W. (2003). *The role of men and boys in achieving gender equality*. United Nations, Division for the Advancement of Women.

Davis, D. E. (1994). The harm that has no name: Street harassment, embodiment, and African American women. *UCLA Women's Law Journal, 4*(2), 133–178.

De Benedictis, S., Orgad, S., & Rottenberg, C. (2019). #MeToo, popular feminism and the news: A content analysis of UK newspaper coverage. *European Journal of Cultural Studies, 22*(5–6), 718–738.

DeGue, S., DiLillo, D., & Scalora, M. (2010). Are all perpetrators alike? Comparing risk factors for sexual coercion and aggression. *Sexual Abuse, 22*(4), 402–426.

Eilermann, W. (2018). *Constructing #MeToo—A critical discourse analysis of the German news media's discursive construction of the #MeToo movement* (Master's Thesis, Malmö University).

Fabiano, P. M., Perkins, H. W., Berkowitz, A., Linkenbach, J., & Stark, C. (2003). Engaging men as social justice allies in ending violence against women: Evidence for a social norms approach. *Journal of American College Health, 52*(3), 105–112.

Fairchild, K. (2010). Context effects on women's perceptions of stranger harassment. *Sexuality & Culture, 14*(3), 191–216.

Ferguson, M. A., & Ford, T. E. (2008). Disparagement humor: A theoretical and empirical review of psychoanalytic, superiority, and social identity theories. *Humor: International Journal of Humor Research, 21*(3), 677–691.

Fitzgerald, L. F., Gelfand, M. J., & Drasgow, F. (1995). Measuring sexual harassment: Theoretical and psychometric advances. *Basic and Applied Social Psychology, 17*(4), 425–445.

Flood, M. (2011). Involving men in efforts to end violence against women. *Men and Masculinities, 14*(3), 358–377.

Flood, M. (2019). Men and #Metoo: Mapping men's responses to anti-violence advocacy. In *#MeToo and the politics of social change* (pp. 285–300). Palgrave Macmillan.

Flood, M., & Pease, B. (2006). *The factors influencing community attitudes in relation to violence against women: A critical review of the literature*. Victorian Health Promotion Foundation (VicHealth).

Flyvbjerg, B. (2006). Five misunderstandings about case-study research. *Qualitative Inquiry, 12*(2), 219–245.

Foubert, J., & Newberry, J. T. (2006). Effects of two versions of an empathy-based rape prevention program on fraternity men's survivor empathy, attitudes, and behavioral intent to commit rape or sexual assault. *Journal of College Student Development, 47*(2), 133–148.

Gardner, C. B. (1995). *Passing by: Gender and public harassment*. University of California Press.

Gavey, N. (2005). *Just sex? The cultural scaffolding of rape*. Routledge.

Gill, R. (2011). Sexism reloaded, or, it's time to get angry again! *Feminist Media Studies, 11*(1), 61–71.

Gladwell, M. (2010). Small change. *The New Yorker, 4*(2010), 42–49.

Grazian, D. (2007). The girl hunt: Urban nightlife and the performance of masculinity as collective activity. *Symbolic Interaction, 30*(2), 221–243.

Guha, P. (2021). *Hear#Metoo in India: News, social media, and anti-rape and sexual harassment activism*. Rutgers University Press.

Hearn, J. (1998). *The violences of men: How men talk about and how agencies respond to men's violence to women*. Sage.

Hearn, J., & Pringle, K. (2006). *European perspectives on men and masculinities*. Palgrave Macmillan.

Heiner, R. (2012). *Social problems: An introduction to critical constructionism*. Oxford University Press.

Katz, J. (2006). *Macho paradox: Why some men hurt women and and how all men can help*. Sourcebooks.

Kaufman, M., & Kimmel, M. (2011). *The guy's guide to feminism*. Seal Press.

Kidd, D., & McIntosh, K. (2016). Social media and social movements. *Sociology Compass, 10*(9), 785–794.

Kunst, J. R., Bailey, A., Prendergast, C., & Gundersen, A. (2018). Sexism, rape myths and feminist identification explain gender differences in attitudes toward the #Metoo social media campaign in two countries. *Media Psychology, 22*(5), 818–843.

Kvale, S., & Brinkmann, S. (2009). *Interviews: Learning the craft of qualitative research interviewing*. Sage.

Larkin, J. (1997). Sexual terrorism on the street: The moulding of young women into subordination. In A. M. Thomas & C. Kitzinger (Eds.), *Sexual harassment: Contemporary feminist perspectives* (pp. 115–130). Open University Press.

Loney-Howes, R. (2019). The politics of the personal: The evolution of anti-rape activism from second-wave feminism to #MeToo. In *#MeToo and the politics of social change* (pp. 21–35). Palgrave Macmillan.

Luthar, H. K., & Luthar, V. K. (2008). Likelihood to sexually harass: A comparison among American, Indian, and Chinese students. *International Journal of Cross Cultural Management, 8*(1), 59–77.

MacKinnon, C. A. (1979). *Sexual harassment of working women: A case of sex discrimination*. Yale Fastback Series No. 19. Yale University Press.

McDonald, P. (2012). Workplace sexual harassment 30 years on: A review of the literature. *International Journal of Management Reviews, 14*(1), 1–17.

McMahon, S., & Dick, A. (2011). "Being in a room with like-minded men": An exploratory study of men's participation in a bystander intervention program to prevent intimate partner violence. *The Journal of Men's Studies, 19*(1), 3–18.

Mendes, K., Ringrose, J., & Keller, J. (2018). #MeToo and the promise and pitfalls of challenging rape culture through digital feminist activism. *European Journal of Women's Studies, 25*(2), 236–246.

Messner, M. A. (1997). *Politics of masculinities: Men in movements*. Altamira Press.

Naik, M. G. (2020). Mainstream media's framing of #Metoo campaign in India. *Multidisciplinary Journal of Gender Studies, 9*(1), 79–106.

Noy, C. (2008). Sampling knowledge: The hermeneutics of snowball sampling in qualitative research. *International Journal of Social Research Methodology, 11*(4), 327–344.

O'Donohue, W., Downs, K., & Yeater, E. A. (1998). Sexual harassment: A review of the literature. *Aggression and Violent Behavior, 3*(2), 111–128.

Page, T. E., & Pina, A. (2015). Moral disengagement as a self-regulatory process in sexual harassment perpetration at work: A preliminary conceptualization. *Aggression and Violent Behavior, 21*, 73–84.

Pascoe, C. J. (2005). 'Dude, you're a fag': Adolescent masculinity and the fag discourse. *Sexualities, 8*(3), 329–346.

Pease, B., Pringle, K., & Kimmel, M. (Eds.). (2001). *A man's world? Changing men's practices in a globalized world*. ZED Books.

PettyJohn, M. E., Muzzey, F. K., Maas, M. K., & McCauley, H. L. (2019). #HowIWillChange: Engaging men and boys in the #MeToo movement. *Psychology of Men & Masculinities, 20*(4), 612–623.

Phipps, A. (2017). (Re)theorising laddish masculinities in higher education. *Gender and Education, 29*(7), 815–830.

Pina, A., Gannon, T. A., & Saunders, B. (2009). An overview of the literature on sexual harassment: Perpetrator, theory, and treatment issues. *Aggression and Violent Behavior, 14*(2), 126–138.

Quinn, B. A. (2002). Sexual harassment and masculinity: The power and meaning of "girl watching." *Gender & Society, 16*(3), 386–402.

Reinicke, K. (2020). First-time fathers' attitudes towards, and experiences with, parenting courses in Denmark. *American Journal of Men's Health, 14*(5), 1–13.

Reinicke, K., Søgaard, I. S., & Mentzler, S. (2019). Masculinity challenges for men with severe hemophilia. *American Journal of Men's Health, 13*(4), 1–11.

Salter, M. (2016). 'Real men don't hit women': Constructing masculinity in the prevention of violence against women. *Australian & New Zealand Journal of Criminology, 49*(4), 463–479.

Salter, M. (2019). Online justice in the circuit of capital: #MeToo, marketization and the deformation of sexual ethics. In *#MeToo and the politics of social change* (pp. 317–334). Palgrave Macmillan.

Schneider, K. T., & Carpenter, N. J. (2019). Sharing #MeToo on Twitter: Incidents, coping responses, and social reactions. *Equality, Diversity and Inclusion: An International Journal, 39*, 87–100.

Serisier, T. (2020). Speaking out, public judgments, and narrative politics. In L. A. Gray-Rosendale (Ed.), *Me Too, feminist theory, and surviving sexual violence in the academy* (pp. 167–180). Lexington Books.

Shirky, C. (2008). *Here comes everybody: The power of organizing without organizations*. Penguin.

Smith, M. D. (1988). Women's fear of violent crime: An exploratory test of a feminist hypothesis. *Journal of Family Violence, 3*(1), 29–38.

Stanko, E. A. (1995). Women, crime, and fear. *The Annals of the American Academy of Political and Social Science, 539*(1), 46–58.

Strauss, A., & Corbin, J. (1990). *Basics of qualitative research*. Sage.

Thomae, M., & Pina, A. (2015). Sexist humor and social identity: The role of sexist humor in men's in-group cohesion, sexual harassment, rape proclivity, and victim blame. *Humor, 28*(2), 187–204.

Tuerkheimer, D. (1997). Street harassment as sexual subordination: The phenomenology of gender-specific harm. *Wisconsin Women's Law Journal, 12*, 167–206.

Valiente, C. (1998). Sexual harassment in the workplace: Equality policies in post-authoritarian Spain. In T. Carver & V. Mottier (Eds.), *Politics of sexuality: Identity, gender, citizenship* (pp. 169–179). Routledge.

2

The Concept of Sexual Harassment

Although sexual harassment is one of the most widespread forms of dysfunctional behaviour in the labour market (Lucero et al., 2006), has existed for centuries and is probably the type of harassment that affects the most people in the world (Bargh et al., 1995; Spitzberg, 1999), no commonly agreed concept was available to describe the phenomenon until the end of the 1970s (Belknap & Erez, 1997). It was the women's movement in the USA that first identified the problem and brought it onto the political agenda at the end of the 1970s. In particular, MacKinnon (1979) and Farley (1978) have been credited with bringing the term 'sexual harassment' into everyday language. In the EU, sexual harassment came onto the agenda in 1986, when it was included in the resolution on violence against women (McCann, 2005).

Most research on sexual harassment has addressed labour market contexts where the offender and the victim know each other and where the offending man is often (but not always) in a position of power over the woman (Ilies et al., 2003). Street harassment has not received as much attention in studies of sexual harassment (Vera-Gray, 2016). Likewise, online sexual harassment also appears understudied compared to offline sexual harassment, which is a major concern because more people are using online communication methods such as online dating apps and social media platforms (Buchanan & Mahoney, 2021). The reason for this discrepancy is that much effort has been devoted to developing laws and policies in the area of workplace harassment.

> The ordinary interruptions women experience from men in public space, such as wolf-whistling, cat-calling, staring, and comments, are frequently dismissed as irrelevant or harmless, expressions of free speech or a minor annoyance. This trivialization has led to a gap in the literature, with these forms of "everyday sexism" rarely acknowledged as a legitimate area of study. (Vera-Gray & Fileborn, 2018: 78)

Street harassment often takes the form of accidental meetings between strangers which are hard to follow up legally (Fileborn & Vera-Gray, 2017).[1] Legal consequences do not typically follow from street harassment. Consequently, street harassment has not been perceived as a 'real' problem (Logan, 2015). Nevertheless, a number of jurisdictions in different countries, such as France, Portugal and Belgium, have introduced legislation which addresses street harassment in various forms (Fileborn, 2017).

It has been difficult to agree on definitions of sexual harassment. O'Donohue et al. (1998) state that definitions of sexual harassment are in agreement on only one issue, which is that sexual harassment is improper behaviour which has a sexual dimension. It is difficult to conceptualize the nature of sexual harassment because it is not clear what sexual harassment is, when it occurs and how it should be understood (Davis, 1994; Gailey & Prohaska, 2011; Vera-Gray, 2016; Tuerkheimer, 1997). Sexual harassment is a research area that is characterized by several methodological challenges, which has made it difficult to answer even the most basic questions, such as: What is sexual harassment? How many people are exposed to sexual harassment?

---

[1] In this book, I use the term street harassment to address sexual harassment taking place in public space. However, women's experience of intrusive men in public space has also been named 'public harassment' (Gardner, 1995), 'public sexual harassment' (Thompson, 1994) and 'everyday stranger harassment' (Fairchild & Rudman, 2008).

The question of when behaviour should or should not be labelled sexual harassment is extremely complex. Cleveland and Kerst (1993) have emphasized that what we can most confidently say about sexual harassment is that there is a marked difference in how men and women define it. Men are more likely to focus on incidents such as harmless flirting and attempted sexual conquest, while women more often see it as harmful sexual harassment.

There is great uncertainty about the extent of the problem, and it is assumed that there are large numbers of unreported incidents. Definitions of sexual harassment have also diverged as to whether inequality in power is necessary for an occurrence to constitute sexual harassment. There has also been disagreement regarding the importance that should be attached to whether the victim perceives the behaviour as problematic or not, whether an act can be defined as harassing in and of itself, and whether further negative consequences are necessary for an act to be a case of sexual harassment. Finally, scholars have disagreed on whether only women can be victims of sexual harassment and whether *one* act in itself is enough to meet the requirements defined as sexual harassment (O'Donohue et al., 1998).

Most studies on sexual harassment have been concerned with defining what harassment consists of and how often harassment occurs, and have studied statements from women regarding their perception of and response to sexual harassment (O'Donohue et al., 1998). The question of when a given behaviour can be characterized as sexual harassment has primarily been studied through experimental surveys. In these, participants have often been asked to evaluate whether different hypothetical scenarios could be described as sexual harassment, who was responsible for the occurrence of the incident and what were the consequences of the incident (Quinn, 2002).

Sexual harassment can be both something that is effected through language—for example, in the way a person is spoken to, or in what is being said about someone—but it can also take the form of physical action perceived as offensive by the victim. A victim of sexual harassment should always have the right to define whether it is an intrusion or not. This means that it is the perception of the victim that determines if an event is harassing or not (Fairchild, 2010). Nevertheless, as Gruber

(1992: 447) has expressed it, there has been 'substantial confusion over definitions of sexual harassment as well as over operationalizations of these definitions into meaningful, empirical harassment categories'.

In order for an incident to be defined as sexual harassment, it must have involved unwelcome physical, verbal or non-verbal behaviour. Sexual harassment can take place either quite openly or in more subtle and secret ways. If we look at how, when and under what circumstances sexual harassment occurs, there are many contextual factors that come into play. Sexual harassment is a combination of sexual behaviour and abuse of power. It can involve unwanted touch or sexual invitations, questions about sexual topics, and tasteless jokes. Several studies have shown that sexual harassment most often takes the form of verbal comments or suggestive looks (Pina et al., 2009). It is often a challenge to contest such actions because strong forces are often at play in communities, especially in workplace environments where harassment is accepted. If social life and work are combined and there are few organizational agreements, codes of conduct or guidelines, there is a greater chance of sexual harassment.

McDonald (2012) thinks that behaviours that define sexual harassment are heterogeneous and categorized in different ways. They often, however, represent a continuum, from requests for socialization or dates, personal insults and ridicule, leering, offensive comments and non-verbal gestures, to sexual propositions, and sexual and physical assault. Due to its complex nature, it is not surprising that there is no single and all-encompassing definition of sexual harassment. This uncertainty about the concept makes it difficult to study how widespread sexual harassment is, and in several contexts is still such a taboo that investigations of it bring about considerable upset.

Regarding initiatives that either work against or facilitate harassing behaviour, organizational climate (tolerance of sexual harassment) is often mentioned as playing an important part in making sexual harassment possible (Pina & Gannon, 2012). It has also been emphasized that vague or absent organizational policies and procedures for dealing effectively with sexual harassment lead directly to negative employee experiences, which in turn lead to health and job-related outcomes (Williams et al., 1999; Willness et al., 2007).

2.1 Basic Definitions

Back in the late 1970s, MacKinnon (1979) argued that one should distinguish between harassment as 'something for something' ('quid pro quo') or as resulting from workplace conditions or a hostile environment ('hostile environment'). 'Something for something' refers to a situation where a superior sets sexual conditions, for example in connection with employment or promotion, and where a refusal will lead to the superior using retaliation in terms of the victim's situation in the workplace. Sexual harassment is related to the overall workplace conditions when constant or overarching sexual approaches make the workplace environment hostile and create discomfort among employees (Borchorst & Agustin, 2017).

Sexual harassment is a combination of sexual behaviour and the exercise of power (Farley, 1978; MacKinnon, 1979; McDonald, 2012). Nevertheless, many contextual factors come into play and a discursive struggle continues regarding the definition of sexual harassment (Fairchild & Rudman, 2008; Fitzgerald et al., 1995).

Sexual harassment has various forms and functions, depending on the context and the men involved. For example, it may be used by men as a deliberate act of power directed at a particular woman or group of women. Fitzgerald et al. (1995) point out that sexually harassing behaviour can be divided into three categories, based on the type of harassment and the severity of it:

> *Gender harassment*: A series of verbal and non-verbal acts that express insulting, hostile and degrading attitudes towards women in general. Derogatory and insulting comments on behalf of the sex. Creates an intimidating, offensive and hostile environment. These acts are most often not aimed at initiating a sexual relationship.
>
> *Unwanted sexual attention*: A wide range of unwanted verbal and non-verbal acts, non-reciprocal requests for dates, intrusive letters, phone calls, etc.

Sexual coercion: Bribes and threats that are either explicit or imply that job-related benefits will follow from consent to a sexual relationship. The victim's job or rewards are contingent on sexual cooperation.

Thus, gender harassment may either consist in more general expressions of degrading and negative attitudes towards women, or it may involve unwanted sexual attention and sexual coercion directed at getting access to and control over the victim. Likewise, where 'quid pro quo' sexual harassment is more specific, a hostile work environment is more ambiguous and open to different and directly opposing interpretations (Pryor & Fizgerald, 2003).

2.2 Who Is Violated by Sexual Harassment?

Victims of sexual harassment can belong to any gender and come from any social stratum/class or background (Pina & Gannon, 2012). Although this is not always the case, sexual harassment is most often an act committed by men against women (Pina et al., 2009; Pryor et al., 1995). Therefore, a decisive factor is the victim's gender. In relation to age and seniority, it seems clear that it is disproportionately young people with low seniority who are exposed to sexual harassment. In terms of employment conditions and social background, studies show that sexual harassment more often affects people in fixed-term employment and people who have a low position in the employment hierarchy. Studies indicate that women in less powerful positions are particularly vulnerable to harassment. This includes young women, women new to the labour market, women in precarious employment, women who have been unemployed, women in non-traditional jobs, women in stereotypically masculine professions, women with disabilities, women with few economic resources as well as women belonging to ethnic minorities.

Gay men, men of colour, men working in traditional women's professions and young men are also more exposed to sexual harassment than are other men (McCann, 2005). There is often a connection between branches of trade or work and the likelihood of experiencing sexual harassment. Thus, some of the job groups that are most affected are social and health care assistants, nurses, special educators, physiotherapists and occupational therapists, as well as hotel and restaurant staff. Care workers are more frequently exposed to unwanted sexual attention than all other professional groups, which is often due to close physical contact with their clients/the people they are looking after. Seniority often plays a bigger role than age. A new employee is more exposed than colleagues who have been in the workplace for a long time, as they do not yet know each other and each other's boundaries. Newcomers often do not know the culture in the workplace and may be unsure of their own boundaries in relation to the tone of conversation among colleagues. Sexual harassment seems to have better prospects in workplaces with a large turnover in the workforce than one with long-term employees (McDonald, 2012).

2.3 The Consequences of Sexual Harassment

Research on sexual harassment has revealed that the experience of sexual harassment has substantial effects on employees' health and well-being as well as on organizational variables such as job satisfaction, long-term sick leave and organizational/work withdrawal (Fairchild & Rudman, 2008; Friborg et al., 2017; Lee et al., 2003).

The greatest difficulties seem to result from sexual harassment among colleagues at work. Different from street harassment, where the harassment mostly happens without any prior contact between the people involved, sexual harassment among workplace colleagues often takes the form of an escalating process, where it can be difficult to pinpoint exactly when and how the harassment began. Sexual harassment often builds up slowly. It can be mentally stressful for a victim, who has to be constantly on guard against being left alone with the harassing person. Likewise, having to spend energy on considering how to respond to unwanted comments or how to avoid physical attention affects the victim negatively. Typically, women who have been subjected to sexual harassment do not remain in their employment. Either they terminate the agreement themselves, or they get fired (Pina & Gannon, 2012). Research has shown that women who are exposed to sexual harassment are at greater risk than other women of developing anxiety and depression (Willness et al., 2007). A survey by the Danish trade union FOA (2016) showed that among public employees who have been subjected to sexual harassment, 37 percent stated that they felt stressed to a high or very high degree. The same is true for only 18 percent of those who have not been sexually harassed. Similarly, the study showed that employees who have been subjected to sexual harassment generally have a poor estimation of their work environment and feel less job satisfaction than employees who have not been subjected to sexual harassment. Studies have also shown that employees who have been exposed to sexual harassment from a manager or colleague are more likely to report depressive symptoms than employees who have experienced sexual harassment from, for example, home care clients (Friborg et al., 2017).

Naturally, women can also sexually harass men and men can also sexually harass other men. However, research shows that when men report being exposed to sexual harassment, the perpetrator is often another man. This is, among other things, due to the traditional female gender role socialization that reduces the risk of women being perpetrators of sexual harassment (Berdahl et al., 1996). It is far less common that a man is exposed to sexual harassment, and this may make it more stigmatic (Vogt et al., 2005). Research also shows that men are less likely to tell others about it when they are subjected to sexual harassment, and they are also less likely to seek help (Kime, 2014; McDonald, 2012). A Danish study (Hogh et al., 2016) showed that men who experience unwelcome sexual attention from colleagues or bosses are more at risk of going on long-term sick leave. This may be because it is more of a taboo for men to talk about being violated.

2.4 Societal Explanations of Sexual Harassment

No single explanation can adequately describe why sexual harassment occurs in society, but a number of general theories and models have tried to describe from different angles and perspectives why the phenomenon occurs (Pina et al., 2009).

2.4.1 The Biological Model

According to the *biological model*, sexual harassment is a 'normal' phenomenon in human interaction. The biological model emphasizes that sexual harassment occurs due to men's natural and innate urge to be sexually aggressive and that 'real' sexual harassment (violent sexual abuse, rape, etc.) is committed by only a limited number of 'sick' men. According to the biological model and its evolutionist assumptions, men's aggressive and persistent sexual interest in women—even if unwanted—is a consequence of men's greater sex drive. Sexual harassment should therefore in many cases not be characterized as such, but should instead be described as a natural expression of male desire and of the need for sexual gratification (Tangri et al., 1982). The biological approach also points out that men in powerful positions 'just' exploit their greater sexual drive in order to gain sexual access to as many women as possible. It sees sexual jokes, sexual allusions, and sexual comments as also natural in the interplay of the sexes. Critics of the biological model have pointed out its highly simplified and generalizing view of men's sexuality and the trivialization it involves of sexual harassment as part of natural everyday encounters between men and women.

Bargh et al. (1995) argue for an 'automatic power-sex relationship' in which the harassing behaviour of the male perpetrator does not have a conscious goal. They point out that the sexuality of certain powerful heterosexual men is automatically activated by human interaction with women but that the connection between their position and their sexual harassment is beyond their own consciousness—they are therefore unaware of the inappropriateness of their behaviour. O'Donohue et al. (1998) emphasize that if the biological standpoint were to be true and if sexual harassment is just one of many facets in the normal process of romantic attraction, then one would expect the male–female relationship to be more similar in terms of age, race/ethnicity and status, which applies to many couples. The man should also, as a starting point, mainly only focus on a single woman, just as it should not have any negative consequences for the woman. They also point out that sexual harassment should not be as widespread as it is now, and that sexually abusive behaviour should be spread across men of all ages and would be seen in all industries without any systematic patterns.

2.4.2 The Sociocultural Model

Sociocultural theories concerning sexual harassment are often feminist inspired and directed at the broad social and cultural context in which sexual harassment occurs and originates. Sociocultural theorists suggest that sexual harassment serves to perpetuate patriarchal gender relations through the sexual exploitation and oppression of women (Farley, 1978; MacKinnon, 1979). Sociocultural theories consider sexual harassment as a logical consequence of the gender inequality and sexism that is widespread in society. Sexual harassment occurs because men and women are socialized in a way that makes it natural for men to appear aggressive and outgoing and for women to be passively accepting. In this way, sociocultural theories emphasize that sexual harassment is largely predictable and almost inevitable. As a result, many men are convinced that their actions are legitimate, and many women will blame themselves when subjected to sexual harassment (O'Hare & O'Donohue, 1998).

The sociocultural explanatory model emphasizes that sexual harassment is symptomatic of a patriarchal society and can be interpreted as an abuse of male power in a male-dominated society. It points out that sexism is omnipotent and present everywhere: in schools and workplaces, on public transport, in the city and in close relationships. According to the sociocultural approach, sexism is almost a foundation of our culture, an element of a unified system of oppression, and it is present everywhere in the form of established norms, stereotypes and uses of language. The approach sees a link between sexism, transgressive behaviour, sexual harassment, stalking, revenge porn, violence, sexual assault and rape. Furthermore, the sociocultural model points out that sexism is also rooted in gender constructions, which are reproduced in popular culture through advertisements, films, and mainstream media. For example, Logan (2015) argues that street harassment, the tendency to transfer guilt and shame onto the victim, and the derogatory and sexualized vocabulary used by men against women are rooted in a culture that sees men's harassment and oppression of women as legitimate.

2.4.3 The Organizational Model

Regarding workplace harassment, the organizational model explains the prevalence of sexual harassment as based on a range of organizationally related issues. These include power and diversity in position and status, which result in an increased risk of sexual harassment. Unlike sociocultural explanations, the organizational model focuses primarily on organizational power as an explanation of why sexual harassment occurs in specific and immediate contexts of work. As an explanation of why particularly powerful people exercise sexual harassment against subordinates, the organizational model will emphasize that since some people have power and others do not, and since organizational hierarchies exist, it is to be expected that people without power accept behaviour to which people in power expose them. The model therefore largely sees sexual harassment as an expression of the exploitation of hierarchical relationships, authority and power in the workplace (O'Donohue et al., 1998).

As pointed out by Pina et al. (2009), one strength of the organizational approach is that it seeks to bring together a number of factors that are important for the possibility of sexual harassment. It seems credible that the organizational climate and collegial relations are of great importance for whether sexual harassment occurs or not.

According to organizational theories, it is not only the hierarchy and relations of power, status and authority within the organization that are significant. The professionalization of the workplace can also be of great importance—as can a sexist atmosphere in the workplace—when working conditions are discussed, if there are demands for weekend work and overtime, and if there are expectations and indulgence of sexualized behaviour at work. Similarly, the presence of 'playboy' calendars and pin-up girls on workplace walls may encourage and legitimize a sexist conversation. The organizational model highlights that the presence of anti-sexism policies and grievance procedures has a major impact on whether sexual harassment occurs.

2.4.4 Sex-Role Spillover Model

The sex-role spillover model is an extension of sociocultural and organizational theories and points out that sexual harassment represents an extension of traditional gender roles to the labour market. The sex-role spillover model points out that when the sex ratio is unequal at the workplace, there is a greater risk of sexual harassment. Gutek and Dunwoody (1987) emphasize that there is a transfer of expectations concerning gender-based behaviour to the workplace; in addition, both the workplace context and the individual gendered expectations must be taken into account in order to explain why sexual harassment takes place. The point is that employees most often come to the workplace already having gendered expectations of it being natural for men to be leaders and for women to be subordinate and be assessed according to the ways in which they live up to their role as sex objects. These expectations are culturally created and are rooted in women's traditional roles in society and in typical patterns of interaction between men and women. Employees bring these expectations of specific gender roles with them to work, regardless of the actual practice in the workplace (Borchorst & Agustin, 2017; Pina et al., 2009).

2.4.5 The Four-Factor Model

There are also models that try to include several factors. One example is the four-factor model, which analyzes the interplay between the individual, the contextual and the organizational (O'Donohue et al., 1998; O'Hare & O'Donohue, 1998; Pina et al., 2009). The four-factor model is more concrete than the sociocultural and organizational models and incorporates several of the key components from the single-factor models. It emphasizes that four basic components must be present: (1)

the individual must be motivated to engage in sexual harassment (e.g., be motivated by a combination of power, control and sexual attraction); (2) the individual must be able to overcome personal resistance to sexual harassment (e.g., moral inhibitions); (3) the individual must overcome external restrictions, such as organizational directives not to engage in sexual harassment; and (4) the individual must disregard the victim's resistance (O'Donohue et al., 1998). There is no doubt that the victim's reaction and status can have a decisive influence on whether the perpetrator initiates the harassment and whether he carries on exercising it. Without advancing victim blaming it seems that women who are not passive, do not appear to be traditionally feminine, have knowledge of sexual harassment and are of relatively high status are less likely to be targeted for harassment.

2.5 Reading About Women's Experiences

After this presentation of the societal models, I want to dig deeper into the nature of sexual harassment, focusing on women's experiences of it and what men can learn from reading about it. In my book *Mænd som krænker kvinder – refleksioner I kølvandet på #MeToo* [*Men Who Violate Women – Reflections in the Wake of #MeToo*] (Reinicke, 2018), I used the narratives from the Everyday Sexism Project to illustrate the profound difference and contradiction between what popular discourses tell us sexual harassment is about and how it is experienced by its victims. In 2012, UK activist Laura Bates set up the Everyday Sexism Project to raise awareness of the sexist practices facing girls and women in places ranging from schools and streets to universities and workplaces. Beginning with a website on which women were invited to post their experiences, this has become a viral international movement (Phipps et al., 2018). The project has turned into a worldwide phenomenon with more than 100,000 stories. The narratives concern experiences with daily, normalized sexism—from street harassment and workplace discrimination to sexual assault and rape. On the homepage, one can read that:

> The Everyday Sexism Project exists to 'catalogue instances of sexism experienced on a day to day basis'. They might be serious or minor, outrageously offensive or so niggling normalized that you don't even feel able to protest... By sharing your story you're showing the world that sexism does exist, it is faced by women everyday and it is a valid problem to discuss.

On a general level, the Everyday Sexism Project helps women to acknowledge the discomfort they often feel when moving around in public spaces. The philosophy behind the Everyday Sexism Project is that sexual harassment must be seen on a continuum because small sexist and stereotypical prejudices in everyday life excuse, enable and reinforce serious violations of women. Countless women describe how they have not shared their stories before because the doubts make it hard to speak out. Through the collective sharing of personal experiences, women highlight the systemic and institutionalized nature of their subordination and pain.

Women's articulation of everyday sexism can therefore, as Thomas and Kitzinger (1997) have pointed out, become a part of women's attempts to recreate or change their experiences in the world based on their own reflections on how harassment and abuse feel, including the harmful effects sexual harassment causes. The narratives are full of 'it's a bit shit but inevitable' kind of thinking. When reading the narratives, it is noticeable that a recurring motif for many of the women is that they actually want the perpetrator to understand what the harassment has meant to them.

2.6 The Crime Paradox

Several researchers claim that there is a so-called crime paradox in that men are exposed to more crime in public space, but women far more often than men fear being exposed to crime (Vera-Gray, 2016). However, this does not apply to sexual abuse, to which more women than men are exposed (Smith, 1988). The reason for this difference in fear of crime may also be due to the fact that the statistics do not capture when women are exposed to 'non-criminal' abuses such as sexual harassment. Therefore, the lack of understanding of women's fear might be rooted in the larger societal context, in which men historically have had and to some extent still have greater power than women to define the 'nature' of the abuse. This has meant that it is men who have decided whether it is an act that society should recognize as sexual harassment or not. In that regard, Smith (1988) points out that women's life experiences rarely turn into universally accepted considerations of the state of the world. Women are therefore to some extent forced to relate to the importance that men attach to events. This rarely manages to capture the degradation, anxiety and intimidation that sexual harassment can cause. Legal frameworks do not necessarily reflect experience and there might be problems in locating men's sexual harassment solely within a legal paradigm (Vera-Gray, 2016).

When do women feel intimidated, insecure and harassed? Overall, the fear of being exposed to violence and crime is about an individual's diffuse fear of being violently abused (Smith, 1988). It is often associated with the worry of being away from home, alone and vulnerable to personal injury. However, why are women more afraid than men, and what are women afraid of? Stanko (1995) emphasizes that to a large extent women's anxiety is about their vulnerability to men's violence and that the gender difference is indisputably the most consistent finding in studies dealing with the fear of crime. In this context, exposure to sexual harassment contributes to making women insecure about their sexual integrity.

Many women will rightly believe that if they were to be physically attacked by a man, they would be less physically equipped to either escape or defend themselves against the often faster, bigger and stronger man who is probably also more experienced in mastering violence (Smith, 1988). Research also indicates that women's fear of crime is largely about the fear of rape and that verbal harassment alone can cause an increased fear of being raped (Gordon et al., 1980; Warr, 1984). This is again related to the physical dimension. Since a man is often perceived as being physically stronger than a woman—when accounting for other factors—even the 'softer' form of harassment might be frightening. Episodes that do not develop into physical harassment can seem more frightening to a woman than to a man because they build on the already existing fear due to physical superiority.

Bowman (1993) describes how the law often overlooks harms to women and that one such harm is the harassment that women face when they move around in city streets and appear in other public places. Street harassment is an invasion of women's privacy and a violation of autonomy and consent (Thompson, 1994). Kearl (2010) states that despite street harassment being generally dismissed as harmless, in reality it is omnipresent and causes women to feel unsafe in public. There are stories about women feeling dehumanized, objectified and sexualized when they are being catcalled, stared at, whistled at, groped and touched by strangers against their will.

> I get angry and frustrated every single time it happens. My good mood is being ruined and it will be the only thing I can think of for the rest of the day. It's disappointing. In particular, I find it frustrating that the moment a stranger's hand, uninvited, touches my butt or my breasts, I am reduced from a human being to a sexual object. I am thus no longer just a person in the herd of people of different genders, hair colors, clothing styles and ages - I am the woman with the ass to be patted, and no more than that. (Everyday Sexism Project)

The above description shows how women feel when treated as objects rather than human beings. Furthermore, there are narratives about how women talk about the direct line of causation between women's dress and sexual assault. Women describe how they find the experiences of sexual harassment in public by strangers frightening, disruptive and unpleasant.

2.7   Women's Reactions

If one looks at how women react to unwanted touches and approaches in nightlife venues, the reactions generally depend on the nature of the incident and the emotions that the incident evokes. Some of the most commonly used strategies for dealing with unwanted contact are to ignore and try to avoid the person, to make an angry facial expression or to begin speaking to a third person (Cochran et al., 1997; Fileborn, 2019, 2020). Direct anger at and aggressive confrontation with the perpetrator of the harassment occur more frequently when it comes to unwanted physical touching. Fairchild and Rudman (2008) point out that there are four coping strategies that women often use in connection with sexual harassment in a public space: (1) to be passive; (2) to blame themselves: (3) to be polite; and (4) to act out. Gardner (1995) pointed out, however, that the strategy that women most often used to shield against sexual harassment when they were alone in a public space was to be 'on guard'.

Studies show that although women define sexual harassment more broadly than men, many women are reluctant to report 'minor' incidents of sexual harassment. The most common forms of sexual harassment are therefore not captured because they are so normalized that it is rarely perceived as harassment (Larkin, 1997; Tinkler, 2008). A recent study by UN Women UK (2021) showed that 96 percent of women exposed to sexual harassment are not reporting it because of the belief that it would not change anything. This also may be because the most common forms of sexual harassment are typically not criminalized. Such attitudes were also confirmed in the narratives from the Everyday Sexism Project.

> None of what I have experienced I have reported as it either has not been possible, I do not think it will help anything or because most of all I just wanted to get away as soon as possible. (Everyday Sexism Project)

Looking at the narratives on the Everyday Sexism Project website, one finds both short and long ones, where women call out about the harassing incidents that they have been through. The women describe how there is often a condescending, contemptuous and objectifying tone behind the episodes in the public space. Many stories are associated with shame and doubt as well as fear of overreacting. Numerous women complain that their bodies are looked at as a sexual invitation in the street and in order to stay safe they often cannot fight back. Fairchild and Rudman (2008) describe how most incidents of sexual harassment that women experience in public represent low levels of coercion. Many stories are about men who, completely uninvited, start commenting on or physically touching women or exposing them to sexualized body language (e.g., by making sexual gestures with the body and mouth).

There are different degrees of severity, just as the situational contexts are different. Many women describe how they have been subjected to several sexual assaults during their lifetime. Several women report how derogatory remarks and calls for sex can develop into involuntary touching. Likewise, how the rejection of 'offers' and ignoring unwanted approaches can develop into violent and disrespectful outbursts of anger from men in the form of harsh and derogatory remarks. There are countless reports of women who are catcalled at festivals and 'graded' on a scale of 1–10 when they pass a group of young men.

Perpetrators of sexual harassment who start by giving compliments, but who experience being ignored or rejected, may subsequently be inclined to engage in humiliating and demeaning behaviour towards the victim. Abbey (1987) states that men often tend to misperceive women's friendly and outgoing behaviour as conveying sexual interest. Many women describe how quickly comments that they may be a little flattered to receive to begin with can turn into sexual insinuations and then end up in threats of violence and rape.

If you look at the stories of verbal and physical harassment women are exposed to, they are generally about boundaries that are transgressed by everything from annoying 'come-ons' to derogatory comments, anger, heckling and sexual abuse. Some use time frames when stressing the all-pervading character of sexual harassment, for example 'When I was 12, 15, 17 years old', the following experiences occurred, and others categorize the many different places in which the harassing experiences took place, such as on the bus, in the street, in the city/nightlife venues. Here is an example where a woman uses a mixture of time frame and place name to describe the prevalence of sexual harassment:

> It starts already in primary school, where the boys think it's okay to grope one's breasts and crotch, over secondary school with lists of who the gorgeous girls are (it's neither nice to be on the list nor to be left out because you told them that it was not ok) … It continues on the street, where men think they have the right to make naughty remarks, grope one in the bus, train or just in the public space when walking on the street…

> In the workplace where various bosses thought it was ok to smack you on the bum ('You're just a student here, be a little fresh'), tried to kiss someone when they got drunk at parties or business trips with the boss, where he thinks it's ok to ask if you don't want to go up to his room and 'have some fun' after a business dinner. (Everyday Sexism Project)

Many women describe how they wish they could just be completely 'ordinary' neutral people with the freedom to move around in public spaces without always being made aware of their sexual desirability. Gunnarsson (2018) states that our most personal experiences are formed by external forces—not only in the sense that the latter shape the objective situations we are in, but also in the sense that our subjective understanding of these situations is framed by discourses not of our own making. The denial of sexual harassment as a serious problem is not only to be found in an older generation who are out of step with reality, but may also be found among young people and even in the partners or boyfriends of the women who have been sexually harassed. There are several stories where the victim's boyfriend and relatives downplay the episodes and do not take them seriously.

The stories affirm that girls' vulnerability starts early in life. It might be shocking to read about how very young girls too have reached out to the Everyday Sexism Project to share stories of sexism and harassment. Many stories are about being made into a sex object and exposed to unwanted sexual attention all the way down to the age of 11 or 12—and not just by boys of the same age.

> I was on my way up the stairs from the train station, and a guy in his 20s was walking a little too close to me, when I got to the end of the stairs he smacked me on the bum and winked at me. For him, it has probably been innocent flirting, but I was only 14 years old and certainly did not like it. (Everyday Sexism Project)

According to Bates (2014), the many stories testify that girls and women learn the hard way early on that they are not believed and that there is often an alleged causal link between the clothes they are wearing and the legitimation of the violation. When girls and women dress in the clothes that popular culture encourages and almost dictates to them to wear, they are often told that they have no right to complain. Therefore, it can be argued that women are subject to the so-called 'Phyllis Schlafly myth',[2] namely, that no virtuous woman has ever been sexually harassed and that there is a connection between women's reputation, their way of dressing and their likelihood of being sexually harassed (Belknap & Erez, 1997).

Many women angrily say that they do not like to be taught how to deal with the offensive comments. Several women also write that they do not know what is worse, the experience itself or the frequent subsequent comment that they should just take it as a 'compliment', as well as the fact that they do not feel that the experience is something especially noteworthy because it happens so often. There are stories of women describing how they have been exposed to accusations that it was their own fault and have often been told that they should have 'seen it coming' and that they could have told themselves that 'it was bound to happen'. There are several women who wonder why men may think it is okay to touch women's bodies as if they were a kind of 'public property' and about how they are perceived as 'snarky bitches' if they say 'no'. It is also pointed out by many women that they feel that men live in a different reality—an illusion—and that men, because they are so engrossed in their fantasies, are unable to imagine that their harassing behaviour can be perceived as being frightening.

Women with large breasts describe in particular how vulnerable they are to comments and catcalls.

Overall, many of the women describe a society that not only downplays and accepts this sexual harassment, but also in many respects normalizes it by telling the women that they are overreacting and that they should not make a big deal of it. Instead, they are told 'just' to be grateful for the attention. In most narratives, it is possible to see that many women generally distance themselves from being evaluated by comments about their body and appearance.

No doubt, some men feel that they are 'just' doing a woman a favour by telling her that she is good-looking and by making explicit comments

---

[2] Phyllis Schlafly (1924–2016) was an American attorney, activist and author. She was best known for her conservative social and political views and her opposition to the women's movement and the Equal Rights Amendment. She openly opposed feminism, gay rights and abortion.

about her body. However, the vast majority of women do not perceive it as a compliment but as an unpleasant objectification. They describe feelings of powerlessness, humiliation and fear, and they often label sexual harassment as a demonstration of power by men.

We have belief systems in society that justify sexual harassment, and we do not sufficiently support people who experience problems with it. Culturally, we have not been able to accept the severity of the problem, and many women talk about disbelief. Bates (2014) states that society has normalized sexual harassment and allowed it to become so deep-rooted that many people do not notice it or object to it. Society has taught women that they do not have the right to complain. Women are silenced by both the invisibility and the acceptability of the problem. Often the social acceptability of sexism and harassment is so ingrained that the abuse itself appears to come second in importance to the women's desire to avoid a scene. This might have an impact on women's judgement of situations—women learn not to trust themselves and not to make a fuss (Vera-Gray, 2018).

Historically, men have dominated the public space and there are several stories of women who have experienced having their way blocked or being surrounded and groped by several men/boys.

> I was on my way home at 10 or 11 in the evening. When I cycled past the old stock exchange in the direction of Knippelsbro [bridge in Copenhagen], they were doing some excavation work under the pavement, so the pedestrians had to go out on the bike path. I cycled right in front of a group of 10–15 young men in their 20s who, instead of moving aside and making room for me to pass, split into two groups, so I was forced to cycle in between them at a slow pace. As I cycled through their group, they yelled at me and several of them hit me on the bum. It was a very shocking and unpleasant experience and I was scared and shocked.
> (Everyday Sexism Project)

The above episode testifies to the fact that men in groups have a notion that men own public space and that they feel entitled to comment on and disempower women in a very demonstrative way. There are also many stories of men cruising around in hooting cars commenting on women's bodies or making sexual proposals. Sexual harassment carried out by men in cars is extremely risk-free for men who can drive away immediately after the message is 'delivered'. For a deeper discussion of the construction of masculine identities in relation to cars, see Balkmar (2012).

2.8 Sexual Harassment Versus Being Flattered

As mentioned previously, men's sexual harassment of women can originate from both hostile and benevolent motives. Becker and Wright (2011) highlight that one challenge of benevolent sexism is that on the surface, it generally promotes a positive message that women should be respected and cared for. One factor that complicates the issue of sexism is that it is not always perceived negatively. Some women may feel flattered by attention, even if it is unwanted and sexist (Fairchild, 2010; Graham et al., 2017; Sue, 2010). Women may therefore find themselves in a dilemma around feeling flattered by sexual attention while at the same time feeling overwhelmed, afraid, and uncomfortable. Women may not universally despise sexual harassment; understood more accurately, the same behaviours are not universally experienced as harassment in all contexts and sexual harassment by younger and attractive men is often viewed as less harassing (Fairchild, 2010). Grossman (2008) asserts that some women describe sexual attention from strangers as frightening, while others enjoy the attention. Some form of sexism might appear as a positive or well-meaning appraisal, such as positive comments on one's body or appearance.

There are also stories touching the grey areas between harassment and flattery. Some women also write about positive sexism where the woman feels valued:

> I do not mind strangers calling me a beautiful girl. There was a man who in passing said, 'You are such a beautiful girl,' smiled and walked on. It was nice to hear, but it was also clear there was nothing to it but that. (Everyday Sexism Project)

Another example:

> The 'positive' sexism, in the form of whistling and hissing meant as a 'you are so delicious' – I do not feel offended. I just smile at them. I think one can express oneself positively about others, also sexually, without it being offensive. (Everyday Sexism Project)

Looking at the relationship between attractiveness of the perpetrator and severity of the behaviour, we witness that a harassment incident is more often viewed as benign if the perpetrator is an attractive person (Cartar et al., 1996). There are reasons to believe that the context of the situation in which the harassing behaviour occurs can adjust the perception by the target (Fairchild, 2010: 197). Cartar et al. (1996) also suggest that if women feel flattered by comments from men, they may view themselves as objects of seduction and not as victims. In one situation a catcall or comment may be threatening, but in another, it may be complimentary (Fairchild, 2010). Attractiveness of the perpetrators encourages others to ascribe positive traits and behaviours to them (Golden et al., 2001). However, even though some women may feel flattered by unwanted sexual attention, it is crucial to emphasize that many women find the experience of unwanted sexual attention to be frightening, unpleasant and disruptive. Furthermore, women repeatedly describe themselves as 'frustrated, disgusted, and angered by the experience' (Fairchild, 2010: 192). They say that there is often a condescending and objectifying tone behind the sexualized attention, which reduces them to mere sexual objects (Reinicke, 2018).

2.9 Summary

It has been pointed out that the lack of definitional agreement is a problem because it can be difficult to clarify what sexual harassment is and what sexual harassment is not. Sexual harassment is a matter of individual perception. There are multitudes of potential individual and situational variables that can influence the perception of harassment (Fairchild 2010: 193). However, Sundaresh and Hemalatha (2013) point out that regardless of whether we look at cultural, organizational, or individual causes of sexual harassment, power along with gender relations appear to be significant explanatory factors. The vast majority of people perceive sexual harassment as troublesome, but women often perceive sexual harassment as being more severe than men do. Women's perception of sexual harassment is less ambivalent than men's (Ekore, 2012; Madan & Nalla, 2016). Dillon et al. (2015) state that regarding separate lifeworlds and perceptions of truth mean that women are more likely than men to regard quid pro quo (something for something) scenarios as a threat rather than a social interaction.

So what to do to move forward? The difference in how men and women define sexual harassment and the tendency that legal consequences do not typically follow from street harassment reinforces the need to engage men in combating sexual harassment. Thus, we have to approach the cultural belief systems which gave rise to sexual harassment in the first place.

Overall, the narratives from the Everyday Sexism Project say a lot about how men do not feel they have to decode whether women are interested in receiving their comments but just think that they are owed their attention. In the foreword to Laura Bates' book 'Everyday Sexism' (2014), Sarah Brown writes that the Everyday Sexism Project is not verdicts *on* men, but resources *for* men, because it allows men to understand the structure of patriarchy, which they can either replicate or resist in their own lives. In that regard, Tuerkheimer (1997) pointed out more than 20 years ago that the problem of sexual harassment is intricately linked to the fact that men have no understanding of what women go through. Since, due to their own life experiences, men cannot identify with the realities described by women, even men with progressive attitudes towards gender equality can have a tendency to claim that the phenomenon is not really all that widespread. One reason why many men cannot grasp the extent of sexual harassment is because it rarely occurs when women are accompanied by men. Consequently, Tuerkheimer (1997) says, it is crucial to communicate the gender-specific harm to those who do not share it. Reading the narratives from the Everyday Sexism Project homepage reveals just as much about men as it does about women. Therefore, the Everyday Sexism Project might be used as an example of an eye-opener and awareness-raising exercise for men by illustrating the profound contradictions between what popular discourses tell us about sexual harassment and how it is experienced by its victims. The next chapter discusses the arrival of the #MeToo movement in Denmark and demonstrates that this awareness-raising exercise for men did not happen easily.

References

Abbey, A. (1987). Misperceptions of friendly behavior as sexual interest: A survey of naturally occurring incidents. *Psychology of Women Quarterly, 11*(2), 173–194.
Balkmar, D. (2012). *On men and cars: An ethnographic study of gendered, risky and dangerous relations* (Doctoral dissertation, Linköping University Electronic Press).
Bargh, J. A., Raymond, P., Pryor, J. B., & Strack, F. (1995). Attractiveness of the underling: An automatic power→ sex association and its consequences for sexual harassment and aggression. *Journal of Personality and Social Psychology, 68*(5), 768–781.
Bates, L. (2014). *Everyday sexism*. Simon & Schuster.
Becker, J. C., & Wright, S. C. (2011). Yet another dark side of chivalry: Benevolent sexism undermines and hostile sexism motivates collective action for social change. *Journal of Personality and Social Psychology, 101*, 62–77.
Belknap, J., & Erez, E. (1997). Redefining sexual harassment: Confronting sexism in the 21st century. *Criminal Justice Studies, 10*(2), 143–160.
Berdahl, J. L., Magley, V. J., & Waldo, C. R. (1996). The sexual harassment of men? Exploring the concept with theory and data. *Psychology of Women Quarterly, 20*(4), 527–547.
Borchorst, A., & Augustin, L. R. (2017). *Seksuel chikane på arbejdspladsen: Faglige, politiske og retlige spor* [Sexual harassment in the workplace: Professional, political and legal lead]. Aalborg Universitetsforlag.
Bowman, C. G. (1993). Street harassment and the informal ghettoization of women. *Harvard Law Review, 106*(3), 517–580.
Buchanan, N., & Mahoney, A. (2021). Development of a scale measuring online sexual harassment: Examining gender differences and the emotional impact of sexual harassment victimization online. *Legal and Criminological Psychology*, 1–19.

Cartar, L., Hicks, M., & Slane, S. (1996). Women's reactions to hypothetical male sexual touch as a function of initiator attractiveness and level of coercion. *Sex Roles, 35*(11–12), 737–750.

Cleveland, J. N., & Kerst, M. E. (1993). Sexual harassment and perceptions of power: An under-articulated relationship. *Journal of Vocational Behavior, 42*(1), 49–67.

Cochran, C. C., Frazier, P. A., & Olson, A. M. (1997). Predictors of responses to unwanted sexual attention. *Psychology of Women Quarterly, 21*(2), 207–226.

Davis, D. E. (1994). The harm that has no name: Street harassment, embodiment, and African American women. *UCLA Women's Law Journal, 4*(2), 133–178.

Dillon, H. M., Adair, L. E., & Brase, G. L. (2015). A threatening exchange: Gender and life history strategy predict perceptions and reasoning about sexual harassment. *Personality and Individual Differences, 72*, 195–199.

Ekore, J. O. (2012). Gender differences in perception of sexual harassment among university students. *Gender and Behaviour, 10*(1), 4358–4369.

Fairchild, K. (2010). Context effects on women's perceptions of stranger harassment. *Sexuality & Culture, 14*(3), 191–216.

Fairchild, K., & Rudman, L. A. (2008). Everyday stranger harassment and women's objectification. *Social Justice Research, 21*(3), 338–357.

Farley, L. (1978). *Sexual shakedown: The sexual harassment of women on the job.* McGraw-Hill Companies.

Fileborn, B. (2017). Justice 2.0: Street harassment victims' use of social media and online activism as sites of informal justice. *British Journal of Criminology, 57*(6), 1482–1501.

Fileborn, B. (2019). Naming the unspeakable harm of street harassment: A survey-based examination of disclosure practices. *Violence Against Women, 25*(2), 223–248.

Fileborn, B. (2020). Embodied geographies: Navigating street harassment. In *Contentious cities* (pp. 37–48). Routledge.

Fileborn, B., & Vera-Gray, F. (2017). "I want to be able to walk the street without fear": Transforming justice for street harassment. *Feminist Legal Studies, 25*(2), 203–227.

Fitzgerald, L. F., Gelfand, M. F., & Drasgow, F. (1995). Measuring sexual harassment: Theoretical and psychometric advances. *Basic and Applied Social Psychology, 17*(4), 425–445.

FOA. (2016). *Seksuel chikane: Rapport udarbejdet af FOA Kampagne og Analyse* [Sexual harassment: Report prepared by FOA Campaign and Analysis]. FOA.

Friborg, M. K., Hansen, J. V., Aldrich, P. T., Folker, A. P., Kjær, S., Nielsen, M. B. D., & Madsen, I. E. (2017). Workplace sexual harassment and depressive symptoms: A cross-sectional multilevel analysis comparing harassment from clients or customers to harassment from other employees amongst 7603 Danish employees from 1041 organizations. *BMC Public Health, 17*(1), 1–12.

Gailey, J. A., & Prohaska, A. (2011). Power and gender negotiations during interviews with men about sex and sexually degrading practices. *Qualitative Research, 11*(4), 365–380.

Gardner, C. B. (1995). *Passing by: Gender and public harassment*. University of California Press.

Golden, J. H., Johnson, C. A., & Lopez, R. A. (2001). Sexual harassment in the workplace: Exploring the effects of attractiveness on perception of harassment. *Sex Roles, 45*(11), 767–784.

Gordon, M. T., Riger, S., Lebailey, R. K., & Heath, L. (1980). Crime, women and the quality of urban life. *Signs, 5*(3), 144–160.

Graham, K., Bernards, S., Abbey, A., Dumas, T. M., & Wells, S. (2017). When women do not want it: Young female bargoers' experiences with and responses to sexual harassment in social drinking contexts. *Violence Against Women, 23*(12), 1419–1441.

Grossman, A. J. (2008). Catcalling: Creepy or a compliment. *CNN*. Retrieved April 5, 2021.

Gruber, J. E. (1992). A typology of personal and environmental sexual harassment: Research and policy implications for the 1990s. *Sex Roles, 26*(11–12), 447–464.

Gunnarsson, L. (2018). "Excuse me, but are you raping me now?" Discourse and experience in (the grey areas of) sexual violence. *NORA-Nordic Journal of Feminist and Gender Research, 26*(1), 4–18.

Gutek, B. A., & Dunwoody, V. (1987). Understanding sex in the workplace. *Women and Work: An Annual Review, 2*, 249–269.

Hogh, A., Conway, P. M., Clausen, T., Madsen, I. E. H., & Burr, H. (2016). Unwanted sexual attention at work and long-term sickness absence: A follow-up register-based study. *BMC Public Health, 16*(1), 1–10.

Ilies, R., Hauserman, N., Schwochau, S., & Stibal, J. (2003). Reported incidence rates of work-related sexual harassment in the United States: Using meta-analysis to explain reported rate disparities. *Personnel Psychology, 56*(3), 607–631.

Kearl, H. (2010). *Stop street harassment: Making public places safe and welcoming for women.* ABC-CLIO.

Kime, P. (2014). *Incidents of rape in military much higher than previously reported*. Military Times.

Larkin, J. (1997). Sexual terrorism on the street: The moulding of young women into subordination. In A. M. Thomas & C. Kitzinger (Eds.), *Sexual harassment: Contemporary feminist perspectives* (pp. 115–130). Open University Press.

Lee, K., Gizzarone, M., & Ashton, M. C. (2003). Personality and the likelihood to sexually harass. *Sex Roles, 49*(1–2), 59–69.

Logan, L. S. (2015). Street harassment: Current and promising avenues for researchers and activists. *Sociology Compass, 9*(3), 196–211.

Lucero, M. A., Allen, R. E., & Middleton, K. L. (2006). Sexual harassers: Behaviors, motives, and change over time. *Sex Roles, 55*(5–6), 331–343.

MacKinnon, C. A. (1979). *Sexual harassment of working women: A case of sex discrimination*. Yale Fastback Series No. 19. Yale University Press.

Madan, M., & Nalla, M. K. (2016). Sexual harassment in public spaces: Examining gender differences in perceived seriousness and victimization. *International Criminal Justice Review, 26*(2), 80–97.

McCann, D. (2005). *Sexual harassment at work: National and international responses*. Conditions of Work and Employment Series No. 2. International Labour Organization.

McDonald, P. (2012). Workplace sexual harassment 30 years on: A review of the literature. *International Journal of Management Reviews, 14*(1), 1–17.

O'Donohue, W., Downs, K., & Yeater, E. A. (1998). Sexual harassment: A review of the literature. *Aggression and Violent Behavior, 3*(2), 111–128.

O'Hare, E. A., & O'Donohue, W. (1998). Sexual harassment: Identifying risk factors. *Archives of Sexual Behavior, 27*(6), 561–580.

Phipps, A., Ringrose, J., Renold, E., & Jackson, C. (2018). Rape culture, lad culture and everyday sexism: Researching, conceptualizing and politicizing new mediations of gender and sexual violence. *Journal of Gender Studies, 27*(1), 1–8.

Pina, A., & Gannon, T. A. (2012). An overview of the literature on antecedents, perceptions and behavioural consequences of sexual harassment. *Journal of Sexual Aggression, 18*(2), 209–232.

Pina, A., Gannon, T. A., & Saunders, B. (2009). An overview of the literature on sexual harassment: Perpetrator, theory, and treatment issues. *Aggression and Violent Behavior, 14*(2), 126–138.

Pryor, J. B., & Fitzgerald, L. F. (2003). Sexual harassment research in the US. In H. Einarsen, H. Hoel, D. Zapf, & C. L. Cooper (Eds.), *Bullying and emotional abuse in the workplace* (pp. 79–100). Taylor and Francis.

Pryor, J. B., Giedd, J. L., & Williams, K. B. (1995). A social psychological model for predicting sexual harassment. *Journal of Social Issues, 51*(1), 69–84.

Quinn, B. A. (2002). Sexual harassment and masculinity: The power and meaning of "girl watching." *Gender & Society, 16*(3), 386–402.

Reinicke, K. (2018). *Mænd som krænker kvinder—refleksioner i kølvandet på #Metoo* [Men who violate women—Reflections in the wake of #MeToo]. Samfundslitteratur.

Smith, M. D. (1988). Women's fear of violent crime: An exploratory test of a feminist hypothesis. *Journal of Family Violence, 3*(1), 29–38.

Spitzberg, B. H. (1999). An analysis of empirical estimates of sexual aggression victimization and perpetration. *Violence and Victims, 14*(3), 241–260.

Stanko, E. A. (1995). Women, crime, and fear. *The Annals of the American Academy of Political and Social Science, 539*(1), 46–58.

Sue, D. W. (2010). *Microaggressions in everyday life: Race, gender, and sexual orientation*. Wiley.

Sundaresh, N., & Hemalatha, K. (2013). Theoretical orientation to sexual harassment at work place. *Journal of Business Management and Social Sciences Research, 2*(4), 74–81.

Tangri, S. S., Burt, M. R., & Johnson, L. B. (1982). Sexual harassment at work: Three explanatory models. *Journal of Social Issues, 38*(4), 33–54.

Thomas, A. M., & Kitzinger, C. (1997). *Sexual harassment: Contemporary feminist perspectives*. Open University Press.

Thompson, D. M. (1994). The woman in the street: Reclaiming the public space from sexual harassment. *Yale Journal of Law & Feminism, 6*, 313.

Tinkler, J. E. (2008). "People are too quick to take offense": The effects of legal information and beliefs on definitions of sexual harassment. *Law & Social Inquiry, 33*(2), 417–445.

Tuerkheimer, D. (1997). Street harassment as sexual subordination: The phenomenology of gender-specific harm. *Wisconsin Women's Law Journal, 12*, 167–206.

UN Women UK. (2021). *YouGov, Sexual harassment report*.

Vera-Gray, F. (2016). Men's stranger intrusions: Rethinking street harassment. *Women's Studies International Forum, 58*, 9–17.

Vera-Gray, F. (2018). *The right amount of panic: How women trade freedom for safety*. Policy Press.

Vera-Gray, F., & Fileborn, B. (2018). Recognition and the harms of "Cheer Up." *The Philosophical Journal of Conflict and Violence, 2*(1), 78–95.

Vogt, D. S., Pless, A. P., King, L. A., & King, D. W. (2005). Deployment stressors, gender, and mental health outcomes among Gulf war I veterans. *Journal of Traumatic Stress, 18*(2), 115–127.

Warr, M. (1984). Fear of victimization: Why are women and the elderly more afraid? *Social Science Quarterly, 65*(3), 681–702.

Williams, J. H., Fitzgerald, L. F., & Drasgow, F. (1999). The effects of organizational practices on sexual harassment and individual outcomes in the military. *Military Psychology, 11*, 303–328.

Willness, C. R., Steel, P., & Lee, K. (2007). A meta-analysis of the antecedents and consequences of workplace sexual harassment. *Personnel Psychology, 60*, 127–162.

3

The Danish #MeToo Context

To better understand the societal and cultural setting in which the interviewed men are situated, this chapter gives a brief outline of the major events and reactions that the #MeToo movement has set in motion in Denmark. It gives an indication of where the movement has taken us and how it has influenced political agendas and conversations. It discusses whether dominant notions of masculinity have been challenged in the Danish #MeToo debate. Further, it looks at what kind of attention has been given within the last 20–30 years to the issue of men and masculinities seen from an institutional perspective.

3.1 The Nordic Countries

According to the World Economic Forum's annual Global Gender Gap Report, all of the Nordic countries—Denmark, Finland, Iceland, Norway and Sweden—are in the Western European top ten as regards gender equality (Män, 2018). The Nordic countries appear relatively homogeneous in terms of welfare models (Esping-Andersen, 1990).

© The Author(s), under exclusive license to Springer Nature Switzerland AG 2022
K. Reinicke, *Men After #MeToo*,
https://doi.org/10.1007/978-3-030-96911-0_3

From shared parental leave to quotas of representation in the boardroom, the Nordic countries have been at the forefront of public policies designed to bring about gender equality. Regarding issues of gender equality, Scandinavia is often perceived as a homogeneous area, and the so-called Scandinavian model of gender-equal welfare states is an established concept in international scholarship. Statistics regarding the employment, education and representation of women and men respectively show remarkable similarities between the Nordic countries (Dahlerup, 2011).

Despite the similarities in official policy and overlapping developments in the area of policy and political discourse, public debates about gender equality within the countries are very different. Sweden, for example, is known for its significant development of state feminism and qualified consensus of gender equality (Holmgren & Hearn, 2009). A survey among Danish MPs showed that there was a tendency to consider gender equality to be a 'closed case'. This may be due partly to the widespread perception that gender equality has already been achieved (Dahlerup, 2018). Even though there is widespread support for the principle of gender equality in Denmark, there are fundamental disagreements concerning the policy instruments that are seen as acceptable for reaching the goal of gender equality. Using radical policy instruments such as a ban on the buying of sex, earmarking leave for fathers and passing laws on gender quotas for representation on company boards are not widely seen as legitimate actions. In spite of such disagreements, Denmark is often described as the libertarian member of the Nordic family because Denmark has been a forerunner in both the Nordic area and globally in advancing libertarian agendas such as the legalization of same-sex marriages and single women's right to insemination (Dahlerup, 2018). Denmark was also the first country in the world to lift the ban on pornography, and Denmark has for many years been widely considered a sexually liberal country.

3.2   Politics of Masculinities in Denmark

Little attention has been given by research communities and government to the issue of men and masculinity in Denmark. The discussion on men and masculinity has to a large extent been conducted in a non-institutional context. For example, in the 1980s Norway and Sweden had already set up government committees on men and masculinity with the participation of highly influential (male) politicians, whereas Denmark has not had the same tradition of debate in political life (Balkmar et al., 2009). After 30 years of gender equality debate in Denmark, little has been written by men for men, and Danish men have been relatively silent during the process of changes in gender relations, though in the 1970s Denmark actually was the leading country in Scandinavia with regard to critical books about masculinity (e.g., Clausen et al., 1974; Holm, 1975).

However, there have been some attempts to institutionalize the issue of men and gender equality. In 1994 the expert group The Men's Idea Group was set up at the initiative of the Danish Equal Status Council. This group consisted of scholars and representatives of social partners and NGOs. The purpose of the group was to supply the gender equality debate with male perspectives, that is, fatherhood, violence against women, men and work life, and men's relationship to family life. But a constructive cooperation was never established and after disagreements with the Danish Equal Status Council, the group disbanded in 1995. Christensen and Elm Larsen (2007) emphasize that one of the problems with the Danish equality discourse at that time was that it was largely based on the understanding that progress for one gender could only occur at the expense of the other.

In 2000, the strategy of mainstreaming was adopted as a guiding principle in relation to gender equality work in Denmark. Gender mainstreaming means incorporating a gender perspective in all policy areas. As such, within the last 15 years there has been more public debate on the status, roles, and activities of men, even though Danish society as a whole does not have a good record of involving men in gender equality work. The conditions of life for men have come under the spotlight, not only with respect to men's health and men as fathers but also when it comes to more controversial dimensions such as men's violence and men's mental health problems. In 2000, some young men gained widespread media attention when they started to write about the problems and challenges of being a man in contemporary Danish society from a gender perspective in a personal and confessional way. It became especially clear in the book *Pikstormerne* (The Prick Invaders) where the predominant objective of the male writers was to move beyond the emotional limitations of the traditional male role (Sørensen, 2000). They wanted a democratization of the dominating forms of masculinity and challenged the stereotypical male images reproduced through advertising and the commercial media. In 2006, various Danish male scholars wrote a counterpart to the book *Kvinde kend din krop* (literally, 'Woman, know your body', the Danish version of *Our Bodies, Ourselves*), namely the book *Kend din krop, mand* (literally, 'Know your body, man').

There are many popular interpretations of men's nature in Denmark. Gender is often the subject of jokes; moreover, it is often pointed out that there are other and more important factors relating to inequality than gender that society first and foremost should deal with. The allegation that men are the 'oppressed gender' is also currently seen in the Danish gender equality debate. In 2013, a male gender scholar received widespread media attention when he wrote a book which aggressively opposed the idea of gender quotas (Bonde, 2013).

Another reason why it is so hard to have a serious debate about masculinity in Denmark is the peculiar 'laddish culture' that exists in Denmark (Reinicke, 2004). Laddish culture is hard to oppose because the sexist messages are communicated in an often funny and charming way, leaving the audience with a dilemma about what to think. In relation to this, Bom and Bjerke (2002) define a particular group of men as 'angry white men'. This group of men is by no means the 'male losers' who are hit hard by life and therefore want 'revenge' on women. On the contrary, the angry white men are successful, articulate and use laddism to distance themselves from the gender equality project in a sophisticated way, claiming that too many men have subjugated their masculinity in order to fulfil the needs of women. The lad culture often appeals to the ordinary man and may be the cause of some of the inertia and resistance that characterizes the gender debate in Denmark. Likewise, Norwegian gender scholar Jørgen Lorentzen (2000) has stated that nowhere has he seen populist self-help therapists get so much attention as in the Danish media and that the debate on men and masculinity in Denmark has been silenced before it actually began.

If we look in organizational terms at how men in Denmark have responded to some of the challenges that changing gender relations have brought, men's strategic interests in paternity cases and divorce cases have been the area where they have tried to organize themselves systematically. The most influential group is Foreningen Far (The Fathers' Association), which has been in existence for 30 years and is a national membership organization which maintains that children have a right to both parents' care and protection, even when parents do not live together. The Fathers' Association points out that there still exists a strong notion of the mother as the primary caregiver and as being the most competent parent. They also say that numerous men have felt powerless and unfairly treated by public institutions and that men have been victims of a systematic denigration of them as caregivers with consequent loss of parenthood (Kronborg et al., 2011).

In the academic world, the Network for Research on Men and Masculinities (NeMM), formed in 2002, is a research network that brings together and supports scholars engaged in research about men and masculinities. Men's Health Society, Denmark, a multidisciplinary organization dedicated to the field of men's health, has since 2003 arranged a yearly 'men's health week' focusing on different aspects of men's lives.

In the last 10–15 years, policymakers in Denmark have also started to provide economic support for those areas that have to do specifically with men's gender issues. This includes the establishment of shelters for men exposed to violence, treatment programmes for perpetrators and men's access rights to their children. These rights have partly been strengthened by the Parental Responsibility Act of 2007. In the past few years, various think tanks for men (focusing on particular boys' and men's gender issues such as health, labour, education, care, violence and crime) have also been established.

3.3 The First #MeToo Wave: 2017–2018

In Denmark the #MeToo movement did not take off the way it did in, for example, the USA and Sweden. The messages of the #MeToo movement were received very cautiously in Denmark, challenging only to a small extent established notions of the rights of men to indulge in sexual harassment. #MeToo did not get massive attention from politicians and decision makers and was not acknowledged by leading political parties. Media coverage in Denmark did not rely on a framework of understanding sexual violence as a structural rather than a personal problem—and thus as something to be dealt with by the state at policy level. This meant that in 2017–2018, sexual harassment was discussed largely as a minor irritant and a laddish activity, and was not interpreted from a perspective of abuse of power. In addition, there was little focus on the importance of masculinity for understanding sexual harassment (Män, 2018).

The impact of #MeToo was also different in the individual Nordic countries. A comparative analysis of how Danish and Swedish newspapers framed the debate on sexism and gender inequality incited by the hashtag showed that the coverage of #MeToo was much more extensive in Sweden than in Denmark. During the first three months, four leading national Swedish newspapers published 3332 articles on #MeToo, whereas four leading national Danish newspapers published only 594 (Askanius & Hartley, 2019). Furthermore, the analysis demonstrated that the coverage predominantly positioned #MeToo within an individual action frame portraying sexual assault as a personal rather than societal problem in both countries. Nevertheless, the individualizing and delegitimizing action frame focused on a critique of #MeToo was more common in the Danish coverage, and #MeToo was more often framed as an unimportant or even dangerous form of political correctness.

Where men in Sweden supported the organizations that worked with men and gender equality, the debate in Denmark was characterized by efforts to minimize the importance of #MeToo. The debate was not trying to see connections between big and small offences, but highlighted instead the difference between them and the importance of distinguishing between what was innocent and what was serious. Nevertheless, the Danish NGO DareGender—an organization which encourages boys and men to promote gender equality—arranged some debating sessions where politicians were invited to participate under the heading of 'Men Talk', but in general there were very few events and organizational initiatives that focused on the role of men in the debate about #MeToo. It was characteristic of the #MeToo debate in Denmark that very few politicians chose to participate. It is also noteworthy that—in contrast to Sweden—the theme of men's responsibility and commitment was hardly raised by male writers in the press (Askanius & Hartley, 2019).

Also in contrast to Sweden, there were no repeated calls in Denmark for men to take responsibility, and the debate did not direct attention towards how men needed to get involved (Askanius & Hartley, 2019). Therefore, #MeToo in Denmark did not always emerge as a reasonable, just and positive force, and discourse critical of the movement was strong in Denmark (Nilsson & Lundgren, 2020). Danish newspapers often questioned the legitimacy of the movement, partly by framing #MeToo as an unimportant campaign without any effect, or by portraying #MeToo as unfair to men and a witch-hunt against men. The responses revealed anxiety and distress about what #MeToo would bring forth. There was no strong recognition of and opposition to men's privileges.

Social movements are often defined as forms of collective action aimed at bringing about broader social changes and political objectives outside or in collaboration with established channels for political organization. If one looks at the organization of the #MeToo movement, it becomes clear that—unlike the feminist movement of the 1970s—no meetings or demonstrations were held in the streets. A single exception to this in Denmark is represented by the anti-rape group Aldrig Din Skyld (Never Your Fault), which has succeeded in carrying the #MeToo movement's social media messages into the real world by arranging demonstrations against sexual harassment.

There is much stigma in Denmark attached to being a declared feminist or to openly assuming a feminist standpoint as a man (Dahlerup, 2018). It is therefore no surprise that a feature of the debate in Denmark in 2017 was that famous men reacted aggressively to and ignored the seriousness of the #MeToo reports. They launched a counter-offensive and continued to describe sexual harassment as an innocent form of laddish activity. The best-known instance was probably when the film producer Peter Aalbæk Jensen, who publicly called himself 'The Pig', was accused of having committed sexual harassment on the premises of the film company Zentropa by, for example, placing a microphone under the skirt of a young female intern and saying the now famous words: 'Hear the pussy talk'. The movie director Ole Bornedal also managed—despite the #MeToo coverage in the media with stories of abuse and rape—to downplay and ridicule reports of violation by pointing out that 'it is difficult not to laugh when women feel traumatized 25 years after they were given a smack in the bum'. Overall, there was a consensus that people must not feel violated too easily.

A study of how #MeToo was received in the Nordic countries, with a specific focus on the reactions and responses from men, concluded about Denmark:

> 'Don't accuse men!' This was one of the common, negative responses to #MeToo in Denmark. The public debate was very vivid, though, and everyone had an opinion. The consciousness about sexual harassment increased significantly, but there wasn't a collective movement that engaged a lot of people. There was some progress in the discussion on the need to challenge the power balance in society, but not much was seen of the critical discussion on destructive masculinity norms, that took place in other parts of the region. (Män, 2018)

In Denmark, the media coverage was much less extensive (the number of Danish articles was less than a fifth of the number of Swedish articles) and public debate around #MeToo took a rather different turn. In its initial phases during October 2017, the movement was covered extensively in most news media, but political responses and voices were absent from the coverage, and a backlash occurred, as voices that criticized or opposed the movement started to gain a foothold and dominate the debate. In Denmark, there were fewer organized calls for action or pushes to change legislation and only a few street demonstrations, which were all poorly attended.

In another study of the Danish media's coverage of #MeToo on Facebook by nine major Danish news media, Reestorff states that the Danish media's coverage of #MeToo news in 2017–2018 was predominantly negative (Reestorff, 2019). Seven out of nine news outlets had more than twice as many negative as positive updates about #MeToo. This made the proponents of #MeToo an easy target for hate comments and made it harder to stand up and participate in the debate. Reestorff goes on to say that when reading the news on social media in Denmark, it is not always clear that #MeToo demonstrates that abuse is a widespread problem. Reestorff concludes that only a few Danish men were mentioned by name, and that #MeToo was covered as Hollywood and gossip journalism and as an opinion piece (Reestorff, 2019). In the negative comments, words and phrases were frequently repeated. #MeToo was accused of being a 'pathetic culture of abuse', a 'people's court', a 'witch-hunt' and an extreme 'frenzy of bloodlust'. Women who wrote #MeToo were accused of wanting 'fame' and making 'undocumented allegations'. In addition, a distinction was often made between 'real victims' and those who wrote #MeToo.

In general, it can be said of the #MeToo debate in Denmark in 2017–2018 that much of the criticism levelled at #MeToo around the world—notably regarding scapegoating and personal witch-hunts—was not so prominent. The Danish debate was cautious during the first wave and it did not have consequences for individual men's careers. To put it a little crudely, one could argue that much of what was described as harassment and abuse in other countries tended to be written off as free-spiritedness and flirting in Denmark. This may be because there is a strong tendency in Denmark to depict our society as a paragon of equality, where we do not recognize a blind spot regarding power and abuse. One could therefore ask if people are willing to sacrifice their free-spiritedness in order to eradicate abuse and whether—in spite of #MeToo's huge consequences elsewhere—it has failed to make an impact in Denmark. Peter Aalbæk Jensen, for example, was able in 2017 to appear with impunity on the front page of the national newspaper, *Politiken*, claiming that he was not familiar with the new ethical guidelines for his own workplace and could not be bothered to acquaint himself with them.

There has been a very defensive reaction to #MeToo in Denmark, which may be due to the fact that society was very quick to redirect the discussion to the issue of men's legal rights, instead of focusing on the principles and underlying causes of why some people feel they have the right to harass others. Nonetheless, a professor of sexology, Christian Graugaard, pointed out in an interview in 2017 with the Danish national newspaper, *Information*, that for the first time in decades, we are witnessing a debate about gender which is not just about equal pay and parental leave but also about sex, bodies and power. On #MeToo itself, Graugaard had this to say:

> It is exciting, even though the Danish part of the campaign has pretty much fizzled out, even while heads roll in our neighbouring countries. Is that because the problem really is less marked here, because we really are so thoroughly inoculated with free-spiritedness, a sense of humour and a healthy disrespect for authority? Or is it a sign of a peculiarly Danish blind spot for society's gendered power structures? My guess is that both mechanisms are at play. (Information, 2017)

The impact of the first wave of #MeToo in Denmark was not impressive. Unlike in Sweden, there were no immediate changes in laws (shortly after MeToo in 2017, Sweden passed a new sexual assault law in June 2018). Nevertheless, the #MeToo movement evolved from individual stories into collective action. The Danish film and theatre industry has been among those hardest hit by accounts of sexual harassment. As a result, in 2017 a closed group was set up on Facebook where several hundred women from the Danish theatre and film world secretly shared their testimonies of sexual harassment in the industry. In addition, in December 2017, actors at a theatre in Copenhagen read aloud 100 anonymous postings. It was the first time that so many Danish women from the same industry had joined forces to share their testimonies about sexual harassment.

In connection with harassment in the film and theatre industry, the people behind the Facebook group #stopthesilence claimed that a clear pattern had emerged, since all the abuse had been committed by men who had higher positions in the professional hierarchy than the women involved. Most incidents of harassment were carried out by theatre bosses and theatre and film directors, followed by male actor colleagues, schoolteachers, technicians, and a 'leader' category covering producers, school principals, production managers, photographers, and so forth.

In an attempt to improve the work environment and to stop abuse and harassment, an anonymous psychological consultancy unit was set up in 2018 for the film and theatre industry. It offers psychological support both to those who have already been involved in a harassment situation, and also to the harassers themselves, as well as to anyone who—because of the current debate—is unsure whether they may have acted inappropriately towards someone. The same industry has also taken the initiative to develop some ethical guidelines—a *code of conduct*—and instruments that the film and theatre industry can use to work with the existing culture and prevent harassment from happening.

In a Danish 'Time's Up' manifesto in January 2018, over 1000 actors, directors, authors and other employees in Danish theatre and film committed to combating sexual harassment, abuse and the culture of silence in the industry, under the motto: 'It's our industry. Our workplaces. Our shared responsibility.' The signatories called for a new culture of zero tolerance towards sexism, sexual harassment and sexual assault in the Danish film and theatre industry. They emphasized that they wanted to create a culture in which the victims were not shamed but where instead the harassers were held to account in order to put an end to the culture of silence. Another project, called 'No Confidentiality', was started by a group of female doctors and students who aimed to collect and document experiences of sexism and sexual harassment among doctors, medical students and in the health service in general.

Of course, these different approaches to the gender equality debate in Denmark and Sweden do not mean that there has been no political interest in the topic of sexual harassment in Denmark. A hearing was held on sexual harassment in the workplace, involving major employers' associations and labour unions, with the aim of exchanging positive experiences of preventing and tackling sexual harassment, as well as discussing new initiatives. The employment minister and Minister for Gender Equality sent an open letter urging leaders, business and public institutions in Denmark to take sexual harassment seriously, to encourage a proper tone and to break the taboo in the wake of the #MeToo revelations. The Minister for Gender Equality and the employment minister declared that they would break down the taboos surrounding sexual harassment in the workplace, even though this is clearly only one of the places where harassment occurs.

3.4 The Second #MeToo Wave: 2020

Dominant notions of masculinity were not challenged during the first wave of #MeToo. In Denmark, a national conversation about the male causes of sexual harassment only began seriously in August 2020, when the famous TV host Sofie Linde shared her own personal story of sexual harassment. Linde's discussion of sexism and gender equality became the starting point for the second wave of #MeToo in Denmark. Two weeks after the TV host had confessed what she had experienced when she was younger and began work in the media industry, the front page of *Politiken* carried a statement signed by 701 media women in support of Sofie Linde and speaking out against a sexist culture in the media industry. After that, petitions from women in all professional spheres, surveys and thousands of signatures from many other industries confirmed the magnitude of the problem. Media coverage now helped many more people become aware of the prevalence of sexual harassment. The momentum that arose was strengthened when the #MeToo movement hit the political world and leading politicians began to resign. Suddenly, there was a strong sense that no man was safe.

As an indicator of the impact of #MeToo in 2020 and of how much #MeToo in 2020 became a national conversation, it is worth mentioning that between 10 September and 10 December 2020, there were 6131 articles in the Danish media containing the word 'sexism'. In the same period in 2019, the corresponding number of articles was 165 (Politiken, 2020).

Sofie Linde's revelations heralded a change from a focus on the individual incident to more overall cultural and systemic discussions about the causes of sexual harassment. Men in positions of power in private companies promised that they would now support a much-needed cultural change.

Major #MeToo Events 2020–2021
In September 2020, Foreign Minister Jeppe Kofod, of the Social Democratic Party, goes on national TV after a week of controversy about him and apologizes for a case from 2008, when he had sex with a then 15-year-old girl at a seminar in the youth department of the Social Democratic Party.

Later in September 2020, a total of 322 current and former politicians and politically active women sign a petition in which they describe widespread sexism in Danish politics. *Politiken* prints all the women's names on the front page. Among them, seventy-nine choose to share their experiences of sexism and abuse in the political parties anonymously. This gives a decisive push to the growing debate about violations and sexism in Danish politics.

In October 2020, the Danish Social Liberals' political leader, Morten Østergaard, resigns. It happens after a party colleague reveals that Morten Østergaard had sexually harassed her ten years earlier. This causes several other victims to come forward with similar accounts of Østergaard's behaviour.

Also in October 2020, a joint letter signed by 689 researchers appears in *Politiken* stating that they have experienced or witnessed abuse and violations at universities and vocational colleges.

Later in October 2020, Copenhagen's social democratic Lord Mayor, Frank Jensen, resigns after accusations of violations by younger party colleagues. He has previously been criticized for his behaviour towards women at festive gatherings. However, new information in *Jyllands-Posten* (another major Danish newspaper) makes him leave the post with immediate effect.

A few days after the resignation of Copenhagen's Lord Mayor, the first episode of the documentary "Partiernes skjulte overgreb" ("The parties' hidden abuses") is shown on national television. In it, young women from various youth political parties report sexism, sexual assault and threats as an ingrained part of the culture.

At the beginning of 2021, surveys conducted within the governing party and one of the government-supporting parties revealed that a considerable number of women had experienced 'unwanted sexual attention' within the last two to five years.

> At the end of 2021, the prominent politician Naser Khader is expelled from the Konservative party following a sexual misconduct investigation.

Despite these dramatic events and a new and more gender-critical approach to sexual harassment, opposition to #MeToo remains strong in Denmark. As mentioned earlier, a general criticism of #MeToo is that it risks ending up as a people's court and that principles of the central rule of law risk being suspended. The discourse of criticism towards #MeToo was actualized in 2020 when a well-known and popular TV host was fired from his job due to allegations that he had subjected two former journalist trainees to sexual harassment 18 and 20 years ago, respectively. The TV station claimed that he had behaved in an abusive manner to a degree that is irreconcilable with the public image of the TV station. The TV host claimed in response that he was convicted in a parallel legal society, where those who investigate and interrogate choose the rules and judge for themselves. The TV host refused to sign a secrecy clause and won the sympathy of many by appearing on a popular TV show, where he declared his innocence in the case that had led to his dismissal. This event reinforced the argument that the #MeToo debate had gone too far. Further, it led to a fierce subsequent debate in established and social media about what possibilities of defending themselves the accused have in #MeToo cases. Following this, a Facebook group was formed in support of the dismissed TV host. It submitted a citizens' proposal to Parliament in which it was pointed out that the focus should be on providing more justice and legal certainty in the process that employers initiate in #MeToo cases.

3.5 The Debate About the Sexual Assault Law

When Denmark signed the Istanbul Convention—which aims to prevent and combat various forms of violence against women—in 2013, an obligation followed to introduce a consent-based definition of rape.

Nevertheless, it was not until December 2020 that Denmark strengthened its rape laws by criminalizing sex without explicit consent. The new law passed by Parliament widened the circumstances that could constitute rape—under the old legislation, prosecutors had to show the rapist had used violence or attacked someone who was unable to resist.

For several years, before the government passed this law, there had been heated discussion in the Danish Parliament about whether society should implement a law criminalizing sex without explicit consent. The ongoing discussion has focused on men's responsibility and awareness of consent. The climate of debate has been characterized by widespread opposition to the change in the definition of rape to non-consent based. The effort was ridiculed in a number of satirical newspaper articles and cartoons. Opposition to and lack of insight into the long-term potential for cultural change–including that the legislation will be able to create a more democratized culture of sexuality—have dominated the debate on consent legislation.

In the Amnesty International report "Give us Respect and Justice" (2019) about legal practice and barriers to justice regarding legal cases of rape in Denmark, it is mentioned that rape survivors often find the reporting process and its aftermath extremely traumatizing, particularly when faced with inappropriate questions and inadequate communication. Many rape survivors are met with dismissive attitudes, victim blaming, and prejudice influenced by gender stereotypes and rape myths. This echoes similar findings from jurisdictions around the world (see, e.g., Cossins, 2019, 2020; Larcombe et al., 2016; Smith, 2018).

It is not easy to specify when sexual acts should be considered criminal acts—but there is no doubt that the legal rights of perpetrators have historically been weighted more heavily than the legal rights of the violated party and that the victim generally has poor legal standing in Denmark. The legal challenge in rape cases has often concerned the dilemma between what a woman perceives as rape and what the law perceives as rape. Situations have often been assessed and verdicts based on the man's interpretation of the woman's behaviour and response. Old-fashioned legislation, rape myths and gender stereotypes have gone hand in hand and created a gulf between what women experience and the interventions that society can offer. The burden of proof around the issue of consent has been on the victim (Balkmar et al., 2009). One consequence of this has been that less than 2 per cent of all rape cases result in convictions. Therefore, without a doubt many women have felt angry and violated when the police have refused to pursue their cases and prosecute.

The introduction of consent-based legislation has been framed as a question of whether the legislation is weakening the legal rights of all men or is tailored to the small minority of men who cannot seem to respect some reasonably clear signals. The debate about consent is also very much a question about whether men can 'accidentally' rape someone. Opponents of consent-based legislation have expressed concern because both genders often expect the man to be the one taking the initiative for sex and because the accused should have the benefit of the doubt. On the other hand, those who support the proposed law have argued that it will make it easier for many women to prove their case in court, without innocent men being convicted. They emphasize that a consent provision will send a strong message, particularly to younger people, and that it can therefore promote a more democratic culture of sexuality.

The introduction of a rape provision based on consent is not only intended to have an impact on how rape cases are assessed and handled by the police, prosecutors and courts. It is also intended to contribute towards a general change of attitude in society, as it increases the focus on being respectful of other people's boundaries and freedoms, and the right to decide over one's own body. A consent-based rape law balances the considerations of protecting rape victims and the legal rights of those who are accused of rape, as a prosecutor will still need to prove the case.

Whether consent was given for intercourse must be evaluated based on whether the person engaged in intercourse of their own free will. The critical factor is whether the person had the opportunity to freely decide whether they wanted to engage in intercourse. Actions that could be viewed as consenting to intercourse could include, for example, kissing, touching, making sounds of pleasure or relevant movements such as turning towards the other person, helping to take one's underwear off, actively engaging in intercourse, etc.

The law clearly states that it is the behaviour of the people involved in the direct context and time of the intercourse that is the critical factor when evaluating whether there was consent. Flirting behaviour, kisses earlier in the evening or the fact that someone willingly went home with someone cannot by themselves be regarded as consenting to intercourse.

The former law's focus on resistance and violence rather than on consent has had an impact not only on the reporting of rape but also on social awareness of sexual violence, both of which are key aspects of overcoming impunity for these crimes and preventing them from happening. Hence, Amnesty International (2019) has emphasized that there are reasons to believe that changing the legal definition of rape to one based on sexual autonomy and consent has significant potential to bring about broad, systemic societal change and prevent rape in the long term, especially if accompanied by adequate sexuality education and awareness-raising from a young age.

An opinion poll conducted at the end of 2017 for the Danish television channel TV2 showed that Danes are sceptical as to whether Denmark should follow Sweden's example and introduce a sexual consent clause into Danish criminal law. In the poll, 28 per cent of respondents replied 'yes' to a new law that would penalize sex without explicit consent as rape, while 54 per cent said 'no', with 18 per cent of the 1100 respondents replying 'don't know'. There was no political support for the initiative from Denmark's large political parties.

Consent is a tool that can help shift the focus away from the victim and onto the perpetrator by asking the perpetrator to justify the sexual act. Nevertheless, based on how similar provisions in other jurisdictions have been applied, for example in the UK, Australia, and New Zealand (Larcombe et al., 2016), in practice it often means the victims have to demonstrate that they had not consented.

When the bill to change the rape clause was first discussed in the Danish Parliament in 2017, there was very little understanding of the importance of using the new legislation to also send a signal. When the bill was debated again in 2018, there was a noticeable change in the arguments put forward even by its opponents. There was an open attitude towards gaining experience from other countries' legislation in the area. Further, there was a consensus that the legislation should reflect the sexual norms of society.

3.6 Summary

Denmark was without a doubt the Nordic country where there was the greatest opposition to the #MeToo movement, and overall the reception of #MeToo in Denmark must be said to have been highly defensive. The will to change society was not huge in 2017–2018, when the first wave reached Denmark. After the first wave, it seemed obvious to think that #MeToo had already peaked and died out in Denmark and that the movement was just a fleeting, superficial phenomenon which did not create any lasting and irreversible change. Metaphorically speaking, it was like a window that had been opened a little and which had now been closed again tightly. It was in 2020 that the #MeToo wave finally made an impact in Denmark and came to signify the tipping point, particularly in relation to Danish workplaces. The movement started in the media and entertainment industries and quickly spread to other sectors. Looking at some of the trends and challenges in Denmark, it seems clear that after the second wave of #MeToo in 2020 it makes sense to talk about—pre- and a post-#MeToo era. The second wave of #MeToo successfully challenged the impunity of perpetrators. The most beloved people on TV, famous actors or directors, big corporate bosses and important board members in organizations were no longer protected by their status and power. We have not yet seen the long-term consequences of the #MeToo revolution, but for a while at least, the barriers that had made perpetrators untouchable seem to have crumbled away.

During the first wave, it became noticeable that many blind spots regarding dimensions of power and violation did not seem to be well understood (Reinicke, 2018). The debate in Denmark was not so much about those who had been subjected to sexual harassment, but more significantly about reactions in favour of or against the movement. The debate also quickly turned to the issue of men's legal security and did not focus on the underlying reasons why someone could feel entitled to offend against other people. It was also characteristic of the debate in Denmark that it quickly escalated into polemics about the creation of an inappropriate culture of violation.

The reactions to and consequences of the #MeToo revelations have been far more severe in Sweden than in Denmark. This may be because culturally, while political correctness is almost considered an insult in Denmark, in Sweden it is practically a virtue (Ledstrup, 2012). While, for example, in Denmark it is customary to use campaigns and dialogue in attempts to encourage more men to take paternity leave and desist from buying sex, in Sweden these issues are usually tackled through legislation.

Violence and threats of violence were central in the understanding of previous rape legislation. Literally speaking, the earlier Danish rape clause entailed a premise that a person's body was in principle available unless 'no' was clearly given voice and there was resistance. This has meant that men were often acquitted of rape if the woman had not resisted energetically enough. With a consent clause, the burden of proof will still be the same, but the subject of proof changes. This could create a change in the way questions are asked in the courtroom, as the woman will no longer have to prove in the same way that she tried to avert the rape in a determined and resolute manner.

It seems clear that #MeToo has contributed significantly to a shift in public awareness and in debates on sexualized violence and sexual harassment in Denmark. It is now also possible to trace a tendency towards a break with those who claim that the fight against sexual harassment risks destroying a free and flirtatious tone of conversation. Nevertheless, on the other side we still see a kind of pushback against legal consequences for perpetrators of sexual harassment.

References

Amnesty International. (2019). *"Give us respect and justice!" Overcoming barriers to justice for women rape survivors in Denmark.*

Askanius, T., & Hartley, J. M. (2019). Framing gender justice: A comparative analysis of the media coverage of# metoo in Denmark and Sweden. *Nordicom Review, 40*(2), 19–36.

Balkmar, D., Iovanni, L., & Pringle, K. (2009). A reconsideration of two "Welfare Paradises" research and policy responses to men's violence in Denmark and Sweden. *Men and Masculinities, 12*(2), 155–174.

Bom, M., & Bjerke, N. K. (2002). *Udslag: hverdagsfeminisme i det 21. Århundrede* [Effect: everydayfeminism in the 21 century] [Kbh.]: elkjaeroghansen.
Bonde, H. (2013). *Fordi du fortjener det: fra feminisme til favorisme* [Because you earn it: From feminism to preferential treatment]. Gyldendal.
Christensen, A.-D., & Larsen, J. E. (2007). Gender, class, and family: Men and gender equality in a Danish context. *Social Politics, 15*(1), 53–78.
Clausen, C., Lauritzen, P., & Thygesen, E. (1974). *Mænd: Det svækkede køn* [Men:The weak gender] (Kbh.): Tiderne skifter.
Cossins, A. (2019). Why her behavior is still on trial: The absence of context in the modernisation of the substantive law on consent. *UNSWLJ, 42,* 462.
Cossins, A. (2020). Modernisation of the substantive law of consent. In *Closing the justice gap for adult and child sexual assault* (pp. 277–337). Palgrave Macmillan.
Dahlerup, D. (2011). När svenska partier blev 'feminister': Om skillnader i dansk och svensk jämställdhetsdebatt [When Swedish parties became "feminists": On differences in the debate on gender equality in Denmark and Sweden]. In L. Freidenvall & M. Jansson (Eds.), *Politik och kritik: en feministisk guide till statsvetenskap* [Politics and critique: A feminist guide to political science] (pp. 193–212). Studentliteratur.
Dahlerup, D. (2018). Gender equality as a closed case: A survey among the members of the 2015 Danish parliament. *Scandinavian Political Studies, 41*(2), 188–209.
Esping-Andersen, G. (1990). *The three worlds of welfare capitalism.* Princeton University Press.
Holm, E. (1975). *Den maskuline mystik* [The masculine mystique]. Rhodos.
Holmgren, L. E., & Hearn, J. (2009). Framing 'men in feminism': Theoretical locations, local contexts and practical passings in men's gender-conscious positionings on gender equality and feminism. *Journal of Gender Studies, 18*(4), 403–418.
Information. (2017. 28. December). #MeToo er historisk, men ikke i sig selv samfundsomvæltende [#MeToo is historic, but not in itself socially revolutionary].
Kronborg, A., Holmfjord, L., Rasmussen, N., & Koch, I. (2011). *Forældreansvarsloven: når der er vold i familien* [The parental responsibility act: When there is violence in the family]. Nyt Juridisk Forlag.
Larcombe, W., Fileborn, B., Powell, A., Hanley, N., & Henry, N. (2016). 'I Think it's Rape and I Think He Would be Found Not Guilty' focus group perceptions of (un) reasonable belief in consent in rape law. *Social & Legal Studies, 25*(5), 611–629.

Ledstrup, M. (2012). *Hvorfor er svenskerne så feministiske?* [Why are Swedes so feminist?] Videnskab.dk.

Lorentzen, J. (2000). *De tavse mænd* [The silent men]. Kvinfo webmagasin Forum.

Män. (2018). *Men, masculinity and #MeToo.*

Nilsson, B., & Lundgren, A. S. (2020). The #MeToo Movement: Men and Masculinity in Swedish News Media. *The Journal of Men's Studies, 29*(1), 8–25.

Politiken. (2020, December 27). *Hun var påpasselig med ikke at blande sig: Indtil hun skrev årets mest omtalte åbne brev* [She was careful not to interfere: Until she wrote the most talked about open letter of the year].

Reestorff, C. M. (2019). Affective politics and involuntary autoethnography: Backlashes against #MeToo. *Capacious: Journal for Emerging Affect Inquiry, 1*(4), ii–xix.

Reinicke, K. (2004). *Mænd i lyst og nød* [Men for better or for worse]. Det Schønbergske Forlag.

Reinicke, K. (2018). *Mænd som krænker kvinder—refleksioner i kølvandet på #Metoo* [Men who violate women—Reflections in the wake of #MeToo]. Samfundslitteratur.

Sørensen, N. U. (Ed.) (2000). *Pikstormerne* [The prick invaders]. Informations Forlag.

Smith, O. (2018). *Rape trials in England and Wales: Observing justice and rethinking rape myths.* Springer.

4

Why Have Men Not Been Held Responsible?

This chapter looks at some of the general social conditions accounting for why it is difficult and even culturally transgressive to focus on men as a social gender. The rendering of men as invisible in terms of their social gender roles, which results from the 'neutralizing' of the societal and cultural norms that shape men's lives, has an impact on men's thoughts and actions, and influences the *questions* that we, as a society, can ask and the *answers* that we can obtain. In other words, since as a society we are not used to problematizing the socialization that many men receive, it is often difficult to find solutions to men's problems and to the problems they create for others. Hearn (2004) has pointed out that studying men's lives is nothing new. It depends entirely on how one looks at it. History books are replete with accounts of men's lives and deeds. However, these stories of men's achievements as kings, warriors and politicians have seldom problematized men as a social category and a socially constructed gender. Hearn therefore points out the need to study men in terms of gendered power relations—in other words, men must be 'gendered' before they can be studied critically, otherwise one risks taking their behaviours for granted and continuing to think of masculinity as an eternal, timeless essence that cannot be changed. Hence, the focus should not be so much on what women are subjected to but rather on what men *subject* women to. Men must be actively written into debates about violence, rape, sexual assault and sexual harassment.

Why aren't men's attitudes and behaviours towards women the focus of more critical scrutiny and coordinated action? asks Katz (2006). Men's privileges are naturalized and normalized. According to Bourdieu (2001), masculine domination is to be perceived as a paradigmatic form of symbolic violence. It is so deeply ingrained in our unconscious that we barely recognize all of its dimensions, and we struggle to call it into question. Therefore, indirectly, part of the agenda of #MeToo is about making boys and men aware of their privileges. Historically this has been difficult because society has not been used to addressing boys and men as being problematic. We are used to looking at gender equality as about women's disadvantage. Yet we can look at gender inequality as a story of male privilege. Men's privileges are not only the result of men's skills and efforts; instead, they are also the result of unearned advantages of an unequal gender system.

Unlike women, who have been thoroughly studied within gender studies since the 1960s, as a research object men have remained neutral, invisible and genderless, and there is no doubt that many, especially white men, have enjoyed the 'privilege' of getting away with sexual harassment because their behaviour has not been problematized as culturally deviant.[1] This is connected to the fact that there has been little or no tradition of addressing men's behaviour in institutional or professional contexts. Nevertheless, viewing men through a gendered lens has meant that previously taken-for-granted powers and authority of men and ways of being men can now be considered much more problematic (Hearn & Pringle, 2006). Regarding the change in perception of men's practices, Giddens (1992: 59) has stated the following:

---

[1] However, it is crucial to emphasize that black men and men of minority backgrounds have not had that 'privilege', as their behaviour has often been problematized as culturally deviant. See the section 'Ethnicity and violence' in this chapter for a further discussion on the impact of race and ethnicity.

In western culture at least, today is the first period in which men are finding themselves to be men, that is, as possessing a problematic 'masculinity'. In previous times, men have assumed that their activities constituted 'history', whereas women existed almost out of time, doing the same as they had always done.

Hearn (1998) emphasizes that men are often implicitly talked of but rarely talked of explicitly and that men are visible but not questioned. When men are not explicitly talked of and named as men, it is difficult to start to question men's power in relation to women, children, and other men. Newburn and Mair (1996) have stressed how men within social and health work are only seen as problematic *individuals* and not as problematic *men*, which has prevented the development of gender-sensitive treatment strategies. It is not culturally controversial to talk about violence as long as we do not mention it more specifically as 'male violence' (Romito, 2008). Criado-Perez (2019) describes that seeing men as the human default is fundamental to the structure of human society and that the unmarked term is assumed to be male, which often makes masculinity invisible for analysis. Vera-Gray (2016) points out that it is important to understand the lack of conceptualization of men's various forms of violence and abuse if one is to combat the historical silence surrounding sexual harassment.

4.1   Hegemonic Masculinity

As mentioned in the introduction, the theoretical approach used in this book is located within critical studies on men and masculinities, which highlight the importance of patriarchy, hegemonic masculinity, cultural domination and differences between men. A key contribution in the area of masculinity studies is the notion of hegemonic masculinity—that is, the concept that exists in each society defining what it means to be masculine (Connell & Messerschmidt, 2005).

More precisely, hegemonic masculinity refers to the most influential and 'most honoured or desired' ideas about manhood through which heterosexual men assert their dominance over women and other masculinities (Connell, 1995). The dominant form of masculinity in a specific culture at a particular time is hegemonic masculinity (Connell, 1995; Connell & Messerschmidt, 2005).

Connell considers hegemonic masculinity as being culturally promoted and superior and an ideal all men are judged in relation to. Hegemonic masculinity tends to marginalize men who do not perfectly fit the description of a 'real man'. This dominance is clearly seen in the unequal power relations between men and women but also among men as part of a hierarchy of historically specific masculinities. Connell points out that there is more than one type of masculinity; in fact, there is a complete structure of various masculinities. Following on from hegemonic masculinity, Connell takes up the idea of complicit masculinities, which are commonly sustained by or characteristic of men who support the ideals of hegemonic masculinity but are unable to comply with those ideals themselves. Connell also operates with the concept of subordinate masculinities, which often relates to homosexual men or men with feminine traits. The last concept in Connell's (1995) terminology is marginalized masculinities, which refers to, for example, unemployed men, poor men, and men of a different race or skin colour. In developed countries, hegemonic masculinities tend to be composed of a combination of economic success, racial superiority (whiteness) and overt heterosexuality (Ruxton, 2002). Construction of masculinities has a powerful influence on what it means to be a man. Men and boys are not only rewarded when they behave in accordance with 'masculine ideals' but also typically ridiculed and discriminated against when they fail to do so (Mellon, 2013).

Hegemonic masculinity is thus a recognized term which has been used in many settings to identify the ways that men dominate women and other men. However, the concept of hegemonic masculinity has also received criticism due to lack of complexity and nuance. This criticism often concerns what the term specifically refers to and how different forms of masculine hegemony interrelate (see, e.g., Hearn, 2012). Anderson (2010) developed the term *inclusive masculinities* to understand the changing relationship between adolescent males and their masculinities and argued that Connell's theory of hegemonic masculinity was only accurate in settings of high homophobia. Anderson (2002, 2005) asserted that several studies were documenting an increasing inclusion of gay men in young men's peer groups.

4.2 Men and Gender Equality

Gender (in)equality concerns both women and men and has a strong impact on their daily lives. It is crucial that both women and men are aware of the benefits that gender equality brings to them as individuals and as members of communities and societies. However, many men hesitate to get involved in gender equality issues. Has gender equality something positive to offer men? Gender equality debates have, for a variety of reasons, been based on the lifeworlds and experiences of women. Therefore, gender issues have been widely regarded as of no concern to men and boys (Connell, 2003). In some countries, gender equality issues hardly appear on the political agenda or are mainly seen as a 'women's issue'. Not all men the world over have the same attitudes, challenges and problems. Regarding gender roles and norms of communities and cultures, there are higher rates of violence against women in cultures that emphasize male dominance in families and where there are strong beliefs in male honour (Flood, 2018). Men accept gender equality in countries with greater economic and political stability; and men with higher educational attainment and married men have more equitable attitudes (Barker et al., 2011).

Undoubtedly, many men think that gender equality has to do with promoting the rights and interests of women (EIGE, 2012). In addition, women have historically had poorer living conditions and fewer democratic rights than men. However, there is also a need to expand the scope of systematic knowledge about men's lives from the perspective of gender if the object is to find solutions to some of today's gender equality challenges (Holter, 2003). It is of great societal importance that more of an effort is made to engage men in future collaborations to promote gender equality, because continued progress in gender equality depends on men supporting the project. If men's experiences are not taken into account when designing gender equality policies, it is difficult for men to make this topic a priority.

Overall gender inequality is fundamentally men's problem. Therefore, we have to look at the problems men create and the problems men experience. Gender has become both a challenge and a problem for men. Many men feel caught up in a situation where they are expected, on the one hand, to embrace traditional male virtues such as providing for their families and, on the other hand, to be able to critically reflect on their masculinity (Reinicke, 2012).

One of the reasons why we know so little about men's inner thoughts and personal lives, yet so much about their behaviour, is that most men are not brought up to talk about their gender but rather to 'take their gender for granted' (Reinicke, 2004). Men's reflections about gender often seem unwelcome and hard to grasp. With the exception of fathers' rights groups, men also often do not perceive—or do not want to perceive—their problems as political gender issues. The tension between what is *taboo* and what is *ridiculed* is probably the most fundamental obstacle to the development of a serious, deep-rooted and honest debate about men and gender equality. Gender is often trivialized and becomes the butt of jokes, and it is common to hear that there are other more important inequality issues that people should be addressing. But the claim that men are the oppressed gender pops up every now and again in the media, and there is still a tendency to pay a lot of attention to people who ridicule women's issues and defend men's traditional rights.

Some men are unable or unwilling to understand problems from the perspective of gender. Many men are uninterested in gender equality because they associate gender equality with men relinquishing power to women and not as a process of liberation that will benefit men. These blind spots are founded in the male being defined as the norm—as the neutral, public, genderless person. Consequently, many men tend to 'tune out' when they hear the words 'gender equality' (Katz, 2006).

It is often difficult to motivate men to participate in gender debates. Whitehead (2002) has pointed out that before a significant change can take place in men's practices, a transformation of men's perceptions of their own gender identity must take place, and he indicates that many men are not able to understand the gendered reality that surrounds them.

4 Why Have Men Not Been Held Responsible?

He asks provocatively, 'Do men even know that they have a sex?' Though men are also gendered and shaped by norms and expectations, it has been particularly difficult to get politicians to discuss the controversial aspects of men's life at the political level. The silence around men as a political category acts as a mixture of something universal and something non-existent. The debate about men is thus placed between the *obvious* and the *unmentionable*. Eduards (2002) points out that it is difficult to name men as a political category, and she claims that the core of the male norm is that it does not 'exist in politics'. This may seem to be a remarkable claim. However, often the political, institutional, and bureaucratic 'language' does not operate with men as a group or social analytical category alongside neutral demographic categories. This has made the development of national care plans and policies difficult. Therefore, society often lacks a language to understand men's social problems in a gendered way. According to Hearn (1998), men are a socially powerful category to be explained like other social phenomena. However, it is difficult to make men's power and domination an issue for study and critique because men have been invisible to critical analysis and somehow been absent from explicit inquiry and deconstruction. Connell (1995) has described how the project of transforming masculinity has almost no political weight at all and that men's interest in patriarchy is defended by a broad cultural machinery which exalts hegemonic masculinity.

The founder of the White Ribbon Campaign, Michael Kaufman, has stated that we have to simultaneously challenge men's patriarchal assumptions and privileges, and reach out to them with respect and compassion (Kaufmann, 2001). We have to address both the social problems that men *cause* and the problems that some men *experience*. We need to talk about 'how bad things are' in order to understand and deal with the problem while also understanding that men are not always motivated to participate in gender equality discussions by talking about 'how bad things are'. Men and boys are most likely to support change towards gender equality when they can see positive benefits for themselves and the people in their lives (Connell, 2003). The focus simultaneously needs to be on how men can help reduce or eliminate gender inequalities rather than on how they are the problem. At the same time, men need space to become their own social innovators in the area of gender equality.

Nevertheless, why should men start to think and act differently? The key to getting men interested in changing is to convince them that they have more to gain by embracing modern forms of masculinity and that the price of hanging on to the old masculine order is too high.

4.3   Men and Feminism

While feminism is primarily a social movement for women, it has obvious implications for the lives of men (Digby, 1998; Edley & Wetherell, 2001). Egeberg Holmgren and Hearn (2009) highlight that feminism has always been partly about men and what to do about men. Looking at men's relationship to feminism, it seems clear that to make men examine and redefine masculinity with feminist principles is not an easy sell. Feminism can make things uncomfortable for men and unsettles assumed positions (Hearn, 1987). Therefore, some men think that feminism is detrimental to men.

There are many misconceptions about feminism being anti-male and hostile to men, and undoubtedly many men have a troubled relationship with feminism. There are also many misconceptions of women's accomplishments. Some men think that men are only pushed backwards while women have progressed. They think feminism is not about them, they remain distant and confused about feminism, and often think it might be potentially threatening to them.

Something in our culture wants us to believe that men and women are fundamentally different. Instead, we have to think that women's and men's interests are similar. Gender equality is not a zero-sum game. Furthermore, it is not only women and girls who benefit from feminism and women's advocacy. There are many reasons why men should be interested in gender equality issues and feminism (van der Gaag, 2014). Feminist activity is not only created in solidarity with women but also with men. Men have also benefited from feminism. Some of the best things that have happened to men are because of feminism. Still, many men tend to wonder what feminism has to do with their lives. It might have everything to do with them, and it is crucial to educate men about feminism in order for them to fully understand just how important and positive these changes have been for them. Feminism allows men to live the life they say that they want to live (Kaufman & Kimmel, 2011). Ruxton (2020: 4) defines the benefits as follows:

> For men, feminism can provide the inspiration for personal development, shifting towards more co-operative and equal relationships and friendships, and greater sharing of care and work responsibilities.

We need a new way of thinking about feminism because feminism might also be part of the solution to some men's problem. Feminism might help men to understand how narrow definitions of manhood have harmed men. Men should not be afraid of feminism. Instead, men should support feminism because their liberation as men connects directly to the liberation of women. However, it is not easy to make feminism comprehensible to men.

Whitehead (2002) points out in that regard that it is important for men to find resources they can use to help them move on. He further argues that men's *empowerment efforts*—in other words, men's attempts to avoid situations of powerlessness—are important but can also be dangerous if they involve an unnecessary rejection of women. He remarks that it is by supporting women's empowerment that men can create the conditions for their own change and that the changes in societal conditions for women actually give men an unprecedented degree of freedom.

Flood (2014) argues in a very thought-provoking way that society will not make progress towards gender equality without men's support because gender inequality is a problem for and about men. Flood goes on to say that feminism needs men and men need feminism. Thus, men are in a double position. They need to change and to make change. Women will not experience gender equality unless and until men change. On the other side, men need feminism because without it, men risk being stuck in narrow, suffocating gender roles, which are unhealthy and limiting for men, and harmful for women. Many of the actions that men carry out to prove their masculinity can engender respect among other men and consequently be used to gain prestige and power. However, these achievements also contain an element of recklessness and can have serious human costs. Therefore, it is crucial to realize that feminism is not anti-male but anti-sexist. Feminism calls for gender justice and gender equality. Feminism gives men choices and may free men from expectations that they must be the dominating breadwinners, that men are to give priority to career before family, that men are expected not to work in caring professions, and that men are expected to leave the responsibility for housework and childcare to women. Feminism can also enrich men's friendship with each other and make it possible for them to be more supportive and intimate. Therefore, feminism is not the cause of men's problems; instead, it might be the solution to some of men's problems. Nevertheless, while there are no doubt men who want to be involved in feminism, there are just as surely also men who want to fight against it.

4.4 Men's Negative Health Outcomes

It seems crucial that men learn to acknowledge and address men's own gendered needs and vulnerabilities, and the ways that they suffer under patriarchy (Kaufman, 2003). In today's Western society, there is an increasing focus on men's health and on viewing men's health issues as gender related. Men have significantly shorter life expectancies than women, men are more often involved in accidents and more men than women commit suicide. Hence, there are many issues that disproportionately or exclusively affect men. However, it is not the same for all men, and men's health issues are to a high degree influenced by class, race, education, employment and other social determinants (Bates et al., 2009; White et al., 2011). There are grounds to presume that one of the reasons that men live shorter lives than women is found in men's gender-role socialization processes, which can have a negative impact on a man's physical as well as his mental life.

The way we train and educate men to deal with pain and sadness is not optimal. Instead of getting in touch with themselves when facing adversity, men often get angry with other people (Möller-Leimkühler, 2002; Pollack, 2005). Men must understand that their life also encompasses vulnerability and sadness and must be better at managing grief, disappointment and hurt without projecting it onto other people. However, men often feel that they do not have cultural permission to admit their vulnerable situation. They find it difficult to acknowledge their vulnerability and to display weakness due to fear of being denigrated as feminine or gay (Pollack, 1998). Some men also tend to suppress empathy and compassion. Back in 1978, James Harrison wrote an article provocatively entitled 'Warning: The male sex role may be dangerous to your health'. The punch line was that one of the reasons why men have a shorter life expectancy than women was to be found in men's gender-role socialization, and it emphasized that a strong belief in traditional ideas of masculinity has a negative effect on men's physical and mental life. It is crucial to address men's own experiences of gender, including perceived and actual disempowerment (Flood, 2018). In that regard there is undoubtedly a group of men that are vulnerable both in the labour market and in the family and who have difficulty taking advantage of social and health services. Andersen and Elm Larsen (1998), who studied the 'gender profile of social exclusion', point out that unemployment has a large negative impact in regard to men and family dissolution and that, in comparison with women, men face more difficulties in developing coping strategies to manage everyday life. The idea that men have specific health needs, experiences and concerns related to their gender as well as their biological sex is relatively new, and the psychosocial aspects of male health are still not accepted, or even understood, by many health practitioners and policymakers (Baker, 2001; Courtenay, 2000; WHO, 2018).

Men's mental health problems, especially depression, are under-detected and under-treated. This is due to men not seeking help and the lack of appropriate mental health services for men (Brooks, 2010). Likewise, there are reasons to believe that men's higher suicide rates are linked to undiagnosed mental health problems (Madsen, 2008). Men are often more reluctant than women to face up to and respond to physical and mental problems, and men's position of tension between autonomy and attachment is different from that of women (Beynon, 2001). Men's depressive symptoms are often characterized by aggressiveness, withdrawal from relationships, low impulse control, over-involvement with work, low stress threshold, alcohol abuse, denial of pain and rigid demands for autonomy (Madsen, 2008). Nevertheless, as Courtenay (2000) emphasizes, if society can take advantage of the knowledge that exists about men as socially gendered persons, it can improve the development of male-friendly policies including treatment offers, which may appeal positively both to men in general and in particular to men in vulnerable positions.

Class and socioeconomic parameters play a central role for both genders, but the impact is greater for men than for women (Christensen & Elm-Larsen, 2007). For instance, it is healthy for men to be married, because married men generally have a lower morbidity rate than single men. Men's lifestyles and their risk and health behaviours lead to unnecessary sickness, a decline in well-being and premature death. This is especially true for vulnerable and socially disadvantaged men, because men's health is impacted more by social inequality than women's health is. Most of the health-related issues experienced by men are found in single, uneducated and relatively impoverished men (World Health Organization, 2018).

4.5 The Invisibility of Men's Destructive Behaviour

Messner (1997) points out that there are many white, heterosexual middle-class men who take their social privileges for granted and remain ignorant of the social structures that privilege them, even if these clearly come at the expense of other people. Therefore, without making too absolute a statement, it makes sense to say that society as a whole does not critically interrogate the dominant group. Morgan (1992) has pointed out how difficult it is to undertake a critical examination of men's practices. He emphasizes that powerful people rarely want to take a critical look at their position and privileges in society, and if they are confronted with their own power, they will try to describe their position as being normal, fair and inevitable. This separation serves a function for individuals with privilege by offering them a sense of morality, while not demanding any changes to their own behaviour (Whitt, 2016). In particular, topics such as violence, prostitution and rape are in many ways characterized by a systematic disregard of men's gender socialization (Reinicke, 2004). It is not easy to make a critique of contemporary masculinity because there exists a kind of cultural legitimacy apparatus ready to make the abusive behaviour acceptable and socially recognizable (Søndergaard, 2000).

Katz has pointed out that when talking about violence against women, we tend to focus on the *against women* part of the phrase and not on the fact that men are the ones doing it (Katz, 2006: 3). We are inclined to say 'violence against women' instead of 'men's violence against women'.

Katz points out that gender and masculinity have not received sufficient attention. This is a problem because gender is at the heart of almost all types of violations of human rights. Language is so deeply embedded in culture that we are tempted to forget that the words and phrases we use in our everyday lives shape our reality. We have to change our focus point, because on an unconscious level our cognitive structure is set up to blame victims. In his inspiring TED talk, Jackson Katz uses an exercise that illustrates at sentence-structure level how the way that we think, literally the way that we use language, conspires to keep our attention off men. Inspired by Julia Penelope's language of sexism (1990), Jackson Katz describes how the passive voice effectively triggers a shift in responsibility from male perpetrators to female victims.

He starts with a very basic English sentence: 'John beats Mary.' In this sentence, John is the subject, beat is the verb, Mary is the object. Then he moves to the second sentence, which says the same thing in the passive voice: 'Mary was beaten by John.' A whole lot has happened in this sentence, because there is a shift in focus in one sentence from John to Mary and because John is very close to the end of the sentence. This changes the meaning of the sentence. In the third sentence, John is dropped; we have 'Mary was beaten' and now it is all about Mary. John is no longer present in the sentence; it is totally focused on Mary. The final sentence in this sequence, running from the others, is 'Mary is a battered woman.' So now, Mary's very identity—Mary is a battered woman—is what was done to her by John in the first instance. However, John is no longer part of the conversation.

The development of the phrases shows how the dominant discourses about violence are framed and how the way we talk about these issues is vital for being effective in tackling them. The point of this lineup is to demonstrate how the way we usually talk about violence in society entails that the male subject 'John' quietly disappears from the discourse/narrative about the violence he stands for. The focus shifts from the perpetrator to the victim to eventually deal in general with abused women. Thus, language is important when articulating men's destructive actions and maintaining an analytical view of men as social gender. Our language encourages people to think that violence just happens without any perpetrator. We are asked to think that no one is doing it—violence just happens, it has no active agent, it is just something women experience. There is, so to speak, no accountability built into the language. We say 'violence against women' without problematizing who is committing the violence. This is a problem, because men commit the overwhelming proportion of violence.

4.6 The Gender-Neutral Approach

Katz (2006) posits that mainstream commentary about gender violence and other forms of interpersonal violence is remarkably degendered. We rarely have a national conversation about the way our culture teaches boys and men to think about and act towards women (Katz, 2006: 103). There is often a tendency to reduce violence to individual tragedies and psychologically deranged persons (Flood & Pease, 2009; Ronkainen, 2001). This is a reduced perception of violence. It is important to include gender and power in the analysis and understanding of violence. Discussions about men and violence are still characterized by a systematic downplaying of the relationship between male socialization and violence. Katz asserts that we cannot reduce men's sexual harassment against women until we can at least name the problem correctly.

> The shift needs to begin with language. Language structures thought, which means that for us to change our thinking about gender violence, we have to change the language we use to think about it. And in order for us to make room for new language, we have to critically reexamine the old language; the words, phrases, and usages that serve to maintain and perpetuate the status quo. (Katz, 2006: 92)

Katz (2006) goes on to say that the current language about sexual harassment hides men's responsibility and keeps many people stuck in the old paradigm: the passive and gender-neutral language that dominates the national conversation about rape, domestic violence, sexual harassment and related problems.

Furthermore, Katz (2006) elaborates that we get nowhere if we continue to ignore the way masculine socialization helps to produce abusive boys or boys who grow into abusive men. Nevertheless, he admits that if we spoke about it as a men's problem, for example if we explicitly asked why men commit these crimes, the critical spotlight would make many men uncomfortable. I experienced this tendency in 2020 when experts on gender issues, myself included, were invited to speak in a Danish Parliament seminar about #MeToo. The title of my presentation was 'Why do some men conduct sexual harassment?' Two weeks before the seminar, I was asked to change the title of the presentation to 'Why do some men and *women* conduct sexual harassment?' The reason was that a member of the Danish Parliament wanted to stress that women also harass men now and then. That, of course, is true, but the gender-neutral approach risks overshadowing the fact that sexual harassment is mainly carried out by men against women. Whether the victims are women or men, men are overwhelmingly the perpetrators. It is important not to lose sight of the much larger problem and not to create a false imagination about a notion of symmetry, for example by claiming that men's experiences of harassment are equal to women's (Ruxton, 2020). This would be a denial of the deeper structural analysis. The effect of this subjectification is that sexual harassment, typically, is referred to in a gender-neutral manner, which implicitly downplays men's structural power.

Feminist perspectives have been demonized and marginalized in the mainstream media. Therefore, it seems crucial to open up the discourses, widen them and encourage the mainstream media to report on violence in a better way. It is important to include the gender and power aspect in the analysis and understanding of violence.

It is also remarkable that when girls and women commit crimes and behave violently, their gender becomes the story (Katz, 2006). When men commit crimes, however, gender is often invisible. Stories come and go in the daily news cycle. We are constantly reminded of the gender of the victims while we rarely emphasize men's role clearly. For example, we hear that women are being assaulted, harassed, raped and abused, but men are nowhere to be found in these accounts. The active agents are often missing. It happens to women, but nobody is doing it. They are just experiencing it. This makes us see it as a women's issue. Violence and homicide are not committed by *men*, but by criminals, motorcycle gang members, drug addicts and minority groups, and so on, but rarely just by *men* (Reinicke, 2004). We hear about the 'people' who commit these crimes but there is a lack of attention to the socialization processes which are at the root of some men's aggressive behaviour. Men and masculinity often remain unspoken in the media presentation of what are known as 'family tragedies' (Køster, 2011). This makes these 'family tragedies', which are most often about a man killing his partner, possibly his children and perhaps ending up taking his own life, seem inevitable, like something that comes 'out of the blue'. It is just perceived as something that unfortunately occurs, which again entails that there is no discussion of how these tragedies can be avoided and prevented. The question seldom raised in connection with such 'family tragedies' is why it is overwhelmingly men who commit these acts. There should be far more questioning of why the media and society consciously or unconsciously 'forget' the gender aspect of these tragic events.

Reinicke (2012) analyzed how the media often 'forgets' to name men when dealing with controversial aspects of men's life. A Danish television news programme from 2012 included a feature about young people being involved in car accidents on Danish roads. The build-up to the programme was that four young men had been badly injured involved in a car accident the night before, and two months earlier, four men were killed in a car crash. The newsreader says: 'The dry figures show that it is disproportionately young people who are involved in car accidents.'

In the news feature, it was further emphasized that *young people* are behind a third of all car accidents in Denmark. Likewise, it was mentioned that *young people* do not have the same experience of traffic, that *young people* are more willing to take risks and that they are less worried and, lastly, that they drive more dangerously. It is interesting that the feature contains no problematization of gender. At no time in the feature were the words 'young' or 'young people' replaced with the more appropriate term 'young men'.

Reinicke (2012) also used another example to demonstrate the invisibility of controversial aspects of some men's sexuality. In March 2004, some 300 Danish police officers carried out raids in the biggest child pornography case in Danish history, known as 'Operation Mjølner'. A total of 101 men aged 26–64—engineers, doctors, schoolteachers, educators, unskilled workers and others—were arrested. The accused had paid for child pornography over the internet with their credit cards, which enabled the police to track them down. In connection with the raid, the then national police chief stated that it should be a warning to the *population* and that *Danes* who were travelling this dangerous road could see how horribly wrong it could go. In the electronic media coverage of the event the same evening, there was a psychologist who presented different types of people who were inclined to search for child pornography: paedophiles, the hyper-sexual and the curious. At only one point in the interview with the psychologist was anything said about 'outgoing male sexuality'. However, seen from a gender perspective, these 101 people were not just neutral persons, they were all *men*, which nevertheless was not explicitly problematized or discussed.

4.7 Stories from Popular Culture That Defend Sexual Harassment

It is not only in daily interaction between people that women become objectified and victims of sexism. One of the reasons it may be difficult for some men to find out what consent truly means is that it is possible to find many examples from popular culture that defend both the objectification of women, and men's insistence and belief that they know better when it comes to women's erotic desires. Rape-affirming beliefs are embedded in our language and part of popular song lyrics. Objectification is normalized in pop culture and media. Just think about the famous Dean Martin song 'There's Yes! Yes! In Your Eyes', which includes the lines: 'Your lips tell me no no – But there"s yes yes in your eyes.'

In movies and TV series, a 'No' can also mean 'Yes' if the man is just insistent for long enough, even if he has been given a clear rejection. In most societies there is a strong narrative saying that it is the men who have the power to decide when it comes to where and when sexual actions should take place and that men know what women really want.

In terms of objectification and men's insistence and belief that they know better, the James Bond character is a prime example. The James Bond movies are filled with male chauvinist actions and comments where the charming and humorous agent does not always accept a 'No' and where the agent's flirting *is near* to being sexual assault without being called such.

One of the most convincing examples of this tendency is from the movie *Goldfinger* from 1964, where James Bond is in a barn and gets into a clumsy and semi-erotic struggle with the female star of the movie, Pussy Galore (who is the captain of an aerial acrobatics team working for the villain, Goldfinger) after she has very directly *told* him that she is not interested. It ends with him having her pinned down by her arms in the hay while he presses his head down against her. She is desperately trying to get away and turns her head. In the end, James Bond succeeds in getting the kiss he wants.

An iconic image which to a great extent ends up indirectly defending the sexual harassment of women in public spaces is the 1951 photograph called 'American Girl in Italy', taken by Ruth Orkin. It shows the then 23-year-old Ninalee Craig who was travelling alone through Europe and was wearing a long dress while strolling down the streets of Florence. As she is walking, there are about fifteen men pursuing her with longing in their eyes and some are whistling at the beautiful woman gliding by. It is very telling in terms of accepting and ignoring sexual harassment that such a powerful objectification of a woman can end up being a mainstream work of art.

However, there are also trends that indicate that it is becoming less socially acceptable to act in a sexually harassing manner. As a consequence of the #MeToo movement, the Miss America beauty contest announced in 2018 that the contest would no longer focus on the female participants' bodies. As a result, they were dropping the part of the contest involving the women performing in bikinis or swimsuits. Also in 2018, the Tour de France bicycle race dropped the so-called 'podium girls' who give shirts and kisses on the cheek to the winners after each stage of the race, as this was part of maintaining a sexist stereotype. The Formula 1 management also chose to get rid of the scantily clad girls in 2018, the so-called 'grid girls' who hold numbers and welcome the drivers in the starting area of the race, as they were incompatible with 'contemporary social norms'.

4.8 The Man Box

There is often a contradiction between the guidance that young men need and the ready-made rules they have to obey (Kimmel, 2008: 22). One term that has been widely used to describe the dominant form of masculinity in the United States is the 'man box' (Greene, 2013). It refers to a set of beliefs, expectations and pressures placed on men to conform to harmful masculine norms which require young men and boys to be self-sufficient, act tough, take risks, be in control, be heterosexual, enforce rigid gender roles and use aggression to resolve conflicts (Heilman et al., 2017). The glue that keeps the 'man box' together is a rigid set of expectations, perceptions and behaviours seen as 'manly'. Research indicates that men and boys who adhere to rigid, traditional notions of masculinity are more likely to report having used violence against a partner (World Health Organization, 2018).

What kind of masculinities are implicated in sexual harassment, assault and violence? Pascoe (2005) highlights that boys and men often feel pressure to engage in or be complicit in the degradation of women in order to conform to standards of hegemonic masculinity. Support for this interpretation of a rigid construct of cultural ideas about male identity also comes from Glickman (2012), who states that the 'man box' is one of the main reasons why men harass women on the street and why catcalling and violence tends to escalate when men are in groups. Since the man box is hierarchical as well as performative, the men at the bottom of the hierarchy are at risk of being cast out. Therefore, men have to compete with others in order not to be the one who is outside the box.

Moreover, as each one's performance becomes more vigorous, it forces the others to do the same. It is not easy to say: 'I can't be part of this if it's going to be abusive and sexist.' Therefore, Glickman goes on to say, men must be ready to join the escalation of 'the performance of manhood' without hesitating, or they risk being cast out. This is of course a very simplistic and generalized perception of the dynamics between peers. Nevertheless, it indicates how sexual harassment might be interpreted as manly. Further, it shows that engaging in sexual harassment is also about impressing other men. In line with this, Grazian (2007) studied how male students employed the power of collective rituals of homosociality to show their sexual competence and masculine identity by 'girl hunting' in the context of urban nightlife. Grazian (2007) emphasized that the young man's peers 'are the intended audience for competitive games of sexual reputation and peer status, public displays of situational dominance and rule transgression, and in-group rituals of solidarity and loyalty' (Grazian, 2007: 224).

The practice of a more sensitive kind of manhood is the path out of the man box, and it is essential to preventing violence and pursuing equity in our society. In the man box, men are expected to be strong, successful, powerful, dominating, fearless, in control and emotionless. In the man box, women are viewed as objects, as the property of men and as having less value than men. These messages limit men and hurt women because the 'act like a man' mentality can result in abuse and mistreatment of women. The man box perpetuates a heterosexist norm that devalues all those who do not conform to a gender binary. The harmful effects of the man box are severe, real and troubling. The majority of men who adhere to the rules of the man box are more likely to put their health and well-being at risk, to cut themselves off from intimate friendships, to resist seeking help when they need it, to experience depression and to think frequently about ending their own lives (Heilman et al., 2017; Hill et al., 2020).

Empirical studies with a conceptual starting point in the man box have been conducted on young men's attitudes, behaviours, and understandings of manhood. A study with a representative random sample of young men aged 18–30 in the USA, UK and Mexico reveals that most men still feel pushed to live in the man box. This comprises being self-sufficient, acting tough, looking physically attractive, sticking to rigid gender roles, being heterosexual, having sexual prowess and using violence to resolve conflicts (Heilman et al., 2017). However, the study also shows that social norms and ideals about manhood are complex, and many men hold contradictory views about them. Many young men support both gender equality and some 'tough-guy' version of manhood.

Another study from Australia, also with a conceptual starting point in the man box, showed that a majority of young men agreed that there are pressures to be a 'real man'. The study also revealed that men inside the man box (those who have most internalized society's rigid messages about manhood) are also far more likely to report having perpetrated sexual harassment against a woman (The Men's Project and Flood, 2018).

4.9 Non-Hegemonic Masculinities

Notions of masculinity shape different men in different ways and not all men absorb these rigid messages about masculinity. Not all men live within the narrow constraints of the man box, and the significance of the 'bro' code is not the same in all men's lives. While gendered sexual scripts are hegemonic at the cultural level, it does not need to be so at the individual level (Masters et al., 2013). Ruxton (2002: 14) emphasizes that boys and men negotiate their own way of being male and that masculinities are actively produced by individuals in particular settings rather than being programmed by genes or fixed social structures. Different groups of men identify and associate with different types of masculinities or behaviours. Research dealing with men and masculinity points to the need for boys to be able to take a stand against traditional stereotypical gender roles (Mills, 2001). Thus, there is no lack of studies that point out the inadequacy of striving for rigid masculinities and the need to develop more healthy constructions of masculinity (see, e.g., Frosh et al., 2001; Skelton, 2001). Rather, less is written about the possibilities of living out or performing alternative masculinity identities. Based on an ethnographic study of children's play at break time in two English primary schools, Epstein et al. (2001) posit that boys mainly express their masculinity through football and fights. However, there is scope to introduce their masculine identities and power relations into the discussion, and it is possible for the boys to find other, more peaceful ways to create and live out their masculine identity.

Have the definitions of masculinity changed or remained consistent? Phipps (2017: 818) posits that even though contemporary forms of masculinity continue to be constructed in relation to women and sexuality, analyses that focus only on these dimensions risk being monolithic and determinist. In the article '"Other" boys: Negotiating non-hegemonic masculinities in the primary school', Renold (2004) analyzes the experiences of boys who choose not to cultivate their masculinities through hegemonic discourses and practices. Renold describes how white working- and middle-class boys in the UK create and seek out spaces from which they can resist, undermine and actively challenge prevailing hegemonic (heterosexual) masculinities within a peer group pupil culture. Renold (2004) distinguishes between undertaking new and 'different' activities—something that even the hegemonic boys sometimes do without being stigmatized—and being markedly 'different', which to a much greater extent exposes the boys to becoming victims of bullying and teasing.

Edley and Wetherell (1997) have also described, based on the English school environment, how some boys aged 17–18 try to define themselves as sensitive 'new men' who at the same time are also able to perform elements of the traditional hard and emotionally closed masculinity. The boys whom Edley and Wetherell interviewed tried to create a masculine identity for themselves where they were not appearing too feminine, while also distancing themselves from the school's macho-influenced rugby players, whom they described as ridiculous and caricatured. They perceived the macho style of rugby players as stupid rather than cool and desirable. They wanted to be men—but not that kind of men. They valued a diversity of gender expressions, and they did not want to prove their masculinity through physical strength and courage but instead through masculine contemplation and reflection. The study shows the complex construction of young men's identity projects and how they constantly negotiate their positions within the peer group. However, it is rare that a direct confrontation takes place between the boys who try to live out more alternative forms of masculinity and the more traditional boys. The 'alternative' boys are aware that they may come to pay a high and painful price, in the form of degrading teasing and bullying, if they break too openly with the traditional norms (see also Blazina et al., 2007). The definition of young men's attempts to appear masculine does not take place via unreflected automatism but is the result of concrete negotiations about which kind of gendered subject the boys want to appear as. Contained herein is a complex relationship between distancing from and approval of traditional forms of masculinity (Renold, 2004). Therefore, it seems crucial to move away from one-dimensional notions about masculinity and avoid reproducing narrow and stereotypical understandings of gender roles.

4.10 Ethnicity and Violence

Regardless of race and ethnicity, perpetrators are mostly men. We rarely ask questions about the gendered factors causing crime and violence when men are the perpetrators of violence, rape or sexual harassment, whether as individuals or as a group. Nevertheless, this is only true when the perpetrators are white men. Race and culture move to the front page when men from minority backgrounds commit rape or violence, particularly when it is perpetrated against white women.

The Swedish gender researcher Inger Lövkrona has pointed out that when the men of the majority culture commit violence, the violence is explained for individual reasons, whereas when men with an immigrant background or descendants of immigrants commit violence, the violence is explained with cultural dimensions (Lövkrona, 2001). This form of culturalization of the violence of ethnic minorities helps to perpetuate the blindness to similarities in different forms of violence by different men, and it often results in an inappropriate essentialist generalization about ethnicity and crime. The same is true of sexual assault. Here, the events from New Year's Eve in Cologne in 2016, when some eighty German women were assaulted and sexually abused by large groups of men with diverse immigrant backgrounds, gave rise to highly simplistic and generalizing presentations of the sexuality of male ethnic minorities.

The media's discourses about violence are not only male, they are also white. Andreassen (2006) highlights that descriptions of violence and rape are an essential aspect of the perception of Danish nationality and Danish gender constructions. Every time the media present ethnic minorities in a certain way, ethnic-majority Danes become indirectly presented in the opposite way. By projecting gender equality issues onto ethnic minorities, ethnic Danes will often appear as liberated and equals. Jensen (2007) has highlighted that the issue of ethnicity, violence and crime has fundamentally changed the social differentiation mechanisms and forms of inequality in Western societies. This often gives rise to young men with ethnic minority backgrounds being linked with gang crime and portrayed as a marginalized and dangerous social group.

4.11 Summary

It has been difficult and sometimes culturally provocative to focus on men as socially gendered, especially when it comes to the more controversial aspects of men's everyday lives. The key messages of the #MeToo movement are that gender is an integral part of power structures and subject to the exercise of power. This is crucial, since there is a widespread tendency to view sexual harassment as an individual problem disconnected from broader social and cultural factors, and many excuses are still made for sexual harassment by men. The latter is often shrouded in denial, and there is a tendency to minimize the nature and scope of the harassment inflicted.

In that respect there has been an invisibility of men's destructive behaviour, often due to the propensity to use social and gender-neutral explanations when dealing with different kinds of men's violence, including sexual harassment. Popular culture defends the objectification of women in many ways, and boys and men often feel pressure to engage in or be complicit in the degradation of women in order to conform to standards of hegemonic masculinity. The next chapter will therefore look more deeply into the reasons why some men find it appealing to engage in sexual harassment.

References

Anderson, E. (2002). Openly gay athletes contesting hegemonic masculinity in a homophobic environment. *Gender & Society, 16*(6), 860–877.

Anderson, E. (2005). Orthodox and inclusive masculinity: Competing masculinities among heterosexual men in a feminized terrain. *Sociological Perspectives, 48*(3), 337–355.

Anderson, E. (2010). *Inclusive masculinity: The changing nature of masculinities*. Routledge.

Andersen, J., & Larsen, J. E. (1998). Gender, poverty and empowerment. *Critical Social Policy, 18*(2), 241–258.

Andreassen, R. (2006). Intersektionalitet i voldtægtsnarrativer [Intersectionality in rape narratives]. *Kvinder, Køn og Forskning, 2–3*, 93–104.

Baker, P. (2001). The international men's health movement has grown to the stage that it can start to influence international bodies. *British Medical Journal, 323*, 1014–1015.

Barker, G., Contreras, J. M., Heilman, B., Singh, A. K., Verma, R. K., & Nascimento, M. (2011). *Evolving men: Initial results from the international men and gender equality survey (IMAGES)*. Washington, D.C.: International Center for Research on Women (ICRW) and Rio de Janeiro: Instituto Promundo.

Bates, L. M., Hankivsky, O., & Springer, K. W. (2009). Gender and health inequities: A comment on the final report of the WHO commission on the social determinants of health. *Social Science & Medicine, 69*(7), 1002–1004.

Beynon, J. (2001). *Masculinities and culture*. McGraw-Hill Education.

Blazina, C., Cordova, M. A., Pisecco, S., & Settle, A. G. (2007). Gender role conflict scale for adolescents: Correlates with masculinity ideology. *Boyhood Studies, 1*(2), 191–204.

Bourdieu, P. (2001). *Masculine domination*. Stanford University Press.

Brooks, G. R. (2010). *Beyond the crisis of masculinity: A transtheoretical model for male-friendly therapy*. American Psychological Association.

Christensen, A.-D., & Larsen, J. E. (2007). Gender, class, and family: Men and gender equality in a Danish context. *Social Politics., 15*(1), 53–78.

Connell, R. W. (1995). *Masculinities*. Polity.

Connell, R. W. (2003). *The role of men and boys in achieving gender equality*. United Nations, Division for the Advancement of Women.

Connell, R. W., & Messerschmidt, J. W. (2005). Hegemonic masculinity: Rethinking the concept. *Gender & Society, 19*(6), 829–859.

Courtenay, W. H. (2000). Constructions of masculinity and their influence on men's well-being: A theory of gender and health. *Social Science & Medicine, 50*(10), 1385–1401.

Digby, T. (1998). *Men doing feminism*. Routledge.

Edley, N., & Wetherell, M. (1997). Jockeying for position: The construction of masculine identities. *Discourse & Society, 8*(2), 203–217.

Edley, N., & Wetherell, M. (2001). Jekyll and Hyde: Men's constructions of feminism and feminists. *Feminism & Psychology, 11*(4), 439–457.

Eduards, M. (2002). *Förbjuden handling: om kvinnors organisering och feministisk teori* [Prohibited action: On women's organization and feminist theory]. Liber ekonomi.

EIGE. (2012). *The involvement of men in gender equality initiatives in the European Union*.

Epstein, D., Kehily, M., Mac An Ghaill, M., & Redman, P. (2001). Boys and girls come out to play: Making masculinities and femininities in school playgrounds. *Men and Masculinities, 4*(2), 158–172.

Flood, M. (2014, March, 28). *Feminism needs men and men needs feminism*. www.ourwatch.org.au

Flood, M. (2018). *Engaging men and boys in violence prevention*. Springer.

Flood, M., & Pease, B. (2009). Factors influencing attitudes to violence against women. *Trauma, Violence, & Abuse, 10*(2), 125–142.

Frosh, S., Phoenix, A., & Pattman, R. (2001). *Young masculinities: Understanding boys in contemporary society*. Macmillan International Higher Education.

Giddens, A. (1992). *The transformation of intimacy: Sexuality, love and eroticism in modern societies*. Polity Press.

Glickman, C. (2012). *Escape the 'Act Like a Man' box*. The good men project.

Grazian, D. (2007). The girl hunt: Urban nightlife and the performance of masculinity as collective activity. *Symbolic Interaction, 30*(2), 221–243.

Greene, M. (2013). *The man box: The link between emotional suppression and male violence*. http://goodmenproject.com/featured-content/megasahd-man-box-the-link-between-emotional-suppression-and-male-violence/

Hearn, J. (1987). *The gender of oppression: Men, masculinity and the critique of Marxism*. Wheatsheaf.

Hearn, J. (1998). *The violences of men: How men talk about and how agencies respond to men's violence to women*. Sage.

Hearn, J. (2004). From hegemonic masculinity to the hegemony of men. *Feminist Theory, 5*(1), 49–72.

Hearn, J. (2012). A multi-faceted power analysis of men's violence to known women: From hegemonic masculinity to the hegemony of men. *The Sociological Review, 60*(4), 589–610.

Hearn, J., & Pringle, K. (2006). *European perspectives on men and masculinities.* Palgrave Macmillan.

Heilman, B., Barker, G., & Harrison, A. (2017). *The man box: A study on being a young man in the US, UK, and Mexico.* Promundo-US and Unilever.

Hill, A. L., Miller, E., Switzer, G. E., Yu, L., Heilman, B., Levtov, R. G.,... & Coulter, R. W. (2020). Harmful masculinities among younger men in three countries: Psychometric study of the Man Box Scale. *Preventive Medicine, 139,* 106185.

Holmgren, L. E., & Hearn, J. (2009). Framing 'men in feminism': Theoretical locations, local contexts and practical passings in men's gender-conscious positionings on gender equality and feminism. *Journal of Gender Studies, 18*(4), 403–418.

Holter, Ø. G. (2003). *Can men do it?* Nordisk Ministerråd.

Jensen, S. Q. (2007). *Fremmed, farlig og fræk: Unge mænd og etnisk/racial andenhed-mellem modstand og stilisering* [Stranger, dangerous and naughty: Young men and ethnic/racial otherness—Between resistance and stylization]. Aalborg universitet.

Katz, J. (2006). *Macho paradox: Why some men hurt women and how all men can help.* Sourcebooks.

Kaufman, M. (2001). *The seven Ps of men's violence, in recommendations of the E.U.* Expert Meeting on Violence against Women, Ministry of Social Affairs and Health, Finland.

Kaufman, M. (2003). *The aim framework: Addressing and involving men and boys to promote gender equality and end gender discrimination and violence.* UNICEF.

Kaufman, M., & Kimmel, M. (2011). *The guy's guide to feminism.* Seal Press.

Kimmel, M. (2008). *Guyland: The perilous world where boys become men.* Harper.

Køster, A. D. (2011). *Familietragedier og æresdrab—en analyse af maskulinitetsfremstillingen i mord-selvmord og mord pa en intim partner i de danske medier* [Family tragedies and honor killings—an analysis of the masculinity portrayal in murder-suicide and murder of an intimate partner in the Danish media]. Specialeafhandling. (Master thesis) Københavns Universitet.

Lövkrona, I. (2001). *Den våldsamme mannen: Mord, misshandel och sexuella övergrepp, historiska och kulturella perspektiv på kön och våld* [The violent man: Murder, assault and sexual assault, historical and cultural perspectives on gender and violence]. Nordic Academic Press.

Madsen, S. A. (2008). *Mænd i psykoterapi* [Men in psychotherapy]. *Psykolognyt, 62*(19), 3–9.

Masters, N. T., Casey, E., Wells, E. A., & Morrison, D. M. (2013). Sexual scripts among young heterosexually active men and women: Continuity and change. *Journal of Sex Research, 50*(5), 409–420.

Mellon, R. C. (2013). On the motivation of quid pro quo sexual harassment in men: Relation to masculine gender role stress. *Journal of Applied Social Psychology, 43*(11), 2287–2296.

Messner, M. A. (1997). *Politics of masculinities: Men in movements*. Altamira Press.

Mills, M. (2001). *Challenging violence in schools*. Open University Press.

Möller-Leimkühler, A. M. (2002). Barriers to help-seeking by men: A review of sociocultural and clinical literature with particular reference to depression. *Journal of Affective Disorders, 71*(1–3), 1–9.

Morgan, D. H. (1992). *Discovering men* (Vol. 3). Taylor & Francis.

Newburn, T., & Mair, G. (1996). *Working with men*. Russell House.

Pascoe, C. J. (2005). 'Dude, you're a fag': Adolescent masculinity and the fag discourse. *Sexualities, 8*(3), 329–346.

Penelope, J. (1990). Speaking freely: Unlearning the lies of the fathers' tongues. Pergamon. Perpetrator, theory, and treatment issues. *Aggression and Violent Behavior, 14*(2), 126–138.

Perez, C. C. (2019). *Invisible women: Exposing data bias in a world designed for men*. Random House.

Phipps, A. (2017). (Re) theorising laddish masculinities in higher education. *Gender and Education, 29*(7), 815–830.

Pollack, W. (1998). *Real boys: Rescuing our sons from the myths of boyhood*. Henry Holt and Company.

Pollack, W. S. (2005). 'Masked men': New psychoanalytically oriented treatment models for adult and young adult men. In G. E. Good & G. R. Brooks (Eds.), *The new handbook of psychotherapy and counseling with men: A comprehensive guide to settings, problems, and treatment approaches* (Rev. ed., pp. 203–216). Jossey-Bass.

Reinicke, K. (2004). *Mænd i lyst og nød* [Men for better or for worse]. Det Schønbergske Forlag.

Reinicke, K. (2012). *Drenge og mænd i krise? Perspektiver og indsatsområder* [Boys and men in crisis? Perspectives and focus areas]. Hans Reitzel.

Renold, E. (2004). 'Other' boys: Negotiating non-hegemonic masculinities in the primary school. *Gender and Education, 16*(2), 247–265.

Romito, P. (2008). *A deafening silence: Hidden violence against women and children*. Policy Press.

Ronkainen, S. (2001). Gendered violence and genderless gender—A Finnish perspective. *Kvinder, Køn & Forskning, 2*, 45–57.

Ruxton, S. (2002). *Men, masculinities and poverty in the UK*. Oxfam.

Ruxton, S. (2020). *Men and gender equality: Challenges and opportunities*. ICMEO.

Skelton, C. (2001). *Schooling the boys: Masculinities and primary education*. Open University Press.

Søndergaard, D. M. (2000). *Tegnet pa kroppen—køn: Koder og konstruktioner blandt unge voksne i Akademia* [Drawing on the body—gender: Codes and constructions among young adults in academia]. Museum Tusculanums Forlag.

The Men's Project and Flood, M. (2018). *The man box: A study on being a young man in Australia*. A Jesuit Social Service.

Van der Gaag, N. (2014). *Feminism and men*. Zed Books Ltd.

Vera-Gray, F. (2016). Men's stranger intrusions: Rethinking street harassment. *Women's Studies International Forum, 58*, 9–17.

White, A., McKee, M., Richardson, N., de Visser, R., Madsen, S. A., de Sousa, B. C.,... & Makara, P. (2011). Europe's men need their own health strategy. *BMJ, 343*.

Whitehead, S. M. (2002). *Men and masculinities, key themes and new directions*. Polity.

Whitt, M. S. (2016). Other people's problems: Student distancing, epistemic responsibility, and injustice. *Journal of Student Philosophy Education, 35*, 427–444.

WHO. (2018). *Fact sheet—Men's health and well-being in the WHO European region*.

5

Who Perpetrates Sexual Harassment and Why

To understand sexual harassment, it is necessary to provide in-depth knowledge of what causes it. Until we move beyond seeing sexual harassment as being committed by a 'few bad apples', we will fail to understand the reasons and to address them accurately. We need to challenge the culture and address the structural and systemic gender inequality that fortifies it, rather than respond only to individual episodes as they occur.

As mentioned earlier in the introduction, the book is based on the notion that we must understand the construction of masculine identities and the role that sexually harassing behaviours play in bringing them about. Further, I have underlined the sociological link between traditional attitudes of masculinity and the practice of sexual harassment. Likewise, I have stressed that sexual harassment must be viewed along a continuum of behaviours that could result in sexual violence (Dobash et al., 2000; Kelly, 1988). Yet, I will start this chapter by looking at research focusing on the individual and psychological characteristics of sexual harassers. I will then turn my attention to the collective socialization of men and the production of male identities through male bonding, peer culture and 'lad' culture. We will also meet the voices of the interviewed men for the first time.

Despite the fact that the consequences of sexual harassment for its victims are well documented, there is still very little research that has focused on the characteristics of men who sexually harass (Pina et al., 2009). The international literature has debated whether developing typologies of men who carry out sexual harassment might make it possible to describe how and why some men do this. There have been discussions of whether, by comparing men who carry out sexual harassment with those who do not, it might be possible to gain insight into the processes and behavioural patterns at the root of the phenomenon (Lengnick-Hall, 1995; Lucero et al., 2003, 2006; O'Donohue et al., 1998; O'Leary-Kelly et al., 2000; Pryor et al., 1993).

Lee et al. (2003) posit that although many years of research on sexual harassment have greatly improved our understanding of the consequences of sexual harassment victimization and of the contextual variables that increase sexual harassment, relatively little has been learned as to individual characteristics of sexual harassment perpetrators other than some demographic characteristics such as age, marital status and education. This might reflect the difficulty of obtaining participant samples that consist of actual sexual harassment offenders. Men's self-awareness of having engaged in sexual harassment has also been absent in many contexts. Studies show that even when doing anonymous, quantitative surveys, hardly anybody will admit to sexually harassing behaviour (O'Donohue et al., 1998). Logan (2015: 203) suggests that there are two broad overlapping categories of rationalizations for harassment, both shaped by masculine entitlement: male bonding and control. Some men legitimize their harassment as human nature, harmless demonstrations of sexual attraction, and sometimes as a way to bond with other men. Others obviously are set to intimidate, shame, terrorize, control or assault their targets. This is in line with Page and Pina (2015) who, in their review of the motives behind sexual harassers, state that a dichotomy exists in which motives for sexually harassing behaviour are rooted in either sexual attraction or hostility. Lucero et al. (2003) indicate that sexual harassment is not a monolithic construct and that not all perpetrators are the same. They emphasize that two dominant themes emerge around the number of targets and the nature of the harassing behaviour. Some harassers appear to target a small number of victims persistently, while others appear to harass all targets whenever possible.

5.1 Socio-demography

Researchers have also looked at how individual differences play a powerful role in facilitating sexual harassment (Pina et al., 2009). Just as with people using violence and purchasing sex, the most certain thing to say about somebody who perpetrates sexual harassment is that they are very likely to be a man (Pryor & Stoller, 1994; Perry et al., 1998). It becomes more difficult when trying to say something about the perpetrator's marital status, age and educational level, because there are not many reliable socio-demographic indicators. Regarding workplace harassment some studies point out that the man who practises sexual harassment tends to be married, older and more educated than the victim, just as he is often in a higher hierarchical position (Pina et al., 2009). Other studies have questioned the hierarchical aspect and emphasized that sexual harassment is also practised by subordinates but especially among peers (Cleveland & Kerst, 1993).

5.2 The Social-Psychological Model

Whether a person is reluctant or willing to harass other people depends on several factors. Studies show that sexual harassers appear to have problematic ideas of power and sex, unfavourable attitudes towards women and poor empathy, and are likely to blame their own victims for their harassment (De Judicibus & McCabe, 2001; Pina et al., 2009; Pryor & Stoller, 1994). Psychologist John Pryor of Illinois State University is often referred to when it comes to the development of social-psychological explanations of why sexual harassment is practised by *some* people (mainly men) at *some* point in time. Pryor's point is that some men are more likely to practise sexual harassment, just as there are some situations and environments where it is considered more legitimate to practise harassment. Thus, Pryor argues that the incidence of sexual harassment is influenced by a combination of individual differences in propensity to practise sexual harassment (personal factors) and the norms that affect the person's social environment (situational factors).

Most people, to varying degrees, are raised to respect the rights and dignity of others and will, by default, therefore have considerations about exploiting and harming others. Therefore, even if a person wants to offend or harass another person, there are often personal boundaries and inhibitions that need to be crossed first. However, not all people have incorporated these considerations. Sexual harassment is most often perpetrated by men with a propensity for transgressive behaviour in a context where there is a set of norms that are tolerant, ambiguous, or even supportive of conducting sexual harassment (Pryor et al., 1995). Pryor developed what he called a 'likelihood to sexually harass' (LSH) scale, which measures readiness to behave in a sexually exploitative manner. The scale is based on the argument that individual characteristics and the situational context interact to increase the likelihood that sexually harassing activities will occur. The scale is the most widely used measuring instrument and has been used to analyze the hypothetical inclination to practise sexual harassment. The LSH scale has been used in many contexts to understand the attitudes and personality traits of men who are highly likely to sexually harass, and to predict sexual harassment behaviour and how men respond when confronted with their behaviour. The proclivity score scale assesses likelihood to sexually harass by using ten different hypothetical scenarios and a series of self-report measures. These self-report measures ask respondents to indicate how likely it would be for them to behave in a sexually harassing manner if their behaviour were not to result in reprisals (Pryor, 1987).

It is a widely held feminist view that sexual harassment is only to a small extent about sexuality, and mainly about power and control. Pryor et al. (1993) point out that it is wrong to claim that sexual harassment has nothing to do with sexuality because sexual harassment at the psychological level may be closely linked to notions of power and sexuality. Malamuth (1986) has also emphasized that the desire to dominate women is a major motive for sexual harassment. Pryor et al. (1993) state that this is of course true if viewed from the victim's point of view only. However, if viewed from the perpetrator's point of view, the search for power and the need for social dominance may be closely linked to the person's sexuality. Pryor argues that the proclivity to engage in sexual harassment in a cognitive way is related to the ability to associate sexuality and social dominance (Pryor & Stoller, 1994). Pryor (1987) also points out that there appears to be a significant overlap in characteristics between men who commit sexual harassment and other sexual offenders such as rapists. Furthermore, Pryor argues that some sexually harassing men maintain problematic attitudes towards women, have a rigid perception of power and gender and tend to blame sexual harassment on the victim by attempting to legitimize the social context of the act. Other studies, again, have shown that in terms of more antisocial personality characteristics, perpetrators of sexual harassment have been found to lack social conscience and engage in irresponsible behaviour or manipulative and exploitative behaviours (Kosson et al., 1997). Research has also supported the link between LSH and acceptance of interpersonal violence against women (Begany & Milburn, 2002; Malamuth & Dean, 1991; Pryor, 1987). Begany and Milburn (2002) indicate that sexual harassment (non-physically violent sexual aggression) is a part of the same continuum as physically violent sexual aggression.

5.3 Typological Descriptions

Attempts have been made to develop different typologies of men who practise sexual harassment based on knowledge of both the behavioural and the individual characteristics of the sexually harassing man. These studies show that men's sexual harassment of women can originate from both hostile and benevolent motives (Fiske & Glick, 1995). Several researchers have tried to develop typologies based upon different archetypes of male harassers. They focus on the duration of the sexual harassment, the emotional attachment to the victim, the number of victims and the nature of the sexual harassment (Dziech & Weiner, 1984; Lengnick-Hall, 1995; Lucero et al., 2003, 2006). These typologies might help us to understand why and when perpetrators harass. Lengnick-Hall (1995) describes both character traits and behaviours and distinguishes three types of men who commit sexual harassment:

- 'Hard-core' harassers are the most conscious violators and are individuals who seek situations that enable them to harass. They are resistant to stopping when confronted. They often harass in a carefully chosen and strategic way. They practise sexual harassment in an open and direct manner for the purpose of intimidating and controlling the victim. These men often have personality traits that distinguish them from most other people in that they often practise other forms of dysfunctional behaviour.
- The 'opportunist' does not look for opportunities to harass but will harass when the opportunity is presented. It is often a person who seizes an opportunity without having in any way planned it. This type of offender exhibits a more inconsistent pattern of harassment.
- 'Insensitive' harassers are unaware of the impact of their behaviour on others, for instance the bungler, who is simply unable to behave properly. This kind of sexual harassment is often woven into an attempt to create an emotionally romantic relationship with the victim. Regarding the way men respond when confronted with their behaviour, both 'opportunists' and 'insensitive harassers' are likely to stop if confronted.

In the actor-based dynamic perspective proposed by O'Leary-Kelly et al. (2000), harassers are viewed as decision makers who choose behaviours based on their goals and the reactions of their target(s). O'Leary-Kelly et al. (2000) criticized previous research on sexual harassment as providing little guidance as to when or how perpetrators might harass. To better address these fundamental issues, they proposed the use of an actor-based perspective grounded in the interpersonal aggression literature to provide a more useful and dynamic model of the sexual harassment process. The approach is interactive, in that the authors discuss the effects of sexually harassing actions on the target's perceptions, motives and behavioural response choice.

There is reason to believe that the majority of men who expose women to sexual harassment are not pathological harassers. There are, of course, men who deliberately harass women physically and sexually to assert power over them. Thompson (1994: 327) explained that 'strategic harassers deliberately intimidate women to maintain a particular social, economic, or political privilege'. However, the majority of men who practise sexual harassment are probably 'ordinary' men who do not think about or have enough empathic sense to understand how degrading it is to be subjected to sexual harassment. Often, if they are made aware of their sexual harassment, these men will try to explain away their behaviour saying that they are just trying to be fun and charming ('it is just a bit of banter') and that what they do is part of culturally accepted behaviour (Reinicke, 2018).

5.4 Social Bonding

Why do men act out sexual harassment if they are, to a certain extent, aware that it is not correct to do so? To answer the question, we have to look into the phenomenon of male bonding and how the collective socialization of men takes place. The social norms associated with manhood and the social organization of men's lives and relations play a crucial role in shaping men's sexual harassment of women. Homosociality between men has a huge impact on the construction of masculinity (Flood, 2018; Schwartz & DeKeseredy, 1997). In the article 'Sexual harassment and masculinity: The power and meaning of "girl watching"', Quinn (2002) sets out to describe how sexual harassment may be explained to some extent by the requirements of masculinity. Through a process-oriented understanding of sexual harassment, Quinn (2002) attempts to describe the social logic of the phenomenon of 'girl watching' and what it has to do with the production of male identities as well as the creation of social relations. Quinn's main point is that men's refusal to see their behaviour as harassing may be partly explained through the objectification and reduced empathy that the production of masculine identities may require (see also Grazian, 2007).

'Girl watching' refers to the kind of activity that occurs when men together with other men 'evaluate' women's sexual value. It can take the form of, for example, either verbal comments or gestures that indicate that you are 'checking out' something. It can be expressed through explicit comments about the woman's body or imagined sexual activities with the woman. The attention may be on an individual woman or a group of women or simply a photograph or other representation. The woman may be a stranger, co-worker, supervisor, employee or client (Quinn, 2002).

The practice of girl watching is, of course, easier to do in public spaces and especially in nightclubs, where there is a broader acceptance of aggressive and harassing behaviour (Grazian, 2007). However, Quinn (2002) argues that girl watching is widely used in many workplaces and that it easily becomes normalized and trivialized as a game or play between men, which can be defended with versions of the phrase 'boys will be boys'. There is considerable evidence to support that men engage in sexually harassing acts because of ambiguity regarding the appropriateness of that behaviour (Fiske & Glick, 1995; Glick & Fiske, 2011). The fact that men engage in sexual harassment together can create an enjoyable and funny atmosphere, which again might create unity and a strong feeling of 'us' and 'them'. Social bonding among men is a primary factor when sexual harassment takes place in public. Benard and Schlaffer (1984: 71) state that most men perceive street harassment as harmless and a cure for boredom and that it gives them a 'feeling of youthful camaraderie'.

'Checking women out' is often accepted by men as a natural and everyday activity, especially when several men are gathered together. Overall, girl watching can lead to sexual harassment and often creates barriers for men to understand the harm and fear that the phenomenon can cause in the victim. Nevertheless, the phenomenon of girl watching, as Quinn puts it,

> sits on the blurry edge between fun and harm, joking and harassment. An understanding of the process of identifying behavior as sexual harassment, or of rejecting this label, may be built on this ambiguity. (Quinn, 2002: 387)

As stated at the beginning of the book, sexual harassment can represent both a form of power and a source of humour for men. If we look at the literature on sexist humour and its role in male bonding, there is evidence that when a man tells a sexist joke, it may serve the social function of strengthening male in-group cohesion and solidarity (Thomae & Pina, 2015). Sexist humour can be perceived as a social 'lubricant' for the male in-group and as a social 'abrasive' in intergroup relations between men and women (Martineau, 1972). This is consistent with work by Kehily and Nayak (1997), who explored the role of humour in young men's school cultures. They found that the use of humour between men might strengthen their heterosexual masculine identities. Jokes blurring the line between humour and harassment helped the young men to establish a heterosexist status hierarchy.

Girl watching is a game that is played by men for men and where participation and awareness of the game on the woman's part is relatively irrelevant, as she is reduced to an object. Girl watching can have many different forms of expression, depending on the context and the men involved. A prerequisite for being able to participate and thrive in the activity (play or harassment) is that, to some extent, the men involved are able to primarily objectify the woman and the suppression of empathy for her. Gardner (1995) has also highlighted that when men talk about their sexual harassment of a woman, they rarely mention her reaction. This can be either because men have no knowledge or empathic sense to familiarize themselves with the woman's situation and feelings, or because they are not motivated to try to put themselves in her place. Men perceive women as the target of their gaze, as objects rather than participants, and thus women are not the intended audience for the game. In its most serious form, girl watching can serve as a deliberate power strategy in which men want all the potential audience, including the targeted woman, to be made aware that they are looking at her based on the notion that they have every right to sexually evaluate her.

Men's disregard for women's subjectivity and men's tendency not to consider the consequences of their behaviour means that, when women confront them with their behaviour, men are likely to be confused but often also aggressive. Thus, men can be surprised or baffled by the woman's response if they are caught staring at or commenting on her and she aggressively approaches them and shouts, for example, 'What do you think you are doing?'

When men collectively comment on women's bodies, in addition to being play it can also be a way for men to consolidate their masculinity and establish intimacy between them, as well as help to display a heterosexual desire. The fact that social relations are also created through men's assessment of women's bodies and sexual value, coupled with some men's ability not to feel empathy for the victim, are two reasons why men and women often do not view sexual harassment in the same way. Research shows that increasing men's knowledge about sexual harassment will only make a difference if this awareness is paired with recognition that sexism is unjust (Becker & Swim, 2011; Flood, 2018). Quinn (2002) highlights from her interview study of male engineers that when asked how they thought the women who were the objects of their 'game' perceived this playing, they said that they were well aware that being the object of the game could be perceived significantly differently from participating in the game. Interestingly, Quinn points out that none of the men were able to describe the game 'girl watching' from the woman's point of view while maintaining its masculine significance of being play. When they were forced to consider the subjective position of a woman, they had to admit that it was no longer an innocent game but rather something which should be avoided. This is a very interesting point because it indicates and gives hope that the more aware men become of women's experiences, the greater the understanding they will develop of the negative consequences of sexual harassment.

That women tend to see harassment where men see harmless fun or normal gendered interaction is one of the more robust findings in sexual harassment research (Cleveland & Kerst, 1993). Quinn (2002) argues that these differences may be partially explained by the performative requirements of masculinity. Some theorists argue that men are more likely to discount the harassing aspects of their behaviour because of a culturally conditioned tendency to misperceive women's intentions. Looking at the subjectivities of the perpetrator, Stockdale (1993: 96) argued, 'patriarchal norms create a sexually aggressive belief system in some people more than others, and this belief system can lead to the propensity to misperceive'. Gender differences in interpreting sexual harassment, then, may be the outcome of the acceptance of normative ideas about women's inscrutability and indirectness and men's role as sexual aggressors. Men see harmless flirtation or sexual interest rather than harassment because they misperceive women's intent and responses.

5.5 Peer Pressure and Lad Culture

Which aspects of male culture provide active support for some men's abusive behaviour? In her groundbreaking work on sexual harassment in public space, Gardner (1995) demonstrated that many episodes of sexual harassment are performed by men in groups. The peer culture is central in policing men and boys to conform in accordance with traditional masculinity norms (Dempster, 2009). We must not underestimate how powerful the world of peer culture is in policing masculinity. Many men may go along with a behaviour they are not comfortable with, but they hesitate and stay silent.

Therefore, if we are to understand the social meaning of sexual harassment and how constructions of masculinities motivate men to engage in sexual harassment, we must look at how men act in groups. With regard to sexual harassment as culturally accepted behaviour, it is crucial to look at the prevalence of the phenomenon of 'lad culture' and laddish masculinities and the implications it has for the creation of young men's gender identity. Laddism is both an identity performance and a social practice and has been associated with concerns about sexual harassment and violence (Phipps, 2017). It is difficult for teenage boys not to develop gender attitudes inspired by lad culture. Lad culture is a youthful ideal for many men; it functions as a group mentality often articulated through activities such as sport, partying and heavy alcohol consumption, and is characterized by sexist and homophobic 'banter' (sexualized humour) (Phipps & Young, 2013; Phipps et al., 2018).[1] Lad culture in its sexist variant can have broad cultural appeal and is a highly prized and recognizable cultural phenomenon. It is difficult to oppose because it often appears politically incorrect in a provocative but also 'charming' way. The term 'banter' appears to be very central to the driving force behind young men's attempts to diminish the perception of their aggressive and harassing behaviour (Nichols, 2018). Dempster (2009) emphasizes that lad culture can serve as a kind of template for

---

[1] I am aware that 'lad culture' is a British phenomenon. However, as shown in Chapter 3 a strong 'lad culture' does also exist in Denmark. The Danish word for 'lad' is *drengerøv*. The term is often used to describe a young man who is behaving immaturely.

the hegemonic masculinity of many young men. Nevertheless, Dempster also points out that it is not innocent, because it encompasses a certain kind of sex-discriminatory humour that contributes to the acceptance of sexual harassment in society.

Perkins (2003) has stated that according to social norm theory, people behave the way they see others behave. Group norms can be defined as informal behaviour guidelines, a code of conduct that delivers a kind of conformity to group activities and might have a major impact on the prevalence of sexual harassment (Pryor et al., 1993). These notions often function as hidden peer pressure and cause the individual member of a group to conform to the group's norms and attitudes, even if they do not necessarily agree with the norms. Membership of the group can mean that many young men try to avoid creating polarization and conflict. Of importance for the practice of sexual harassment among men in groups is that the practice of sexual harassment is a significant factor in creating a sense of male bonding.

Hegemonic masculinity is often constructed in relation to women and sexuality (Sweeney, 2014), and derogatory statements about women and girls can play a part in confirming men's gender identity. There are reasons to believe that many men who engage in sexually harassing behaviour may not be consciously aware that they are doing so and that their actions are inappropriate or a misuse of their power (Fitzgerald, 1993). Bates (2014) posits that the vast majority of those men who are occasionally sexist are not deliberately, hatefully trying to hurt women or put them down. Instead, they just perform a role they have learned is acceptable. Therefore, much of men's sexist behaviour is 'not intentional or deliberately prejudiced, but simply the result of being immersed in a very patriarchal culture' (Bates, 2014: 328).

Wesselmann and Kelly (2010) analyzed the attitudes, behaviour and motivation of American male college students both when alone and when with other men in groups. The study showed that men were more likely to engage in sexual harassment in groups and that anonymity and male bonding played a significant role (see also Schwartz & DeKeseredy, 1997). If the members of the group perceive the norms as acceptable, it will increase the risk that they are tempted and encouraged to practise sexual harassment. The notion of anonymity can play a crucial role.

Namely, the actual or indirect physical presence of other consenting persons can create a sense of anonymity that can facilitate the manifestation of certain forms of inhibited behaviour, including sexually harassing comments and behaviours (Barak, 2005). Jordan (1995) also emphasizes that the pressure to act in conformity with traditional gender perceptions and many of the most important experiences about what it means to be a real 'man' come from all-male social group arenas, where boys are only in the company of other boys. In these arenas, many rigid notions of masculinity are established, including the justification of harassing behaviour.

Some harassers explicitly set out to anger or humiliate their victims (Benard & Schlaffer, 1984), and wanting to humiliate women through sexual harassment can give status in peer groups. In that respect, the offensive practice of 'hogging' is interesting. Hogging can be defined as sexually degrading behaviour where men deliberately look for women they consider fat or unattractive for the purposes of sexual gratification and/or sport (Gailey & Prohaska, 2006). Hogging practices exist on a continuum, from gang rape at the most extreme to betting who can dance with the fattest woman at a night club or party. Gailey and Prohaska (2011) state that regardless of the severity of the hogging activity, the phenomenon can be interpreted as a misogynistic practice aimed at harming or mocking the victim as a form of homosocial bonding.

5.6 Youth and Rape Culture

What does it mean to have been raised in a rape culture and when does it make sense to claim so? Rape culture can be defined as social attitudes, policies and laws that normalize and trivialize sexual violence or blame women for their own sexual victimization (Loney-Howes, 2019: 23). Victim blaming is an attitude that suggests a victim rather than the perpetrator bears responsibility for an assault. Victim blaming is a crucial element in rape culture because it directs attention towards the actions of survivors, such as what a woman is wearing, what and how much she has been drinking, where she stayed, and so forth.

Nevertheless, it is culturally important to emphasize that the term 'rape culture' is seldom used in a Danish context to describe the social environment that allows sexual violence to be normalized and justified. In contrast, the term 'score culture', which gives credit to the man, is often used to describe the messages circulating between peers about how 'no' does not always mean 'stop' but might also be interpreted as 'try harder'. Seen in a broader perspective, it says something about how different kinds of violence against women in Denmark are not always seen as an expression of men's power over women.

The thinking behind the boastful aspect of scoring is that women are just an object to be won. It is a common cultural belief that it is the man who must conquer the woman. A scoring culture thus includes the idea that the woman should be passive and that it is the man who, with his charm and gentlemanly demeanour, should score with the woman. By courting her, he can convince her that he is worth giving in to, so that it ends up that she wants to have sex with him. This perception may give some men an idea that when the woman says no, it will still be possible to score with her and that she just says 'no' to 'play hard to get' or just needs to continue to be pursued.

It has long been the general view that it was the woman's own responsibility to say 'no' and take care of herself—for example, by not getting too drunk, not wearing provocative clothes and never walking alone at night (see, e.g., Koss, 2018). Likewise, the same attitudes often apply to more serious sexual assaults, including rape. We see widespread victim blaming when making remarks to the victim about what she could have done differently, or questioning her with comments such as 'are you sure it happened?' Another common misperception about rape is that a woman reports rape because 'she has regrets and wants revenge' (Everyday Sexism Project.dk).

Slut-shaming is another form of victim blaming where girls and women in particular are criticized for breaking the norm of how a woman 'should' look and behave. The term refers to the practice of putting down women who dress defiantly and have a sexual expression that falls outside what is socially accepted. If a woman has been raped while wearing a short skirt, she risks being blamed and told that 'she asked for it'. Therefore, slut-shaming supports a mindset that it is women's own fault because they must have sent some kind of welcoming signal to attract the attention (Herriot & Hiseler, 2015). In addition, women who have lots of consensual, casual sex are often being told that they are 'deserving' of being raped and that they generally are engaging in 'shameful' behaviour.

A large proportion of the norms and expectations that are associated with flirting, sex and boundaries are about gender. There are particular expectations of which roles and positions men and women are expected to assume when they meet or become interested in each other. There is a widespread norm that heterosexual boys or men must take the initiative and the lead when it comes to flirting, pick-ups or having sex, while heterosexual girls must take a passive stance and are responsible for saying 'yes' or 'no' to the boy's initiative (Dahl et al., 2018).

Society in many ways worships sexually aggressive masculinity and normalizes the degradation and objectification of women (Katz, 2006). Many young men are socialized to be persistent and to focus on their own desires and ignore the needs of others, and some are searching for an identity of their own by attempting to violate the boundaries of others (Budde, 2009). A study of New Zealand and British adolescents' narratives concerning sexuality, sexual practices and coercion within heterosexual dating relationships demonstrated that sexual coercion operates through 'normal' heterosexuality (Hird & Jackson, 2001). Further, Tolman et al. (2003) have shown that male aggression is to a certain extent expected and normalized, and that there is a strong pressure among boys to behave in a sexually aggressive way. One of the men in my study states it as:

> It was almost a sport, being a bit sexually aggressive and harassing girls… and you could almost say that doing what was not allowed was viewed positively in some groups of boys.

Mac an Ghail (1994) has emphasized that boys often perceive all-male friend groups as a place where they need to prove their masculinity. In these group settings, it is difficult to express vulnerability, and there is a big difference in how boys talk about their relationships with girls depending on whether they are alone with girls or together with boys in all-male groups. Several of the men in my study describe their teenage years as a time when it was about outperforming your peers. Some had personal experiences of this among their group of close friends, while others noted that they had only seen this in acquaintances. What sexual experiences do men then share with each other? One of the men in my study said that one would not tell male friends about unsuccessful sexual experiences involving, for example, erectile dysfunction if one wanted to be respected by them. The sexual stories that were told were mostly about the successes. There may also be embarrassing stories told that highlight how clumsy one was, but the stories are rarely about how difficult sex can be, and vulnerable and sensitive topics are seldom brought up in conversation. Overall, vulnerability is not a big factor in how men see themselves. One of the men described it in the following way:

> It is about outperforming your peers and being able to tell good stories... the stories don't always end up with sex... but there needs to be a climax to the stories that can at least be funny... for example, if you messed up in the worst way possible.

Budde (2009) emphasizes that the male body has to live up to masculine expectations in order to not risk being exposed to mocking and feminizing remarks. He points out that the body is both an actor and an objective in the marginalization and subordination strategies that boys can use against each other. Kehily (2001) also describes how embodiment and strong physical performance are important factors in how boys create and maintain their heterosexual masculine identities. The enactments of heterosexual masculinities demonstrate both the normative power of heterosexuality and the fragility of sex/gender categories. Boys are often encouraged to sexualize intimate relations with women and heterosexual masculinity is therefore reproduced via talk about masturbation, sexual conquests and pornography, and consolidated via sexual relations with girls. Teenage boys are often very focused on sexuality, and their sexuality is often self-centred (Berger et al., 2005).

Boys are in no way pre-programmed from birth to deny their feelings and avoid intimacy. Pollack (1998) claims that the culture of masculinities that requires emotional silence is the reason why many boys are not inclined to develop a language to talk about their vulnerability, insecurity and sensitivity. Levant (1995) has pointed out that boys lose the ability to talk about their emotional life in their early childhood. He states that whereas girls learn not to be aggressive and, later, not to be sexually aggressive, boys learn to hide their feelings, become independent and learn to feel shame when they express their fears, sadness and disappointment. Levant also points out that boys experience how it becomes legitimate to transform feelings of insecurity into anger and aggression. Boys can be told off for being angry and aggressive, but they often do not feel the same shame and humiliation that they risk exposing themselves to if they express feelings of vulnerability. It can therefore be difficult for boys to take responsibility for their emotional lives and be honest about emotional issues, and this can result in an undesirable degree of emotional repression.

The vast majority of the men specified that they had not intended to demean or offend the women who were targeted, but there was no way of knowing for sure if they had done so. Some stated that what could be perceived as a fun remark/joke among 'the boys' could easily be viewed as demeaning by women. This is in line with Tuerkheimer (1997), who argues that women are more willing to define acts as sexual harassment and are more likely to perceive situations as coercive. A number of the men said that the reason they had been harassing was not that they had intended to do harm, but it had just been funny in the specific situation, and they had felt like there was a form of *carte blanche* that allowed the behaviour to continue. Several of the men also pointed out that they had been given credit for it by the other boys. This is supported by Gailey and Prohaska (2007), who state that often sexual harassment is committed by men to amuse and gain status with male friends.

Among some of the men, it is also mentioned that the charming boys, particularly the good-looking ones, could get away with a lot, as the girls, for example, also thought it was funny to be smacked on the bum if one of the good-looking boys did it. One of the men described it in the following way:

> Often the charming boys really profited from that, because they weren't afraid to go the distance.

This corresponds with Fairchild (2010), who posits that there are many individual and situational variables that can influence the perception of harassment, and that harassment by younger and attractive men is often viewed as less harassing, although it should be noted that this is typically from the perception of men, and does not necessarily reflect how women interpret these experiences. This is also to be found in Thompson and Cracco's article (2008) titled 'Sexual aggression in bars: What college men can normalize', where it is stated that the young men most likely to be sexually aggressive in bar settings are also the men who describe themselves as having 'socially attractive qualities'.

Some of the men also emphasize the importance for the internal hierarchy in the male group of picking up women.

> There was definitely some prestige in sleeping with a lot of girls back when I was single… it could be used as a status symbol and help you to advance in the social hierarchy if you had slept with a lot of girls or really attractive girls… it was exciting going out and proving yourself in a way.

They talk about the competitive approach to sexuality and young men's tireless struggle to 'get laid' and then receiving the recognition that comes with it.

> When I was in upper secondary school, I was partying a lot and back then it was the case that if you could pick up the hottest woman on the dance floor, then you were high up in the hierarchy… then you had a story to tell the others when you were back in school on Monday.

The above quote indicates, as Flood (2008: 5) states, that 'sexual activity is a key path to masculine status and other men are the audience, always imagined and sometimes real, for one's sexual activities.' The majority of the men state that they grew up with the notion that they have a different role to play from women when it comes to dating and relationships. Overall, the men said that they often have a responsibility, as neither women nor men expect the woman to take the initiative. Therefore, if something were to happen, it was up to the man to make the first move because they do not expect the women to approach them and say, 'Wow, you're good-looking.'

Most men agreed that it could be dangerous to base one's self-perception on what happens in their sex life and that one could easily end up violating the boundaries of others without intending to or being aware of it, if one's dating practice became a kind of contest and if the contest gets out of hand.

> One of the reasons we hear about rape can also be that some people are so keen on proving themselves... this may be related to a lack of self-esteem and feeling that you have to prove that you can pick up women... and it can be dangerous if they don't want to but you are sexually aggressive or frustrated... no doubt a lot of people's boundaries are violated in such situations.

It was repeated several times that avoiding inappropriate sexual behaviour was about being able to interpret signals and get a feel for the situation and then knowing what to look for and daring to make your move. A substantial number of the men point out that those who picked up the most women were sometimes also those who were not afraid to violate other people's boundaries and that caution was seldom rewarded.

5.7 The Penetration Norm

All the men in the study said that they now treat women and girls with respect and care. None of the men had forced women into sex or sexually assaulted women. However, it is always possible that some of them are lying or are not aware that what they did constitutes sexual assault. Nevertheless, they acknowledged that they had participated in maintaining sexism though they had not been involved in the bluntest forms of men's power against women. Several of the men talked about how they have acted based on masculine ideals, presenting the man as a hunter and the woman as the prey and the man needing to take the risks. Prahl (2018) points out that the penetration norm means that it is not enough to be in love with and fascinated by women. Penetrative sex is the most prestigious activity. Several of the men had subscribed to this ideal and spoke about the pressure of expectations to have penetrative sex. They pointed out how much there was to gain by attempting to 'score' and describe how no street credit was gained from saying that they were in love with or attracted to a woman. As an example of the penetration norm, one of the men spoke about the following dilemma:

> You have taken a woman home but have agreed that there will be no sex. However, you may be faced with the dilemma that you are unsure whether you should attempt to get her to agree to sex or if you should lie about having had sex with her – which comes with the risk of appearing like an idiot if the woman calls you out on the lie… but it may be worth taking the chance, because you also don't want your friends to see you as someone incapable of going all the way… If you haven't had sex, it doesn't count… you can laugh about it and think that's stupid, but that's how it works.

The above quotes indicate how men's sexual storytelling is shaped by homosocial masculine cultures (Flood, 2008) and how peers impose the standards of masculinity to maintain the code of 'acting like a man'. Men's peer relations might have a deep influence on some men's heterosexual involvements. It appears that for some men it is more important to impress their peers than the woman they have sex with. It is therefore essential to understand the dynamics between young men and how men can prove their masculinity to each other. It was stated several times that when it comes to assessing success, it is about taking risks. Participants underlined that sex is not just something that happens between two people. Instead, it is a signal to the world about how successful and attractive a person is. This is in accordance with Kimmel (2008: 172), who states that for many young men it is about having sex with as many women as possible and as frequently as possible, no matter what. Gavey (2005) talks about 'the male sexual drive discourse' which assumes that men always want sex and if they do not, there must be something wrong (see also Meenagh, 2021).

In that context, Paglia (1991) has pointed out that men only become masculine when other men say that they are, and having sex with a woman is one way of being regarded as masculine. Such a view of gender and sexuality increases the risk of sexual assaults and inappropriate sexual behaviour because it urges men to cross the line and act out in a fearless and limit-seeking way.

Dahl et al. (2018) emphasize that traditional gender norms impact boys and girls differently. When boys tell of their sexual escapades, they are praised and get street credit, whereas the most sexually active girls risk being portrayed as 'easy'. They also emphasize that it can be difficult being in a male peer group and being one of those who are unable to brag about sexual conquests. Boys who have not had their sexual debut are more likely to speak about loneliness than boys who are sexually active.

One of the men stated that there was almost an unwritten rule that you had to have had sex with a certain number of girls before you could take it easy and enter into a steady relationship. These problems are also touched upon in the podcast from The Danish daily, *Information*, called 'Grænseland – samtaler med mænd om sex' ('Borderland – Conversations with men about sex'), where a young man in the upper secondary school age group tells how he got a girlfriend that he liked in upper secondary school but this also meant that he could no longer participate in the prestigious contest of picking up the most girls and thus get more 'notches in his belt'.

Masculinity must be won and proven. Masculinity is about challenging and testing other men. The logic behind the creation of masculinity is that men must do or risk something in order to become men. They must be validated by other men (Brannon, 1976; Willis, 1977). In that context, many of the men expressed the importance of what other men say about the sexual experiences that are presented. The competitive element is a key feature of the telling. They test and prove each other by competing around quantitative measures of sexual experiences.

> Having sex was cool, and the first one of the boys to have sex was the coolest.

> It was not the quality of the girl that matters, it was the quantity. I don't think many of the guys woke up the next day and had any regrets... it was just about getting out there and getting high fives from the guys

> when you had slept with a girl… it was some male ego and competition thing and the charming boys really profited from that when they could demonstrate that they were a real player.

Kimmel (2008: 98) states that a person undergoes initiation in order to stabilize a new permanent identity. Several of the men say that it was particularly in the early teenage years where the quality of the intercourse was not important: rather, you just had to 'pass' by proving that you were capable of having intercourse. Even though most men noted that the importance of having had a lot of sexual partners was mainly an aspect of their early youth, there were also some men in their mid-20s who admitted that it was still something that provided status among men.

> There are still some of my friends who are very interested in who and how many they have slept with and who view picking up women as a hard currency.

As the quote indicates, they earned status when they were sexually active. It did not in any way cost them their reputation—rather the reverse, in fact.

5.8 Do Men Know When They Violate Someone's Boundaries?

There can be many contradicting emotions at play when it comes to erotic encounters between the sexes. Some of the men emphasized that you cannot be sure that you will never violate someone's boundaries, but you can get better at avoiding such situations. They state that it is about being open about what you will take part in and where your boundaries and the boundaries of others are. It is important to have a language and a conversation about sexual topics. However, it can be uncomfortable to talk about boundaries. Therefore, it is important to verbalize the dilemmas and paradoxes.

Benard and Schlaffer (1984) emphasize that most men are at a loss to explain their harassing behaviour and that the notion that women do not like sexual harassment was a novel idea to many men. Several of the men look back on their teenage years as a time when they were 'young and horny' and describe how they had a blind spot when it came to the consequences of their aggressive sexual actions in their youth.

> I just wanted to get attention from girls and try to create a connection, and back then I was not thinking that I was trying to dominate. However, with 20/20 hindsight I can see that I tried to dominate... but I felt 100 percent entitled to do so... I just took that right... there was no self-reflection.

> From the age of 16–20, I was not at all aware of the fact that I was perpetrating some kind of sexual harassment. I did not give it any thought at all, I did not know any better.

Sexual boundaries are about what you like and what you do not like in terms of intimacy and sex. Violating your own boundaries can be erotic and exciting, and often you do not know your boundaries before you hit them. Boundaries depend on context and the people you are with. Sexual boundaries are also about many things other than sex; they are about touch, kisses, looks and words, and all the rest that defines intimacy between people when, for example, flirting (Masters et al., 2013).

A substantial number of men have no idea of how profoundly some men's sexual harassment affects women's lives (Cleveland & Kerst, 1993; Herrero et al., 2017). In relation to minor sexually offensive actions such as whistling, groping, rubbing against a girl, staring and speaking loudly about a girl's body, several of the men pointed out that back then they did not think about their harassment as being part of a pattern of abuse and they did not think about what impact their actions had on others.

> When I was in upper secondary school, smacking a girl's bottom or saying something sexist was totally normal. It was part of everyday life, more or less, both for me and the people I hung around with.

They state that they could have done something which they felt did not cross the line, but which in fact did. They worried that something they had done could be seen as sexual harassment.

They spoke about how no one forced them to act in such ways, but there was a kind of pressure of expectation that both men and women gave into. Several of the men pointed out that the #MeToo movement in that context may help to create a mutual understanding of how the way the 'game' is choreographed and set up does not benefit either women or men.

5.9 When Sexual Harassment Is 'Allowed'

Space and location are very important for how sexual harassment is carried out and legitimized (Fileborn, 2016; Nichols, 2018). In terms of the circumstances and in what social contexts sexual harassment takes place in, it appears that nightlife—bars, discos, pubs, concerts, festivals— is a very particular context. Several of the men state that nightlife settings encourage aggressive sexual interaction. Furthermore, they emphasize that the nightlife setting itself also seems to invite a more collective orientation to masculine performance and sexual pursuit than other contexts (see also Grazian, 2007). The reason that these environments are viewed as different is that sexual harassment and unwelcome touches are so internalized that it seems like a natural part of mainstream life for both young men and women. The men often view it as 'normal' to act out sexual harassment and women view it is something they will inevitably be confronted with and something they just have to tolerate (Thompson & Cracco, 2008). The particular thing about that behaviour, which can sometimes seem normative in late-night bar environments, is that it will be perceived as gross sexual harassment or a sexual assault in most other social contexts. Nightlife is thus in some situations viewed as a context in which the normal rules do not apply (Reinicke, 2018).

The reason why sexual harassment in this environment is often viewed leniently and with tolerance is also that the incidents often occur in tightly packed and loud environments where the perpetrator can remain somewhat anonymous and thus run little risk of facing negative consequences (Graham et al., 2017).

The normative codes of behaviour in late-night bar/club environments are to a great extent organized based on an underlying narrative of masculinity that honours and encourages heavy drinking and men's right to take the initiative in sexual interactions (Graham & Homel, 2008). Therefore, an acknowledgement of attention through flirting is often an accepted practice in a bar. Taking into account the victim and abuser's intoxication from alcohol/drugs, research also shows that approximately one-third of the cases where sexual assaults happen involve both victim and perpetrator being under the influence of alcohol (Heinskou et al., 2017).

Thompson and Cracco (2008) studied 264 male American university students and their behaviour towards women in late-night bar/party environments. The study showed that the men to a great extent encourage each other to violate boundaries that would not be tolerated in other contexts. Two-thirds of the men had leant up against a woman from behind and 80 percent had intentionally and without invitation grabbed a woman's behind. Only very few responded that they had never displayed any kind of aggressive and invasive sexual behaviour.

The vulnerability of women is particularly clear in nightlife venues, where the boundaries of socially acceptable behaviour differ from everyday life. This, in addition to the consumption of alcohol, also means that the boundaries for acceptable behaviour are set and controlled by mainly male security personnel who are often proponents of a hyper-masculine and sexist culture (Graham & Homel, 2008; Graham et al., 2017). Dempster (2011) demonstrates the association between heavy alcohol consumption and masculinity and underlines how the consumption of alcohol allows men to prove their manhood to others and facilitate their inclusion in male peer groups. Men often use alcohol as an excuse for their unwelcome behaviour (Abbey & Wegner, 2015). Abbey et al. (2000) have pointed out that alcohol facilitates and makes it easier for men to violate women in nightlife venues but that it is not the *reason* for the violations. They also state that many men claim that misunderstandings can occur when it comes to what women who are intoxicated want in terms of physical contact, including intimate sexual contact.

Ronen (2010) states that the sexualized form of dancing known as 'grinding' is sociologically interesting because it is a public manifestation of contemporary heterosexual scripts, which are a crucial site for the reproduction of gender inequality and which privileges men's pleasure. One of the men stated the following:

> You can also find yourself crossing the line on the dance floor where you are relatively close together… I have tried suddenly beginning a very close dance with a girl without there having been any communication or invitation… here you should probably also be asking for consent, but how? Is it a nod or is it just her not walking away?

Men habitually initiate grinding and acceptance is seldom verbal. Most often, it takes the form of a woman allowing the initiator to continue dancing near her and allowing him to touch her during dancing—that is, not rejecting him.

In terms of how commonly women are victims of unwelcome sexual advances in nightlife venues, Graham et al. (2017) state that based on an American study of 153 women aged 19–29 who frequented bars, 75 percent had been exposed to either unwelcome sexual touching or persistent flirting and 46 percent had been exposed to both. The women responded that they felt violated, disrespected and angry. However, half the women participating in the study also said that they did not take the incidents seriously because they almost always happened and 25 percent stated that they also felt a bit flattered at first, even if almost everyone reported at least one negative emotion associated with the incidents.

The value of women in society has also been closely linked to men's 'approval' of women as sex objects. Women are therefore to some extent socialized to adapt to men's desires. The question of whether unwanted sexual attention can be experienced positively, as the victim may also feel flattered, occurs especially in nightlife venues, where much focus is on sexuality and appearing physically attractive (Fairchild, 2010; Sue, 2010). Studies also show that although some forms of harassment occur because men sincerely believe that women are receptive to these comments, many others are committed by men for their own gain or to entertain and gain status among male friends (Gailey & Prohaska, 2006; Ronen, 2010).

5.10 When Men Are Exposed to Inappropriate Sexual Behaviour

Even though it is mainly women who are exposed to sexual harassment, there is a growing number of reports from men who were exposed to sexual harassment (Quick & McFadyen, 2017). Bates (2014) emphasizes, however, that sexual harassment of men and women is not the same thing and that the overall problem of sexual harassment in public spaces affects women far more often than it does men. Women are more likely to feel afraid for their safety when a strange man shouts at them in the street than vice versa. Bates (2014) claims that there are three factors separating the experiences of men and women with sexual harassment that make them different: frequency, severity and context. Women are far more frequently exposed to sexual harassment and sexism than men, both individually and due to the general gender-cultural environment. The severity of incidents is also often greater when women are the victims. When men are exposed to sexual harassment, it is typically via comments about their appearance and unwelcome sexual attention. Women, on the other hand, often report that in addition to comments about their appearance and unwelcome sexual attention, they are exposed to threats of violence upon refusing to respond, or when having responded negatively to a sexual request, and have been violated physically. They also report having been stalked, men trying to pick them up on the street or having been physically assaulted after rejecting a man's advances or even just having ignored an unwelcome advance. Women are therefore far more likely to be seriously frightened when an unknown man, for example, catcalls them or tries to contact them without an invitation (Bates, 2014).

There is thus a difference between how men and women perceive being violated. Even though men's experiences with sexual harassment are highly likely to be under-reported, and even if women can also sexually harass men, the sexual harassment that men subject women to results in far more serious psychological problems than the sexual harassment women subject men to (Kessler et al., 2020; Rotundo et al., 2001). Without trivializing or undermining men's experiences of sexual harassment, it seems that men are not in the same way afraid of the escalation aspect of sexual harassment when the sexual harassment is conducted by women (Stockdale et al., 1999, 2004). It appears that men feel considerably less threatened than women by behaviours that women find harassing (Berdahl et al., 1996). It is therefore fair to point out that women sexually harassing men has not yet turned into a significant societal problem. Berdahl et al. (1996) posit that the behaviours that men actually experience as sexual harassment need to be determined and that this assessment must be grounded in men's perception and experiences.

A study conducted for Danish Broadcasting Corporation (Epinion for DR, 2017) showed that women generally thought that unwelcome touching in nightlife venues was a problem and that women, when they are touched while in a nightlife setting without having encouraged it, are far more likely than men to feel violated, humiliated and provoked. They are also more likely to become angry, sad, irritated and afraid. Conversely, men seem more inclined to feel flattered, happy, attractive, excited and validated, and they find it humorous when they are touched without having encouraged it. Nevertheless, the construction of hegemonic masculinity might play a role in shaping these responses, as some men may feel unable to admit to feeling scared, violated, etc. The women in the study also said that they were more likely than men to think that it was easy to figure out when it was appropriate to touch someone else in a nightlife setting. Regarding the different perceptions of unwelcome touching, one of the men states:

> Several of my friends have had their penises grabbed while out partying… if the woman is hot, they just think it's cool, and if not, they usually just laugh about it.

Therefore, sexual harassment is often perceived differently when perpetrated by men on women, due to the correlation with and commonality of men's violence towards women (Kelly, 1996; Rotundo et al., 2001). There is therefore reason to believe that much of what women perceive as unpleasant and threatening forms of sexual harassment from men would not be considered as sexual harassment to the same extent by a man if he was exposed to the same from a woman (Rothgerber et al., 2021).

Being viewed as a sexual object often has a different impact on men than on women. When men stare at and comment on women's bodies, the women are more turned into a sexual object, and in this process their other competences and identities as individuals are made irrelevant. Men are not reduced to a mere sexual object to the same extent, and this allows them to maintain their status on other fronts. The bodily objectification of women is often perceived as more demeaning (Reinicke, 2018).

Society tends to first look at and accept a man's talents and merits, that is, to see them first as politicians, business professionals, sports stars, etc., and then only after that to sexualize them. This results in the objectification of men being less extreme and less demeaning. It does not reduce men's worth to their level of physical attraction in the same completely comprehensive way as it does in the case of women.

Kelly (1988) describes how most women recognize the feeling of being secretly watched or stalked and how these realities tend to put women 'on guard' in public spaces; women's fear of rape in particular contributes to a reduced quality of life. In this context, it is important to point out that very few men suffer from fear of rape, if one disregards particular prison environments and war situations (Smith, 1988). Therefore, an investigation of what sexual harassment means for women and men must take into consideration the socio-historical context in which such behaviour takes place (Berdahl et al., 1996).

Overall, the men did not indicate that they had been victims of sexual harassment. However, there was one man who mentioned how, at a former workplace where he was moving some tables wearing a tight T-shirt, he had received a comment from his female superior saying that he had large biceps. The remark had not been unpleasant. However, he claimed that it had imprinted itself on his memory and that it was a form of unwanted sexual attention.

5.11 Summary

Men who perpetrate sexual harassment do not represent a fixed character type. It is more important to understand the situations in which individual men and groups of men come to perpetrate sexual harassment and to understand the consequences of their actions. Studies show that in many contexts, it is culturally acceptable for men to comment on and evaluate women's appearance (Quinn, 2002). It is difficult, on the basis of socio-demographic factors, to generate a typology of men who practise sexual harassment. Men who practise sexual harassment are to be found in all social strata, in all different fields of employment and in all age groups.

There are several different psychological and social factors that may play a role in the development of abusive behaviour. The chapter has shown that some men are more likely to practise sexual harassment than others and that especially men in groups are motivated to act in a sexist manner towards women. Although typologies can say something about which men commit sexual harassment, it is important that they do not draw attention away from broader gender-cultural explanatory models. In general, typologies are based on simple behavioural indicators combined with some personality characteristics that may make it difficult to understand the diversity and plurality of the causes, techniques and motives behind the actions. Complex explanations are required to understand why different men practise sexual harassment. The LSH scale, which measures the readiness to behave in a sexually exploitative manner and which has been used to analyze hypothetical inclinations for sexual harassment, is also doubtful. One possibility might be to design an experiment. Nevertheless, it is almost inconceivable that even a well-written description of an imagined situation is capable of reflecting and capturing the complexity and depth of emotions, interactions and ambivalences that play out in an actual, real-world sexual harassment incident. Additionally, Pina et al. (2009) have emphasized that typologies describing sexual harassers are very simplistic and offer no useful guidance regarding the key characteristics of harassers. Often, they are not able to capture real-world ambiguities. At present, sexual harassment typologies are useful for providing professionals with a broad yet simplified overview of the characteristics of sexual harassers.

It is crucial not to try to establish a pathology of sexual harassers. The focus should be mainly not on individuals but on the culture and the structures that prepare the ground for the harassment. We need an examination of masculine identities and the role of sexually harassing behaviours as a means to their production. We must understand the processes and the underlying social factors that contribute to men's sexual harassment of women and girls. One of the insights that the interviews provided on this point was the ambiguity regarding the appropriateness of the interviewees' behaviour. Social norms among men do not necessarily challenge sexual harassment; they might even accept and strengthen it. It seems that aggressive and competitive sexual conquest and harassment strategies are one of the ideals and practices that are pursued and engaged in by young men, and the main audience is other young men, as their 'performance' is often intended to be observed and confirmed by other men. Several of the interviewees had a blind spot regarding their harassing behaviour as they did not always understand the harm and fear the harassing behaviour might have produced in the victim. They perceived boundaries to be fluid and difficult to identify. Furthermore, they saw their behaviour as a harmless social interaction and as 'the way the game was played'. The interviews also indicate that sexually harassing behaviour may serve the function of proving masculinity to other men and strengthening social bonding among men. This is in line with Grazian (2007) who argued that girl hunting is not always a purely heterosexual pursuit but can also take the form of a fundamentally homosocial activity. Nevertheless, there is no doubt that picking up women makes it possible to advance in the social hierarchy among their friends.

Since #MeToo most of the world has been witnessing a discursive battle over the definition and understanding of sexual harassment. A focal point of this fight is whether men's aggression and violence should be discussed in relation to the masculinity of deviant or normal men. Definitions can have a significant impact on what preventive measures are introduced. It seems reasonable to emphasize the fact that sexual harassment is not a problem that only concerns a deviant minority of men, but rather exists as part of a continuum of sexual violence. There is often a sense of continuum between 'everyday' forms of sexual harassment and more violent sexual assaults (Kelly, 1988). With this knowledge at the back of our minds, the next chapter will discuss how specifically men have responded to the messages from the #MeToo movement.

References

Abbey, A., & Wegner, R. (2015). Using experimental paradigms to examine alcohol's role in men's sexual aggression: Opportunities and challenges in proxy development. *Violence against Women, 21*(8), 975–996.

Abbey, A., Zawacki, T., & McAuslan, P. A. M. (2000). Alcohol's effects on sexual perception. *Journal of Studies on Alcohol, 61*(5), 688–697.

Barak, A. (2005). Sexual harassment on the Internet. *Social Science Computer Review, 23*(1), 77–92.

Bates, L. (2014). *Everyday sexism*. Simon & Schuster.

Becker, J. C., & Swim, J. K. (2011). Seeing the unseen: Attention to daily encounters with sexism as way to reduce sexist beliefs. *Psychology of Women Quarterly, 35*(2), 227–242.

Begany, J. J., & Milburn, M. A. (2002). Psychological predictors of sexual harassment: Authoritarianism, hostile sexism, and rape myths. *Psychology of Men & Masculinity, 3*(2), 119–126.

Benard, C., & Schlaffer, E. (1984). The man in the street: Why he harasses. In A. M. Jagger & P. S. Rothenberg (Eds.), *Feminist frameworks: Alternative theoretical accounts of the relations between women and men* (3rd ed., pp. 70–72). McGraw Hill.

Berdahl, J. L., Magley, V. J., & Waldo, C. R. (1996). The sexual harassment of men?: Exploring the concept with theory and data. *Psychology of Women Quarterly, 20*(4), 527–547.

Berger, J. M., Levant, R., McMillan, K. K., Kelleher, W., & Sellers, A. (2005). Impact of gender role conflict, traditional masculinity ideology, alexithymia, and age on men's attitudes toward psychological help seeking. *Psychology of Men & Masculinity, 6*(1), 73–78.

Brannon, R. (1976). Looking at the male role. In J. H. Pleck & J. Sawyer (Eds.), *Men and masculinity* (pp. 795–796). Prentice-Hall.

Budde, J. (2009). The significance of the body: The construction of masculinity among German students. *Boyhood Studies, 3*(1), 39–49.

Cleveland, J. N., & Kerst, M. E. (1993). Sexual harassment and perceptions of power: An under-articulated relationship. *Journal of Vocational Behavior, 42*(1), 49–67.

Dahl, K. M., Henze-Pedersen, S., Østergaard, S. V., & Østergaard, J. (2018). *Unges opfattelser af køn, krop og seksualitet* [Adolescents' perceptions of gender, body and sexuality]. VIVE – Det Nationale Forsknings- og Analysecenter for Velfærd.

De Judicibus, M., & McCabe, M. P. (2001). Blaming the target of sexual harassment: Impact of gender role, sexist attitudes, and work role. *Sex Roles, 44*(7), 401–417.

Dempster, S. (2009). Having the balls, having it all? Sport and constructions of undergraduate laddishness. *Gender and Education, 21*(5), 481–500.

Dempster, S. (2011). I drink, therefore I'm man: Gender discourses, alcohol and the construction of British undergraduate masculinities. *Gender and Education, 23*(5), 635–653.

Dobash, R. E., Russell, D. P., Kate, C., & Ruth, L. (2000). *Changing violent men*. Sage.

Dziech, W. D., & Weiner, L. (1984). *The lecherous professor: Sexual harassment on campus*. Beacon Press.

Epinion for DR. (2017). *Gramseri* [Pawing]. Epinion.

Fairchild, K. (2010). Context effects on women's perceptions of stranger harassment. *Sexuality & Culture, 14*(3), 191–216.

Fileborn, B. (2016). *Reclaiming the night-time economy: Unwanted sexual attention in pubs and clubs*. Springer.

Fiske, S. T., & Glick, P. (1995). Ambivalence and stereotypes cause sexual harassment: A theory with implications for organizational change. *Journal of Social Issues, 51*(1), 97–115.

Fitzgerald, L. F. (1993). Sexual harassment: Violence against women in the workplace. *American Psychologist, 48*, 1070–1076.

Flood, M. (2008). Men, sex, and homosociality: How bonds between men shape their sexual relations with women. *Men and Masculinities, 10*(3), 339–359.

Flood, M. (2018). *Engaging men and boys in violence prevention*. Springer.

Gailey, J. A., & Prohaska, A. (2006). "Knocking off a fat girl": An exploration of hogging, male sexuality, and neutralizations. *Deviant Behavior, 27*(1), 31–49.

Gailey, J. A., & Prohaska, A. (2007). Bad boys in bars: Hogging and humiliation. *Youth violence and delinquency interventions: Monsters and myths* (pp. 81–91). Greenwood Publishing Group, Inc.

Gailey, J. A., & Prohaska, A. (2011). Power and gender negotiations during interviews with men about sex and sexually degrading practices. *Qualitative Research, 11*(4), 365–380.

Gardner, C. B. (1995). *Passing by: Gender and public harassment*. University of California Press.

Gavey, N. (2005). *Just sex?: The cultural scaffolding of rape*. Routledge.

Glick, P., & Fiske, S. T. (2011). Ambivalent sexism revisited. *Psychology of Women Quarterly, 35*(3). 530–535.

Graham, K., & Homel, R. (2008). *Raising the bar: Preventing aggression in and around bars, clubs and pubs*. Willan Publishing.

Graham, K., Bernards, S., Abbey, A., Dumas, T. M., & Wells, S. (2017). When women do not want it: Young female Bargoers' experiences with and responses to sexual harassment in social drinking contexts. *Violence against Women, 23*(12), 1419–1441.

Grazian, D. (2007). The girl hunt: Urban nightlife and the performance of masculinity as collective activity. *Symbolic Interaction, 30*(2), 221–243.

Heinskou, M. B., Marie, S. L., Friis, C., Ejbye-Ernst, P., & Liebst, L. S. (2017). *Seksuelle krænkelser i Danmark: Omfang og karakter* [Sexual abuse in Denmark: Extent and character]. Det Kriminalpræventive Råd.

Herrero, J., Rodríguez, F. J., & Torres, A. (2017). Acceptability of partner violence in 51 societies: The role of sexism and attitudes toward violence in social relationships. *Violence Against Women, 23*(3), 351–367.

Herriot, L., & Hiseler, L. E. (2015). Documentaries on the sexualization of girls: Examining slut-shaming, victim-blaming and what's being left off-screen. *Children, sexuality and sexualization* (pp. 289–304). Palgrave Macmillan.

Hird, M. J., & Jackson, S. (2001). Where 'angels' and 'wusses' fear to tread: Sexual coercion in adolescent dating relationships. *Journal of Sociology, 37*(1), 27–43.

Jordan, E. (1995). Fighting boys and fantasy play: The construction of masculinity in the early years of school. *Gender and Education, 7*(1), 69–86.

Katz, J. (2006). *Macho Paradox: Why some men hurt women and how all men can help*. Sourcebooks, Inc.

Kehily, M. (2001). Bodies in school: Young men, embodiment, and heterosexual masculinities. *Men and Masculinities, 4*(2), 173–185.

Kehily, M. J., & Nayak, A. (1997). 'Lads and laughter': Humour and the production of heterosexual hierarchies. *Gender and Education, 9*(1), 69–88.

Kelly, L. (1988). How women define their experiences of violence. In K. Yllö & M. Bograd (Eds.), *Feminist perspectives on wife abuse* (pp. 114–132). Sage Publications.

Kelly, L. (1996). It's everywhere: Sexual violence as a continuum. In S. Jackson & S. Scott (Eds.), *Feminism and sexuality: A reader* (pp. 191–207). Edinburgh University Press.

Kessler, A. M., Kennair, L. E. O., Grøntvedt, T. V., Bjørkheim, I., Drejer, I., & Bendixen, M. (2020). The effect of prototypical #MeToo features on the perception of social-sexual behavior as sexual harassment. *Sexuality & Culture, 24*(5), 1271–1291.

Kimmel, M. (2008). *Guyland: The perilous world where boys become men.* Harper.

Koss, M. P. (2018). Hidden rape: Sexual aggression and victimization in a national sample of students in higher education. In *Rape and society* (pp. 35–49). Routledge.

Kosson, D. S., Kelly, J. C., & White, J. W. (1997). Psychopathy-related traits predict self-reported sexual aggression among college men. *Journal of Interpersonal Violence, 12*(2), 241–254.

Lee, K., Gizzarone, M., & Ashton, M. C. (2003). Personality and the likelihood to sexually harass. *Sex Roles, 49*(1–2), 59–69.

Lengnick-Hall, M. L. (1995). Sexual harassment research: A methodological critique. *Personnel Psychology, 48*(4), 841–864.

Levant, R. F. (1995). Toward the reconstruction of masculinity. In R. F. Levant & W. S. Pollack (Eds.), *A new psychology of men* (pp. 229–251). Basic Books.

Logan, L. S. (2015). Street harassment: Current and promising avenues for researchers and activists. *Sociology Compass, 9*(3), 196–211.

Loney-Howes, R. (2019). The politics of the personal: The evolution of anti-rape activism from second-wave feminism to #MeToo. *#MeToo and the politics of social change* (pp. 21–35). Palgrave Macmillan.

Lucero, M. A., Allen, R. E., & Middleton, K. L. (2006). Sexual harassers: Behaviors, motives, and change over time. *Sex Roles, 55*(5–6), 331–343.

Lucero, M. A., Middleton, K. L., Finch, W. A., & Valentine, S. R. (2003). An empirical investigation of sexual harassers: Toward a perpetrator typology. *Human Relations, 56*(12), 1461–1483.

Mac an Ghail, M. (1994). The making of black English masculinities. In I. H. Brod & M. Kaufman (Eds.), *Theorizing masculinities* (pp. 183–199). Sage Publications.

Malamuth, N. M. (1986). Predictors of naturalistic sexual aggression. *Journal of Personality and Social Psychology, 50*(5), 953–962.

Malamuth, N. M., & Dean, K. E. (1991). Attraction to sexual aggression. In A. Parrot & L. Bechhofer (Eds.), *Acquaintance rape: The hidden crime.* New York: Wiley.

Martineau, W. H. (1972). A model of the social functions of humor. In J. H. Goldstein & P. E. McGhee (Eds.), *The psychology of humor: Theoretical perspectives and empirical issues* (pp. 101–125). Academic Press.

Masters, N. T., Casey, E., Wells, E. A., & Morrison, D. M. (2013). Sexual scripts among young heterosexually active men and women: Continuity and change. *Journal of Sex Research, 50*(5), 409–420.

Meenagh, J. L. (2021). 'She doesn't think that happens': When heterosexual men say no to sex. *Sexualities, 24*(3), 322–340.

Nichols, K. (2018). Moving beyond ideas of laddism: Conceptualising 'mischievous masculinities' as a new way of understanding everyday sexism and gender relations. *Journal of Gender Studies, 27*(1), 73–85.

O'Donohue, W., Downs, K., & Yeater, E. A. (1998). Sexual harassment: A review of the literature. *Aggression and Violent Behavior, 3*(2), 111–128.

O'Leary-Kelly, A. M., Paetzold, R. L., & Griffin, R. W. (2000). Sexual harassment as aggressive behavior: An actor-based perspective. *Academy of Management Review, 25*(2), 372–388.

Page, T. E., & Pina, A. (2015). Moral disengagement as a self-regulatory process in sexual harassment perpetration at work: A preliminary conceptualization. *Aggression and Violent Behavior, 21,* 73–84.

Paglia, C. (1991, February 17). Perspective needed—Feminism's lie: Denying reality about sexual power and rape. *New York Newsday.*

Perkins, H. (2003). *The social norms approach to preventing school and college age substance abuse: A handbook for educators, counselors, and clinicians.* Jossey-Bass.

Perry, E. L., Kulik, C. T., & Schmidtke, J. M. (1998). Individual differences in the effectiveness of sexual harassment awareness training 1. *Journal of Applied Social Psychology, 28*(8), 698–723.

Phipps, A. (2017). (Re) theorising laddish masculinities in higher education. *Gender and Education, 29*(7), 815–830.

Phipps, A., & Young, I. (2013). *That's what she said: Women students' experiences of 'lad culture' in higher education.* National Union of Students.

Phipps, A., Ringrose, J., Renold, E., & Jackson, C. (2018). Rape culture, lad culture and everyday sexism: Researching, conceptualizing and politicizing new mediations of gender and sexual violence. *Journal of Gender Studies, 27*(1), 1–8.

Pina, A., Gannon, T. A., & Saunders, B. (2009). An overview of the literature on sexual harassment: Perpetrator, theory, and treatment issues. *Aggression and Violent Behavior, 14*(2), 126–138.

Pollack, W. (1998). *Real boys: Rescuing our sons from the myths of boyhood.* Henry Holt and Company.

Prahl, F. (2018, February 26). Grænsesætning er sexet [Boundary setting is sexy]. *Information.*

Pryor, J. B. (1987). Sexual harassment proclivities in men. *Sex Roles, 17*(5–6), 269–290.

Pryor, J. B., Giedd, J. L., & Williams, K. B. (1995). A social psychological model for predicting sexual harassment. *Journal of Social Issues, 51*(1), 69–84.

Pryor, J. B., LaVite, C. M., & Stoller, L. M. (1993). A social psychological analysis of sexual harassment: The person/situation interaction. *Journal of Vocational Behavior, 42*(1), 68–83.

Pryor, J. B., & Stoller, L. M. (1994). Sexual cognition processes in men high in the likelihood to sexually harass. *Personality and Social Psychology Bulletin, 20*(2), 163–169.

Quick, J. C., & McFadyen, M. (2017). Sexual harassment: Have we made any progress? *Journal of Occupational Health Psychology, 22*(3), 286–298.

Quinn, B. A. (2002). Sexual harassment and masculinity: The power and meaning of "girl watching." *Gender & Society, 16*(3), 386–402.

Reinicke, K. (2018). *Mænd som krænker kvinder – refleksioner i kølvandet på #Metoo* [Men who violate women—Reflections in the wake of #MeToo]. Samfundslitteratur.

Ronen, S. (2010). Grinding on the dance floor: Gendered scripts and sexualized dancing at college parties. *Gender & Society, 24*(3), 355–377.

Rothgerber, H., Kaufling, K., Incorvati, C., Andrew, C. B., & Farmer, A. (2021). Is a reasonable woman different from a reasonable person? Gender differences in perceived sexual harassment. *Sex Roles, 84*(3), 208–220.

Rotundo, M., Nguyen, D. H., & Sackett, P. R. (2001). A meta-analytic review of gender differences in perceptions of sexual harassment. *Journal of Applied Psychology, 86*(5), 914–922.

Schwartz, M. D., & DeKeseredy, W. S. (1997). *Sexual assault on the college campus: The role of male peer support*. Sage.

Smith, M. D. (1988). Women's fear of violent crime: An exploratory test of a feminist hypothesis. *Journal of Family Violence, 3*(1), 29–38.

Stockdale, M. S. (1993). The Role of sexual misperceptions of women's friendliness in an emerging theory of sexual harassment. *Journal of Vocational Behavior, 42*(1), 84–101.

Stockdale, M. S., Gandolfo Berry, C., Schneider, R. W., & Cao, F. (2004). Perceptions of the Sexual Harassment of Men. *Psychology of Men & Masculinity, 5*(2), 158–167.

Stockdale, M. S., Visio, M., & Batra, L. (1999). The sexual harassment of men: Evidence for a broader theory of sexual harassment and sex discrimination. *Psychology, Public Policy, and Law, 5*(3), 630–664.

Sue, D. W. (2010). *Microaggressions in everyday life: Race, gender, and sexual orientation*. Wiley.

Sweeney, B. N. (2014). Masculine status, sexual performance, and the sexual stigmatization of women. *Symbolic Interaction, 37*(3), 369–390.

Thomae, M., & Pina, A. (2015). Sexist humor and social identity: The role of sexist humor in men's in-group cohesion, sexual harassment, rape proclivity, and victim blame. *Humor, 28*(2), 187–204.

Thompson, D. M. (1994). The woman in the street: Reclaiming the public space from sexual harassment. *Yale JL & Feminism, 6*, 313.

Thompson, E. H., Jr., & Cracco, E. J. (2008). Sexual aggression in bars: What college men can normalize. *The Journal of Men's Studies, 16*(1), 82–96.

Tolman, D. L., Spencer, R., Rosen-Reynoso, M., & Porche, M. V. (2003). Sowing the seeds of violence in heterosexual relationships: Early adolescents narrate compulsory heterosexuality. *Journal of Social Issues, 59*(1), 159–178.

Tuerkheimer, D. (1997). Street harassment as sexual subordination: The phenomenology of gender-specific harm. *Wis. Women's LJ, 12*, 167–206.

Wesselmann, E. D., & Kelly, J. R. (2010). Cat-calls and culpability: Investigating the frequency and functions of stranger harassment. *Sex Roles, 63*(7–8), 451–462.

Willis, P. E. (1977). *Learning to labor: How working class kids get working class jobs*. Columbia University Press.

6

Men's Responses to #MeToo

The #MeToo movement challenges men to change and has grown bigger than many had expected. A critical challenge when #MeToo exploded onto the public stage was how to get men interested in the process of change and how to avoid reactions of distrust, shame and resistance (Män, 2018a, b). Two interesting questions are: what exactly does #MeToo seek to change, and how can men relate to the movement? #MeToo encourages men to reflect critically on their own thinking and behaviour and to examine their own biases. Deep self-interrogation, however, may be tough, because it is not easy among other men to be recognized for such a sensitive virtue.

#MeToo constitutes a potential learning moment that gives men the chance to reflect on things that they perhaps did not have to think about before, and for some men this represents an opportunity for change. Flood (2019) describes how #MeToo's call to action among men comprises three key tasks. First, #MeToo requires men to listen to women, in order to recognize men's violence against women as common, serious and wrong. Second, #MeToo urges men to reflect on and change their own behaviour and everyday relations with women and other men. Third, #MeToo asks that men contribute to social change, both by challenging other men and by contributing to wider efforts to shift the systemic gender inequalities that form the foundation of sexual harassment and abuse.

Many men find it difficult to understand the extent and seriousness of the problems. They are reluctant to discuss sexism and want to downplay and ignore the topic (PettyJohn et al., 2019). When men are asked to relate to their own potential use of harassment and violence against women or their involvement in it, many are uninterested or reluctant, and some respond with hostility (Flood, 2019).

Although most men (fortunately) cannot recognize themselves in the worst accounts that have come to light because of #MeToo, a controversial question is whether all men should stop, listen, look inwards and ask themselves if their actions—and lack of actions or reactions—may have unwittingly contributed to the acceptance and condoning of sexual harassment. Some men would undoubtedly answer 'yes' to that question, whereas others would feel extremely provoked.

In terms of men's reactions to #MeToo, one finds many contradictory tendencies. Men have different agendas and points of view when they take part in debates about gender equality, and their reactions to #MeToo can be categorized into several different positions. Some men have reacted to the movement's messages by introspecting, while others have focused on the bad apples. Without underestimating men's cognitive capacities, there is no doubt that some men find it difficult to grasp the extent and gravity of the problem, are reluctant to discuss sexism and prefer to trivialize or ignore the topic.

There is currently not much data available to assess the effect of #MeToo on men's behaviour and attitudes regarding sexual harassment. We do not know how men are responding to and negotiating the cultural conversation about sexual harassment. However, the #MeToo movement seems to have created greater awareness and understanding among men about sexism and gender inequalities. In a US survey conducted in late 2017, nearly half the men (44 percent) agreed that stories about #MeToo and sexual harassment had changed their view of women's condition in society (NBC News, 2017; *Wall Street Journal*, 2017). One indicator of whether a campaign or movement is contributing to creating social change is whether it is being discussed among the general public. In the UK, a nationally representative online panel survey of 2056 individuals conducted in August 2018 showed that young men in the UK were more likely than older men to have had conversations with their peers about #MeToo. Among men aged 18–34, 54 percent had done so, compared to 27 percent of those aged 35–54 and only 16 percent of those aged 55 and older (Fawcett Society, 2018). Furthermore, the survey demonstrated that the majority of young men are likely to challenge sexual harassment since #MeToo. In addition, the survey showed that while older men in the UK felt that there had been a change in *other* people's ideas about what is and is not acceptable, they were far less likely than younger men to say that *they themselves* thought differently about such things. In Denmark, a representative survey among 1735 Danish men in 2020 showed that for six out of ten men, the #MeToo debate has made it harder to be a man, while three out of ten men declared that the #MeToo debate has made them more apprehensive of women and that they flirt less. There were also many men who stated that men were not sufficiently heard in the debate (Alt for Damerne, 2020).

A comparative study about attitudes toward #MeToo in the USA and Norway showed that men were less positive toward #MeToo than women and perceived it as substantially more harmful and less beneficial. The study also revealed that men 'were higher than women in hostile sexism, higher in rape myth acceptance, and lower in feminist identification' (Kunst et al., 2018: 22). A survey by the Swedish organization Män (2018a) conducted a year after the emergence of the #MeToo movement showed that a majority of men (85 percent) believed that men together should take greater responsibility for counteracting sexualized violence and harassment committed by men. At the same time, however, 51 percent of men answered that the revelations of the #MeToo movement have not led them to investigate their own behaviour. Only 5 percent agree that #MeToo has made them examine their own behaviour. It is interesting that such a large percentage of men do not think #MeToo has implications for themselves. The men see the problems, but not that they themselves can be a contributing factor. Murphy Austin et al. (2016) stress that men find it easier to externalize problematic behaviour contributing to rape culture to other people than to undertake a personal examination of how they benefit from and perpetuate rape culture. This phenomenon is also well known from research on men buying sex. Kippe (2004) emphasized that men who buy sex buy 'illusions' and do not want the façade to be shattered. Several of the men in her study tried to justify their purchase of sexual services by saying that it did not hurt anyone. At the same time, they depicted the other male customers as perverse exploiters but without assessing the moral aspect of their own actions (Kippe, 2004).

Many varieties of masculinity have existed throughout history and many types can exist in a society simultaneously (Reinicke, 2012). Therefore, it is no simple matter to analyze how men relate and react to changes in gender perceptions, as contradictory attitudes and practices abound. Looking at how men have responded to the #MeToo movement, it seems clear that there are both positive and negative responses (Flood, 2019). This was also the case with the Australian journalist Benjamin Law's attempts to involve men in the debate about sexual harassment. In the wake of #MeToo, he tweeted 'Guys, it's our turn. After yesterday's endless #MeToo stories of women being abused, assaulted and harassed, today we say #HowIWillChange.' The intention of the hashtag was to prompt men to change their behaviour if it contributes to or perpetuates rape culture. Thousands of Twitter users responded using #HowIWillChange, with many praising and many criticizing the movement.

In that regard we must not underestimate what men have to lose if patriarchal privileges are challenged (Flood, 2018). PettyJohn et al. (2019) analyzed the tweets about #HowIWillChange and categorized them into three main groups: (1) users committing to actively engage in dismantling rape culture; (2) users indignantly resistant to social change; and (3) users promoting hostile resistance to social change. Actions suggested by users for dismantling rape culture included the following: examining personal participation in toxic masculinity, teaching the next generation, calling out other men, listening to women's experiences and promoting egalitarianism. Users indignantly opposed to social change used the rhetoric of 'not all men' and promoted benevolently sexist attitudes to assert that men as a group have been unfairly targeted. Other users were hostile towards the notion of social change and their angry comments covered a wide range of attacks on the perceived weaknesses of men supporting #HowIWillChange, hostile sexist attitudes and statements of anti-feminist backlash.

6.1 Positive Reactions

Nilsson and Lundgren (2020) state that because of #MeToo we are also witnessing new discourses of awakening and confession. Some men witness new insight and publicly confess that they have previously behaved in a sexist manner. The positive reactions stem from men who themselves do not feel unfairly caught in the crossfire. On the contrary, they have been prompted to soul-search because of the many testimonies of harassment. They are tired of taking on the traditional patriarchal role and see the #MeToo movement as an opportunity for change. They are using the #MeToo movement as a 'teachable moment' and are opting to perform a 'privilege check' to monitor when they exercise power.

They argue that eradicating harassment culture requires that men learn to listen, try to do some soul-searching, and ask themselves if they have ever harassed another person. They can also tackle the problem by daring to talk to other men about harassment, as well as by becoming 'good bystanders' who take appropriate action should they witness sexual harassment. However, there is no doubt that it can be hard for men to stand up to other men due to, for example, fear of social sanctions and ridicule. It is particularly hard for men to change their behaviour in all-male environments where men tend to egg each other on and thereby reaffirm a sexist culture.

In Denmark in 2020, 41-year-old schoolteacher David Russel took the initiative to start a petition targeted at men with the title 'Men who know we have a problem with sexism and want to do something about it'. The motivation behind his petition was that so many men in the #MeToo debate were busier victimizing women who speak out about sexual harassment than doing something about the problem. In addition to signing the petition, men were also given the chance to state their reasons for supporting the petition. Here is a selection of what they said:

I sign because it is obvious that sexism is a widespread problem. No women I know have avoided it—but few men in my circle of friends admit to having crossed boundaries and make amends.

I sign because I recognize that systemic sexism and discrimination are ingrained in our society, and if we are not able as a society to accept and acknowledge that problem and its scope, we will never get rid of it. Whether it is in the workplace, at the university, or somewhere else, systemic power relations play a huge role, and if we do not articulate and actively distance ourselves from it, we ourselves are complicit in maintaining the status quo.

I sign because it's time that we men say no to those of us who cannot figure out how to behave properly. That we address the root of the problem and change the jargon and culture among us men.

I sign because I have two daughters.

I sign because I want to use my privileges to fight against the sexist, discriminatory and patriarchal structures that our society suffers from.

I sign this as I acknowledge that we have a major problem with sexism. I am a feminist and advocate for equal rights of all people, regardless of gender or skin colour.

I sign because it cannot be the responsibility of women who are being exposed to sexism. They have shouted that it happens, time and time again—and each time they are met with accusations that they are too sensitive and vulnerable to offence and something worse than that. Now that simply must be enough.

I sign because it is in my interest that there is a general cultural change—sexism is a common concern and it can only be resolved in cooperation.

I sign because the debate about sexism is derailed. It's going to be about whether there is sexism, not about how we eliminate it.

I sign because the 'laddish club's hi-hi' has annoyed me all my life, and as a man who says no to it and does not participate in it, I also experience exclusion because of it.

I sign because it is important that men work to abolish sexism. Women are people. Not sex objects.

I sign because no one should be discriminated against, oppressed or denied rights solely because of their gender.

> I sign because I'm tired of powerful men coming up with explanations, questioning women's statements and being busier blaming victims than doing anything about the problem.
> I sign because I know damn well that there is a bit of work to do both for myself and society.

If we look at the arguments put forward in the above statements, one can say that they range from the necessity of calling out other men to the commitment to listening more to women's experiences of being victims of sexual harassment. The need is mentioned to get the debate back on the right track by getting it to be about men's behaviour. It also shows the commitment to demonstrate greater respect towards women and promote gender equality. Furthermore, some indicate that they themselves have been victims of the culture of laddishness. Others are examining their own personal participation, pointing out how they themselves have conducted sexual harassment. In addition, the importance of teaching values to the next generation to help combat rape culture is mentioned.

In the development of hashtag activism and activism more broadly used to denounce rape culture, #HowIWillChange and 'Men who know we have a problem with sexism and want to do something about it' represent an important dialogue on sexual violence against women, encouraged by the #MeToo movement, specifically aiming to engage men and boys.

#MeToo has also drawn public attention to the harassment of men. Hashtags such as #HimToo and #MenToo have tried to make men's experience explicitly visible. Although some of the messages have genuinely been about male victims/survivors, it is important to recognize the extent to which these gender-specific hashtags have been taken up by people protesting against #MeToo. To a certain degree, #HimToo sought to undermine and distort the feminist and gendered discourse around #MeToo. Boyle and Rathnayake (2020) state, in connection with Trump's Supreme Court nominee Brett Kavanaugh, that the usage of the #HimToo hashtag was no longer about the experiences of male victims of sexual assault but a marker of men's alleged vulnerability to false accusations of rape. Therefore, #HimToo became an attempt to derail #MeToo and became disrespectful to female survivors.

In 2018, inspired by the #MeToo movement and the Time's Up movement, a group of actors, writers and producers in the USA came together ahead of the Oscars with an open letter to support survivors of harassment and abuse and demand more accountability and action from men in the entertainment industry. They emphasized that, as men, they had a special responsibility to prevent abuse from happening in the first place. They were using the hashtag #askmoreofhim to highlight that one of the most powerful things that men—and especially men with decision-making power—can and must do is to hold other men accountable by telling them that sexual harassment and abuse are never acceptable. This includes everything from sexist and degrading comments right up to domestic violence and sexual assault.

6.2 Defensive Reactions

Some men react with resistance and hostility towards the notion of social change. In one example, Gillette, the American brand of shaving accessories, caused great controversy and media attention in 2019 after launching a #MeToo-inspired advertising campaign 'The Best Men Can Be' promoting a new kind of positive masculinity in which traditional male culture was criticized from a feminist perspective. The advertising campaign consisted of a short film entitled *We Believe: The Best Men Can Be*, which played upon the previous slogan ('The Best a Man Can Get') to address negative behaviour among men, including bullying, sexism, sexual misconduct and toxic masculinity.

The short film shows men as bullies at school and sexual harassers and includes screenshots of news related to the allegations of sexual harassment launched by the #MeToo movement. It also presents them as arrogant braggarts and encourages them to change. The campaign angered many men and customers of the brand: on YouTube it generated far more negative votes than positive ones (1,600,000 negative versus 826,000 positive at the time of writing) (Gillette, 2019).

Many men viewed the campaign as controversial and accused it of promoting a problematic image of men and masculinity. The Gillette advertisement contained the wording 'this has been going on far too long' and the phrases 'there will be no going back', 'we can't laugh it off' and 'we can't make the old excuses saying that boys will be boys'. The advertisement also encouraged men 'to say the right thing' and 'to act the right way'. The advertisement ends by saying that some men have changed but that some is not enough because 'the boys watching today will be the men of tomorrow'.

The campaign challenged men to do better in the #MeToo era and encouraged them to intervene when they witnessed violence by and among other men. Episodes are shown where men stop other men from being 'bad lads'. The advertisement illustrates how it has become harder to celebrate masculinity without addressing the controversial behaviours exposed by #MeToo revelations. It is interesting to reflect on why this commercial about engaging men in stopping violence and sexual harassment can be perceived as a threat for so many men and has become so controversial. Maybe it is due to the uncompromising way it confronts problems such as sexism, bullying and sexual harassment. The advertisement promotes courage, kindness and responsibility. It speaks directly to its male audience. It challenges men to hold other men accountable and set better role models for the men of tomorrow, and challenges the viewer to think about what kind of behaviour defines manhood. The reactions to the Gillette advertisement show that some men continue to be resistant to the idea of social change, in spite of the campaign not being anti-male but anti-toxic masculinity.

Some men think that focusing so much on women's experiences of sexism might seem biased and unfair (Bates, 2014). These men often remind us that not all men act badly and harass, and that there are plenty of positive aspects of masculinity that are too often overlooked. As a response to the Gillette advertisement, Egard Watches launched a short film titled *What is a man? A response to Gillette*. The short film was dedicated to all 'those who sacrifice everything to make the world safer and better for all of us'. The film starts by asking, 'What is a man?' and then answers this question by posing a series of additional questions ending up with the statement, 'We see the good in men.'

The film shows firefighters putting out a fire, noting that men account for 93 percent of workplace deaths, according to official US data. It shows a man in a military uniform asking, 'Is a man a hero?', noting that men represent 97 percent of casualties in wars, according to the US Department of Defense. It shows parents taking care of their children, noting that nearly half of fathers without any visitation rights still financially support their children, according to the US Census Bureau. It states that men account for 79 percent of homicide victims, according to UN data. Further, it asks whether a man is disposable, showing men working in a mine and in oil prospecting, while noting that the male sex accounts for 80 percent of suicides, according to the WHO. It asks if a man is broken and shows images of the homeless, noting that 75 percent of homeless single people are men. Overall, the film tries to focus on the bravery, stoicism and vulnerability of men. The statistics are meant to remind people about the hidden realities of men's lives and the price some men pay for their masculinity. Although it is fine, of course, to put out a positive message for men and remind us about the positive aspects of masculinity, the film might be perceived as anti-feminist by drawing attention away from women's rights issues.

It is noteworthy that #MeToo has already experienced a backlash and has, for example, been called a vindictive plot against men. Some men find the messages offensive because it blames men. When men are told to address their own potential perpetration of sexual harassment against women or their complicity in this, many are uninterested or reluctant, and some react with hostility (Flood, 2019).

There are also those who claim that, culturally, #MeToo has gone too far and that romantic relationships need a free space that the movement is suffocating. Proponents of this perspective declare that 'seduction' is under threat and that the #MeToo movement makes it difficult to flirt and be gallant and is destroying romantic interaction between men and women. For instance, a media storm arose in 2018 when a letter was published by 100 women in France, signed by actors Brigitte Bardot and Catherine Deneuve, among others, which downplayed the harassment suffered by women. They labelled the #MeToo movement hypocritical and ridiculous. The letter urged society to stop the witch-hunt against men and encouraged women to forget about gropey men in the Metro and defend their right to sexual freedom and men's right to hit on them without obtaining any kind of prior consent. It also argued that wanting to protect women by casting them as eternal victims was a classic puritanical move. However, for a critique of the argument that #MeToo have gone 'too far', see Fileborn and Phillips (2019).

For some men there is a deep resistance to #MeToo's call for them to address their own behaviour and interactions. Greene (2018) asks why #MeToo is such a source of alarm for so many men. He points out that it might be that #MeToo challenges men's sense of control over and confidence in who they are. Bates (2014) remarks that men who denounce the attention given to women's experiences of sexual harassment, and who point out that men also experience this, seldom describe their own experiences of sexual harassment; rather, it seems that they are just against the entire anti-sexism 'project'. Bates further describes how men who have actually experienced sexual harassment seldom have anything against the project per se. The reason why some men feel this way may partly be due to the invisibility of the problem, since for some men who have not experienced sexual harassment themselves, the idea of protecting women from sexism feels like an unjustified and unnecessary offer of positive discrimination towards women. When men are proclaiming that 'not all men' abuse women, the focus might shift away from talking about destructive forms of masculinity and men's responsibility for the problem (Män, 2018a, b).

Have men become victims of reverse discrimination? Some critics assert that the movement has moved away from its original goal to give a voice to victims of sexual violence, and has turned into a vindictive plot against men. If we examine the debate surrounding the #MeToo movement, it quickly becomes clear that there are also defensive reactions that point to men as the ones with the gender equality problem and claim that it is *men's* legal rights that are at stake. A common response among men is that sexual harassment towards women is a problem of 'other' men. Men may insist that 'not all men' harass and that they are one of the 'good guys' (Flood, 2019).

Flood (2019) emphasizes that the phrase 'not all men' can express men's rejection of the feminist insight that perpetration and perpetrators are common in society, but also a more personal rejection of the request that they critically examine their own behaviour. #MeToo cannot include all men. Some men experience a loss of privilege. Some men also feel threatened. They see it as an existential threat when they witness the world change from patriarchy and structures of male control, and may feel a loss of control when the balance of power between men and women is shifting in a frightening and irreversible direction. The defensive reactions point to the statement that it is men who face a gender equality problem, and claim that it is *men's* legal rights that are at stake. Typically, they do this by ridiculing the movement or trying to derail the debate, calling it a 'moral crusade' against masculinity.

Another example of men's defensive reaction was on 3 March 2021, when British woman Sarah Everard disappeared in the evening on her way back home in London. A few days later, Sarah was found dead. Following Sarah Everard's murder, women in England and all around the world began posting the hashtag #textmewhenyougethome. The killing of Sarah Everard sparked a debate on women's safety and was accompanied by testimonies from women who all have in common that they feel insecure about walking alone in the evening. They shared their own stories about the steps they take in order to try to remain safe (e.g., making fake phone calls, sharing their location and crossing the street to avoid someone) and demanded that violence against women be taken more seriously.

One week after the death of Sarah Everard, #Notallmen was trending on Twitter. It was mainly men who voiced that they refused to change their behaviour when out at night because they felt that unnecessary suspicion fell on them. They felt frustrated at being categorized as perpetrators and described that by launching #textmewhenyougethome, women were demonizing all men.

In Denmark, many letters to newspaper editors were published including the argument that we must also think about all the 'good men' who know how to behave properly. However, the argument was also put forward that even though, of course, not all men are perpetrators, when women are assaulted, it is almost exclusively men who commit the crime. Therefore, the issue of why it should be the actions of women that were regulated and not the actions of men was problematized. Overall, the reactions to the hashtag indicate how quickly feminist messages can spread on social media and also how difficult it still is for many men to support them without feeling unnecessarily demonized.

6.3 Men's Overall Responses in Denmark

When looking at Danish men's reactions to and relationship with the #MeToo movement, opposing tendencies can be traced. While a discourse emphasizing 'not all men harass' was strong in Denmark, for some men the message of the movement established a space for learning and reflection. These men tended to look inward and conduct a 'privilege check' as to whether some of the actions they had maybe performed before, and which they often perceived as innocent, should in fact be categorized as violations (Reinicke, 2018). Other men, on the other hand, have distanced themselves from the movement and tried to undermine the power residing in the many testimonies of abuse and sexual harassment it has brought to the fore—typically by ridiculing the movement or by trying to derail the discussion. Instead of accepting the notion that sexual harassment used to be widespread and considered normal in society, as demonstrated in the many testimonies of sexual harassment, this knowledge was quickly neglected and 'shot down' in favour of claims that the debate was out of proportion and had stigmatized men. Groes-Green (Kvinfo, 2017) remarks that:

> This division is interesting in several ways. First because we're actually witnessing quite a few men who are willing to embrace new forms of masculinity. Masculinities characterised by a greater degree of respect for women, which can embrace a caring man or father role without being patronising, and which are ready to stand up to the harassment culture to some degree or other. But in connection with #MeToo we also see men who are not at all ready to embrace these new forms of masculinity – not even when they are confronted with the many stories about sexual abuse and harassment.

Are men as a gender being portrayed negatively, or only those men who have been officially accused of harassment? If individual men are the problem, should men as a whole be called to account for harassment? The #MeToo movement has, to a large extent, been 'playing with half a team' in the sense that the majority of men are still silent on the topic of sexual harassment. In an article entitled 'Men, join the #MeToo fight' and published in the political magazine *Altinget*, Rosenbeck (2017) wrote that she was surprised that it is almost exclusively women who are debating #MeToo and the problems that the movement seeks to address. She likewise points out that it seems to be only women who are sharing their experiences and reflecting over the relationship between the sexes, leading her to ask, 'Where the hell are the men in this debate?' Some men reacted by saying they cannot recognize the image that is being presented of men in general and therefore do not feel motivated to take part in the debate. PettyJohn et al. (2019) highlight that such reactions do not necessarily mean that such men absolutely deny that women face mistreatment in society, but these men emphasize that they themselves should not be held responsible or be called to take action for violence or disrespect which they do not believe they have committed. Here are a couple of examples of comments and *attitudinal resistance* (Flood, 2018) by men who disagree with Rosenbeck on *Altinget*'s blog and which indicate how non-harassing men might be tempted to think and say 'I'm a good guy—this isn't my problem':

> I want to be judged for my own acts, not for acts committed by a bunch of idiots who happen to belong to the same sex as me.

> Yes, maybe there has been a sick culture in the film and theatre world. But I refuse to stand to account for that. It has become a kind of mass hysteria to decry all sorts of serious or minor violations of various women's uniquely individual, implicit, invisible boundaries … Any attempt to differentiate or put things into perspective is met by #MeToo's self-referential universe as yet another piece of evidence of men's lack of respect for women and their general, latent tendency to harass. End of discussion.

Critiques of #MeToo have also pointed out that it is hard to speak openly about the movement, that #MeToo has tried to encompass too many things and that opinions have become so streamlined that men find it hard to stand up to the movement. Here is another example from *Altinget*'s blog:

> Like other social media campaigns, #MeToo is extremely unnuanced. Basically, rape is treated the same way as an uninvited hand on a woman's thigh at a dinner party. That muddies the debate. At the same time, the whole debate is framed in terms of 'women vs men'. And if a man tries to nuance the debate he is quickly accused of defending the harassers.

The above quote is claiming that #MeToo has given rise to a moral panic and that men can no longer express any scepticism towards it. A major point of contention, at least according to some critics, is the way the movement mixes up serious and minor infractions, leading to a general shaming of men. These defensive reactions were typical for the first wave of #MeToo in Denmark. As highlighted in Chapter 2, there were few calls for men to take responsibility, the legitimacy of #MeToo was often questioned and the debate escalated into polemics about the creation of an inappropriate culture of violation. Let us look into how the interviewed men think about the #MeToo movement.

6.4 The Attitude of the Interviewed Men Towards #MeToo

All the men in the study stated—even though not all agreed strongly— that they sympathized with the #MeToo movement, and that inappropriate sexual behaviour was an important societal issue. All the men had learned something from the #MeToo movement, as practically all of them recognized that before the emergence of #MeToo in 2017, they had not given serious thought to inappropriate sexual behaviour. They knew it existed but not that it was such a big and far-reaching problem. They had no idea how deeply some men's sexual harassment affected women's lives.

> The issue of sexual harassment never did pop up among me and my peers …we never talked about the pain that sexual harassment may have caused women … I was of the belief that it was about a few rotten apples … therefore I did not feel personally affected and I did not feel tempted to look at my own privileges or to speak up.

The importance of making visible to men the experiences and feelings of significant women in their lives is crucial (Ruxton, 2020). One of the men described how it first became an issue for him when he discovered that one of his closest female friends had written about how she had been subjected to sexual harassment on Facebook. Askanius and Hartley (2019) have demonstrated that within the media coverage of #MeToo there is a tendency to focus on actors within the cultural industries, celebrity producers considered as 'bad apples' and various scandals, rather than on a systemic problem rooted in gender inequality and an uneven distribution of power. All the men in the study said that when the #MeToo movement really took off in October 2017, they did not feel it was about them. They specified that it was interesting to keep up with the news and that they were shocked at how widespread it was, but they did not feel personally targeted. First and foremost, they thought that #MeToo was about men who had systematically abused positions of power and that sexual harassment was mainly related to working life and was about serious transgressions.

> I remember when reading about that guy, Harvey Weinstein, or whatever his name is over in the States, and I was thinking this had nothing to do with my behaviour… it was about the systematic manner in which he had taken advantage of his position of power to exploit women… I thought that he was an extreme sexual predator.

As has been demonstrated in other findings, men tend to become aware and active in relation to gender equality through a slow, gradual process (Messner et al., 2015; Ruxton, 2020). Several of the men emphasized that the awareness of the extent and mechanism of sexual harassment could best be described as being on a long journey or some kind of awakening where you gradually became more aware of it. However, they also emphasized that it took them a long time before they began considering that #MeToo was not just about how some bosses treated their female employees but also about power dynamics between men and women in society in general.

It was especially in the wake of the second #MeToo wave in 2020 that the men expressed that they had been thinking about what kinds of things men do that women find offensive, degrading and sexist. The many examples they found in the press have changed their understanding of the consequences that women suffered from being exposed to sexual harassment.

> It was particularly the events of 2020 that contributed to getting me to start reflecting on this topic—when I began to read the many testimonies in *Politiken* [a major Danish newspaper] about what had happened between colleagues at various workplaces.

When the men had begun opening their eyes to the scope of the problem, one of the results was that more of them also began re-evaluating their own actions. Several of the men expressed that they were pleased that destructive forms of masculinity were finally being confronted. Despite the fact that none of the men perceived themselves as a 'bad guy', several of them—since #MeToo took off—had been considering whether they were part of the problem and recognized that they had engaged in mild forms of sexual harassment in the past. This awareness had turned into an ongoing struggle for some of the men. In line with Essig (2018), they question how their silence had helped enable a rape culture which again derives from an unhealthy form of masculinity.

> I have become open-minded about the fact that there are also other stories that are not just about a few rotten apples but rather about something systematic that I have helped to actively support in the past—but which I have also passively supported by not daring to attempt to correct other men's behaviour.

They emphasized that they had realized it was not just about women being too uptight and hysterical, there was something systematic allowing sexual harassment to occur. Several of them described that both they and their friends reacted a bit hesitantly to the first #MeToo wave in 2017, when the gender politics debate was also more defensive—and where it was not unusual to hear defensive statements like 'It's freedom of speech, dammit.'

6.5 The Debate Is Important, but…

Some of the men were profoundly influenced by the #MeToo movement. They were self-reflexive and stated that they wanted to examine their own role, power and privileges. Others found themselves caught at a crossroads between the past and a new era of masculinity and were more ambivalent, with mixed feelings about the #MeToo movement. Some of the men said they had difficulty positioning themselves in the #MeToo debate. Even though none of the men were reactionary defenders of entrenched privilege, several of them emphasized the importance of distinguishing between deliberately offensive sexual actions and 'unintended' sexual harassment.

Regarding the awareness and assertion of social norms about manhood, some of the men indicated that they had never subscribed to these norms themselves. They stated that they did not 'fit in' with the traditional peer culture. On the other hand, they had not directly opposed the culture. None of the men expressed rigid and reactionary attitudes such as stating that women brought it on themselves if they were exposed to inappropriate sexual behaviour. Likewise, none of them wanted to keep the current situation in place and defend some old order, which is fading. Therefore, they were not 'stuck-in-the-mud' men and did not adhere to the most rigid gender norms. All the men showed awareness and concern about the problem of sexual harassment. Nevertheless, there were some men who pointed out that there might be a correlation between how women dress and their risk of being exposed to sexual harassment, and that women should be aware of this. A small number of the men thought that if women are wearing sexy clothes, it is their own fault that they receive sexual attention from men. It was also possible to trace an attitude towards women that they should become better at expressing their limits because one can always choose to offer resistance, even if someone with power is targeting you. Further, it was occasionally mentioned that women could also sexually harass men. This kind of thinking seems problematic and we need to unpack it critically, since it trivializes sexual harassment and blames women for their own sexual victimization. This is crucial because the goal of #MeToo is not only to hold individual perpetrators to account but also to break down the whole rape culture on which sexual harassment is based. Acquaviva et al. (2021: 24) state that when men disbelieve victims' disclosures they often do so with statements supportive of rape culture.

On a societal level, there has been a call for more men to take part in the debate on sexual harassment and #MeToo. Nevertheless, relatively few men have spoken out about men's perpetration of sexual harassment against women. Likewise, the interviews illustrated that some of the men do not feel they are allowed to state their opinion on #MeToo. Some of these pointed out that they thought the #MeToo debate reflected an aspiration for women to stress their independence and stand on their own two feet and that the general conception was that only women should take part in the debate. Therefore, it often requires double the effort for a man to participate in the debate on sexual harassment and #MeToo. On the one hand, he must be careful not to be laughed at and looked down upon by his male friends, and on the other hand, he must behave carefully in a social environment that has hitherto been dominated by women. A few of the men stated that, due to the explicit focus on #MeToo, what people actually think and feel and what they say in public may differ.

> Some tend to say, 'I support this new culture', even though they are in fact scared of what specifically it will entail.

Generally speaking, one of the strategies of resistance to the #MeToo movement is to claim that it has gone too far culturally and insist that romantic relationships require being free to show your interest and that the movement is strangling this freedom (PettyJohn et al., 2019). Some of the men emphasized that the #MeToo movement had resulted in a lot of confusion. They stated that it could sometimes be difficult being a man these days, given that feminist struggles were getting out of hand

and that one had to be careful not to cross the line and do something which was no longer permitted. In their analysis of the media coverage of #MeToo in Denmark, Askanius and Hartley (2019) found that #MeToo is challenged and brought into question in subtle ways. In some cases, accusations of sexual harassment are described as a 'grey area'. Askanius and Hartley (2019) describe how it might also be questioned whether sexual harassment is a problem proportional to the magnitude of the response and attention #MeToo has received. Such positions tend to weaken #MeToo as an uproar against gendered sexual violence, for example by arguing that 'men also experience sexual harassment' or that explicit discussions about consent will make it difficult for people (men) to know how to behave properly in public space (Askanius & Hartley, 2019: 28).

Several of the men stated that one had to be cautious not to let the discussion about inappropriate sexual behaviour get out of hand or become too much about political correctness. In that context, they emphasized that the political climate after the second wave of #MeToo hit Denmark was unduly negative towards them and had resulted in a campaign against inappropriate sexual behaviour which was out of proportion compared to what actually happens.

> The matter should of course be dealt with if something inappropriate has taken place, but it is important to not let it get out of hand—it is now at the point where you cannot even escort an old lady across the street without being accused of wanting to sleep with her.

Others indicated that the debate milieu continued to be very polarized, even though it had brought with it new societal knowledge. They pointed out the scale and difficulties of communicating the new knowledge to people, while the debate is continually being derailed.

6.6 Has #MeToo Changed Their Views on Sexual Harassment?

Several noted that #MeToo had led to a rush of memories and that #MeToo had been an eye opener, making them re-evaluate their past sexual experiences. One of the men, who now identified as a feminist, described the gender-political journey of learning he had been on as follows:

> Before #MeToo, I hadn't really thought much about sexual harassment, and I would never have considered calling myself a feminist… I actually didn't even know what it meant to be a feminist… I just associated it with the Redstockings movement [the name of the Danish feminist movement in the 1970s] from the past.

Among the men who admitted that they had engaged in some minor forms of sexual harassment, it was characteristic that they all noted that it was something that happened when they were teenagers. When it came to explaining the reasons for them stopping their sexist behaviour and sexual harassment, they said that, generally, it was because they had grown up and become more mature. Others noted that their attitudes and behaviour changed when they got a girlfriend, and some others mentioned the #MeToo debate.

> I can now clearly see the difference between how I behaved when I was 14 or 15 and started taking an interest in girls and how I am now (aged 23)… I have become more decent, in a way. It is hard to be the same flippant kid now.

Often a feminist awakening is fostered by experiences in higher education (Messner et al., 2015). There were also men who highlighted the importance of beginning to study and reading literature on gender issues, which had increased the attention they paid to gender-based forms of inequality.

> Through my studies, I have become better at spotting the subtle mechanisms of oppression that help to maintain men's privileges.

One of the men stated that he had learned a lot about inappropriate sexual behaviour as at one point he had worked at a salad bar with only female colleagues. There he listened to the women talking among themselves about being exposed to unwelcome sexual advances and from that, he had gained explicit knowledge of the many types of sexual harassment that women are exposed to and how hard it could be for women to resist the harassment. In that context, it is worth mentioning that those men who demonstrated the greatest amount of understanding and empathic ability to put themselves in other people's shoes when it came to the impact of sexual harassment were men who stated that they had close female friends and that they had talked to them about #MeToo. The importance of getting heterosexual men to participate in the debate was mentioned by almost all the men.

6.7 Summary

#MeToo is both life-affirming and deeply challenging for men. #MeToo compels men to make a fundamental reassessment of everything they have suppressed, denied or taken for granted about their masculine identities. Therefore, it is not surprising that the #MeToo movement provoked a variety of responses among Danish men. The #MeToo debate has divided Danish men into two camps. One the one hand, there are those who support the movement and who have been prompted to soul-search as a result of the many testimonies of harassment. On the other hand, we find men who disagree with the movement and who are not content just to criticize it but also take part in the debate to try to undermine the many testimonies of sexual abuse and harassment that have emerged.

Nevertheless, there are signs of shifts in social norms in terms of what behaviours are perceived as acceptable or unacceptable. The #MeToo movement may be triggering the most monumental change ever in the rules of the game for men's and women's social and sexual interaction.

Thanks to the #MeToo movement, men have gained insight into a world of experiences about the consequences of harassment, of which they were previously unaware. The #MeToo movement has literally given men a chance to learn more about what it is like to be a woman. However, while it is difficult to find out how Danish men more generally feel about the #MeToo movement and how men relate to society's increasing condemnation of abusive men, the #MeToo movement in Denmark, as in most other places in the world, has created greater awareness of sexism and gender inequality.

Nilsson and Lundgren (2020) speak about how #MeToo might represent a kind of 'fateful' moment where #MeToo becomes a turning point in life for men. However, while fateful moments can be a starting point for a process of change, they can be stressful and full of tension for the individual (Nilsson & Lundgren, 2020: 14). Therefore, because men and women often perceive gender and sexual harassment differently, it might be tough for some men to start exercising deep self-interrogation.

References

Acquaviva, B. L., O'Neal, E. N., & Clevenger, S. L. (2021). Sexual assault awareness in the #MeToo era: Student perceptions of victim believability and cases in the media. *American Journal of Criminal Justice, 46*(1), 6–32.

Alt for Damerne [All for the Ladies]. (2020).

Askanius, T., & Hartley, J. M. (2019). Framing gender justice: A comparative analysis of the media coverage of #metoo in Denmark and Sweden. *Nordicom Review, 40*(2), 19–36.

Bates, L. (2014). *Everyday sexism.* Simon & Schuster.

Boyle, K., & Rathnayake, C. (2020). #HimToo and the networking of misogyny in the age of #MeToo. *Feminist Media Studies, 20*(8), 1259–1277.

Essig, T. (2018). Examples of straight men grappling with the #MeToo movement. *Contemporary Psychoanalysis, 54*(4), 677–687.

Fawcett Society. (2018). *#Metoo one year on—What's changed?* The Fawcett Society.

Fileborn, B., & Phillips, N. (2019). From 'Me Too' to 'Too far'? Contesting the boundaries of sexual violence in contemporary activism. *#MeToo and the politics of social change* (pp. 99–115). Palgrave Macmillan.

Flood, M. (2018). *Engaging men and boys in violence prevention.* Springer.

Flood, M. (2019). Men and #Metoo: Mapping Men's responses to anti-violence advocacy. In *#MeToo and the politics of social change* (pp. 285–300). Palgrave Macmillan.

Gillette. (2019). We believe: The best men can be | Gillette (Short Film) retrieved from YouTube https://www.youtube.com/watch?v=koPmuEyP3a0

Greene, M. (2018). The little #MeToo book for men. Think play partners.

Kippe, E. (2004). *Kjøper «ekte mannfolk» sex?: en studie av 20 menn som kjøper seksuelle tjenester* [Do "real men" buy sex ?: A study of 20 men who buy sexual services]. Stiftelsen for nors helse-og rehabiliseringsorganisasjoner.

Kunst, J. R., Bailey, A., Prendergast, C., & Gundersen, A. (2018). Sexism, rape myths and feminist identification explain gender differences in attitudes toward the #metoo social media campaign in two countries. *Media Psychology, 22*(5), 818–843.

Kvinfo. (2017, October 30). #MeToo sætter den nostalgiske maskulinitet under pres. Interview med Christian Groes-Green [#MeToo puts the nostalgic masculinity under pressure. Interview with Christian Groes-Green].

Män. (2018a). *Ett år #efter MeToo – En SIFO-undersökning om mäns attityder till #Metoo-opproren* [One year #after MeToo—A SIFO survey on men's attitudes to the #Metoo uprising].

Män. (2018b). Men, Masculinity and #MeToo.

Messner, M. A., Greenberg, M. A., & Peretz, T. (2015). *Some men: Feminist allies in the movement to end violence against women.* Oxford University Press.

Murphy Austin, M. J., Dardis, C. M., Wilson, M. S., Gidycz, C. A., & Berkowitz, A. D. (2016). Predictors of sexual assault–specific prosocial bystander behavior and intentions: A prospective analysis. *Violence Against Women, 22*(1), 90–111.

Nilsson, B., & Lundgren, A. S. (2020). The #MeToo Movement: Men and Masculinity in Swedish News Media. *The Journal of Men's Studies, 29*(1), 8–25.

PettyJohn, M. E., Muzzey, F. K., Maas, M. K., & McCauley, H. L. (2019). #HowIWillChange: Engaging men and boys in the #MeToo movement. *Psychology of Men & Masculinities, 20*(4), 612–623.

Reinicke, K. (2012). *Drenge og mænd i krise? Perspektiver og indsatsområder* [Boys and men in crisis? Perspectives and focus areas]. Hans Reitzel

Reinicke, K. (2018). *Mænd som krænker kvinder – refleksioner i kølvandet på #Metoo* [Men who violate women—Reflections in the wake of #MeToo]. Samfundslitteratur.

Rosenbeck, V. (2017). *Kom nu ind i #MeToo-kampen, mænd* [Now get into the #MeToo fight, men]. Altinget.

Ruxton, S. (2020). *Men and gender equality: Challenges and opportunities.* ICMEO.

7

Flirting After #MeToo

What effect has the #MeToo debate had on men's perceptions of inappropriate sexual behaviour and consent? Nilsson and Lundgren (2020) state that because of #MeToo, men have become aware of their own sexist behaviour and of being part of a problem. What is defined as inappropriate sexual behaviour and what do men need to learn? For some men, it is about being more aware of their own boundaries and the boundaries of others and becoming better at understanding consent and learning when to be careful rather than blindly following their own desires and pushing their own needs on to others. A positive sexual encounter (for most people) is about ensuring that everyone involved has a good experience. Nevertheless, how do young men deal with uncertainty and lack of knowledge concerning what is important when being intimate with another person?

If you look at the phenomenon of 'flirting', one can say that it is about attracting the attention of one or more people. Flirting is often expressed as a romantic or sexual interest, where people tease each other's desires and fantasies in an intimate way. Flirting can take place through conversation, body language or a brief physical contact. Examples of flirting can be smiles, eye contact, winking, teasing, exchanging messages, flattering or giving compliments. Flirting can be defined as an ambiguous and potentially pleasurable social practice that is also risky and fraught (Bartlett et al., 2019). Flirting takes place in the field of tension between 'yes' and 'no' and in the dynamics between consent and the eternal fear of rejection. Flirting is, on the one hand, an extremely pleasurable activity, an opening to the possibilities of the present and the future. On the other hand, it is also a risky occupation, where rejection always lurks around the corner and risks crossing the line to harassment in certain contexts.

For some of the men, dating and flirting in the #MeToo era was seen as a positive challenge, while for others, it became a new source of anxiety. The men who were not concerned about this stated that some things had of course changed, but this did not necessarily mean things had changed for the worse. They agreed that both people agreeing about what is going to happen should characterize sexual relations and that it was the person initiating sex who was responsible for establishing consent. They further stated that maybe it required more talking to each other, but that was also an opportunity to show who they really are.

> I can't see how things have gotten harder. You just have to pay attention to each other's boundaries, but come on, how hard is that… and then obviously you shouldn't have sex with someone who is lying next to you sleeping.

Several of the men also stated that their moral compass was more activated now in the sense that they were careful about respecting the boundaries of others. The issue that several of them referred to was very much the dilemma between not taking the initiative enough and, on the other hand, being scared of violating someone's boundaries.

Fundamentally, it was pointed out by a number of men that the difference between sexual harassment and a compliment was that a compliment makes someone happy while sexual harassment is unpleasant for the target. Several men emphasized that anyone with just a little empathy would be able to quickly read a situation. They underlined that it was about when and how compliments are given and therefore it is important to have a good gut feeling about the situation and think about who you are interacting with. The men who were not concerned also stated that it had in no way become more difficult to be a man and that you could still flirt and approach women without having to worry about it being perceived as violating their boundaries. They noted that they had begun paying more attention to 'the good way of doing things'.

> Decent behaviour and flirting are not contradictions... you can easily hit on someone without harassing them... if you could flirt before #MeToo without causing problems then you can also flirt after #MeToo.

Several of the men said that it was not always easy to gauge someone's interest. They describe how sometimes they were reading the other's body language to see if they were interested, sometimes they tried to make a physical move to see what would happen and sometimes they were asking for a verbal confirmation of consent. One of the men declared how he had begun to ask directly if the woman wanted to kiss.

> Flirting and pickup culture have changed... I don't think people will be dating less, rather I think women will instead be more interested in the men who are less groping and less insistent... it can be difficult to know if a woman wants you to take the initiative, and therefore I have actually begun asking women directly if they want to kiss, and I don't think it's a turnoff, it can actually seem sweet.

In contrast, some of the men were adamant that the new rules of dating that #MeToo had created were confusing and that it was now difficult being an admirer. They claimed that it is not always easy to find out when to take chances and detect the boundaries, because everyone has their own views on when their boundaries are violated. They problematized the uncertainty surrounding where the boundaries now were and what kind of approaches were no longer permitted towards women. Furthermore, it was emphasized that one had to be looking for the small hints that permit one to go ahead and that one needs finely tuned senses in order not to step on anyone's toes. They raised the question of whether it is now indisputably the woman who decides and sets the pace for when the first kiss happens and when a man can put his hand on the woman's thigh. In addition, it was also questioned whether the man should still pay for the food on a date or if such practices were now obsolete.

> Before, you had to buy drinks, but now it is more like the woman needs to show interest first before the man attempts to seduce her.

> I have become extremely careful about avoiding the risk of violating other people's boundaries. I would feel absolutely awful if I felt that I had gotten some signals that indicated it was OK to make a move and then being told the day after that what I had done was not OK.

The men in the study, besides having to deal with flirting and dating in a #MeToo era, also had to deal with initiating erotic relationships in a period where a legal definition of rape based on consent was being introduced, as highlighted earlier in Chapter 3.

7.1 Does No Always Mean No?

Teaching men to talk about consent, respect and sex is challenging, and research on how young people negotiate consent is still rare (Coy et al., 2013; Holmström et al., 2020; Muehlenhard et al., 2016). Looking at how the men make sense of and negotiate the meaning of sexual consent, it was underlined that, particularly when they were younger, they had difficulty decoding where the boundaries were. They highlight that the way a 'No' is spoken can be a factor, and a 'No' cannot always be taken literally. It can be perceived as ambiguous and be part of the game, and in such cases it is not necessarily crossing a line if you keep up with the attempted seduction. Is there a 'virtuous no' that perhaps might mean 'try again'? Is the soft 'No' just part of playing hard to get? One of the men pointed out the dilemma:

If the 'No' does not sound like a resounding negative, you might be unsure about how to respond to it.

It is interesting to see how, in the way they navigate sexual consent, the men are to a certain extent drawing on a construction of the male sexual subject and female passive object which serves to de-legitimatize allegations of sexual assault that are contrary to heterosexual norms (see also Gavey, 2005). It was also pointed out that it was impossible to exclude that there was something erotic about pushing others' boundaries but that one had to be really good at reading the other person and interpreting the situation, tone of voice and body language. Further, it was emphasized that one has to be open to signals, because what does consent mean in practice when a 'Yes' can turn into a 'No' and vice versa?

The idea of the man being the one to take the initiative and that if they do not go far enough, then usually nothing happens, is reflected in the following quote:

> You can't avoid entering the grey zone... you sometimes have to take chances and show that you are interested in the other person, and sometimes, you might go too far.

The above point undoubtedly resonates with many men. Nevertheless, it can be interpreted as problematic because it might play down the importance of negotiating consent. The men largely agreed that being bad at reading signals and showing too much aggression was a dangerous cocktail. It is about the dilemma of taking chances while also wanting to play it safe. The man needs to dare to take the initiative, and some men end up crossing the line. Therefore, for young men it is often about learning about and *confirming* the healthy types of masculinity (which means being able to show vulnerability and express a wide range of feelings) and *challenging* the problematic unhealthy types of masculinity (orientated towards not showing weakness and expecting other men to do the same).

7.2 The Missing Language

The life of young people today includes intimate and sexual situations that some people may find difficult to navigate. These situations often occur in a grey area with unclear sexual rules and boundaries. This makes them difficult for the people involved to navigate and manage, particularly because the interpretation of a situation and what is at stake may vary from individual to individual (Roien et al., 2018).

Both men and woman often lack a language to discuss the registration of boundaries and to express what they want (Holmström et al., 2020). More than a few of the men tell of experiences where they have been unsure whether they have violated others. They state that they could be featuring in some women's #MeToo stories without being aware of it. Several talked of episodes in their past that, in retrospect, they could see might have been offensive or perhaps even a sexual assault.

> I was undeniably part of it, but due to ignorance... I have been part of a sexist culture, but I was not aware of it.

The above-mentioned reasons for engaging in sexist behaviour are in accordance with Essig's (2018) study on how straight men were grappling with #MeToo. They thought that that was how the game was played and how the world works. It is interesting to note that in my study several of the men did express a form of masculinity where it was legitimate to harass and exceed a woman's boundaries but not to physically force her. The majority of the men admitted that they had participated in sexist behaviours on a continuum that ranges from mildly objectifying women to pressuring women but always without using violence to achieve their goal. This is also in line with Essig (2018) who emphasizes that many young men report experiences in adolescence and young adulthood of cat-calling and repeatedly asking for dates or sex from the same woman who said no over and over, to the point of becoming a nuisance, or otherwise being more pushy than they wanted to be because they felt such behaviour was an acceptable part of what it meant to be a man pursuing sex. Essig (2018: 677) goes on to state that #MeToo made previous established ways of conducting themselves sexually such as 'how and when – and when not – to flirt, seduce or otherwise pursue sexual aims, originally crafted and tested during adolescence and young adulthood, back into a problem'.

It is important to understand the stage of a young man's life between adolescence and adulthood. Numerous men noted that there was a need for a cultural change that could ensure that both men and women had more positive experiences and that more people were prevented from seriously crossing the line. They discussed how the fragility of the male role and the fumbling transition from boy to man needs to be brought into the light and become part of the conversation between men. However, they did admit that it is difficult to have such conversations in practice. This is because it requires that both men and women learn to be better at listening to each other. A culture needs to be created where those who feel that their boundaries have been crossed and the ones violating those boundaries understand each other. This is often complicated by the fact that traditional cultural sexual scripts are highly gendered and prescribe often opposite positions for men and women (Masters et al., 2013). Nevertheless, several of the men emphasized that the cultural conflict over boundaries and consent is not a conflict between men and women.

> This is not about 'men versus women'. Everyone can gain from changes. This is because it can also lead to a liberation of men if the talk about sex is not only about bragging or pickup stories and they can also talk about when sex is difficult and when they fail to live up to their responsibilities.

The vast majority of the men agreed that it is important that men become better at focusing on women's reactions to their comments and behaviour. Several of the men also pointed out the importance of not becoming angry or sexist when they feel challenged or powerless. In addition, it was stated that men need to learn that they are not victims when women reject them and that it is all right to feel upset when they get rejected. It is also important to be able to manage rejections constructively, without feeling entitled to be aggressive, yell insults, or be physically or emotionally threatening.

People need to be able to handle rejection. This is part of life. We can get rejected applying for jobs or when trying to get closer to another person.

Besides obviously not tolerating outright inappropriate sexual behaviour, people also need to learn to talk about the experiences that take place on the spectrum where there is some form of mutual consent but where there is still a need to learn how to navigate, listen and ask questions. A number of the men stated that if people could learn to talk openly about how communicating with a potential sex partner has many pitfalls, we may begin to understand why it sometimes goes wrong.

Looking at which characteristics currently define hegemonic masculinity, as Schapiro (*Information*, 2018) emphasizes, there are contradictory aspects to being young. Therefore, it is crucial to embrace paradoxes in sexual encounters, but it is particularly difficult for our young people to decipher the sexual codes in our culture, making them difficult to navigate because there are different sets of moral values that are activated. On the one hand, cultural codes encourage young people to try new things and push others' boundaries, but on the other hand, they are also encouraged to take care of themselves and others. Not all men can handle the complexity of women also seeking compliments and wanting to be admired and desired while at the same time they naturally do not want to be dehumanized, objectified, or undressed with the eyes.

So, what do men need to learn? Several of the men stated that if you want to enter another person's intimate sphere, you need permission. It is still all right to desire women, compliment them and say nice things to them. However, overall, it is about maintaining a form of mutual respect and men being able to make ethical choices. One of the men says that sex should be talked about in an ethically correct way. He puts it this way:

You don't have to say 'I fucked her'; you can instead say 'We had sex.'

The quote shows how they try to become a better version of themselves and how they are wondering about how much they had earlier adopted rigid norms of masculinity. As with Essig's (2018) study of men's responses to #MeToo, the men had lost confidence in behaviours previously taken for granted. This gives rise to personally substantial questions about how to conduct themselves.

7.3 The Consent Law

Consent-based legislation shifts the focus and changes the 'theme of evidence' and the starting point for the presentation of evidence. Consent legislation can thus make a big difference to the way cases are conducted and how the victim is treated in court. The legislation will put the victim in a new and better situation, because it will be more about the right to the victim's body and less about the resistance offered by the victim. Therefore, there are good reasons for believing that this will bring about a change in mindsets. Nevertheless, it is important to emphasize, as stated in Chapter 2, that evidence from other jurisdictions has shown that the law has not been completely successful. Despite the good intentions of the law, often it is for the victims to demonstrate that they had not consented (Cossins, 2020; Larcombe et al., 2016).

Most men pointed out that they believed it was a positive development that the man now had to account for what signals the woman had sent him and that it requires that men be more attentive. In that context, several of them mentioned that the consent law could help create 'common' ground rules and will change the conversational culture. They saw #MeToo as a necessary attack on an outdated patriarchal culture and talked about the necessity of being on the 'right' side of history. Here are some examples:

> It's fine if the consent law can prevent rapes and I think it's a good law, because I only sleep with women who want to sleep with me.

> It's about both parties wanting to have sex... I can't understand at all how you could argue against this law... those who are against it must really see themselves as being on the wrong side of history 20 years from now.

> When one's actions are not reciprocated, it is important to take a step back... It's not about needing someone to sign the dotted line, it's about feeling whether the other part is into it and if you are in doubt, then ask... I'm tired of hearing journalists ask what it sounds like when consenting.

The last of the above quotes indicate how the new law of consent and the associated arguments for and against have been part of extensive public debate about personal boundaries, assaults, rights, and so on. One of the men stated that he was reluctant to engage in conversations about #MeToo for fear of being accused of misogyny. He also stated—referring to the introduction of the new consent law in Denmark—that it could be difficult for the man to prove his innocence with the new consent law but that one had to be careful about expressing such dangers, because then you could be accused of generally being against the consent law.

> When I discuss the consent law, I try to remain as objective as possible, and I generally avoid using the phrase 'I think...' if I am discussing something related to the grey areas that I think are problematic with the legislation. For example, when is it the man's fault, and when should the woman have more clearly objected... if, for example, you say that an innocent man might end up in court, then you are told that men are not brought before a court unless they deserve it.

An aspect of the #MeToo movement that has been brought up many times is men's legal rights. Will a tightening of the law result in men having to do more to prove that they had no ill intentions, thereby paving the way for reduction and prevention of rape, and can such a law prevent people from having sex with others against their will? Nilsson and Lundgren (2020) stress that #MeToo was also positioned as being problematic because the movement legitimizes acts that are legally unsound and punishes individual men who have not been found guilty of any crime. Thus, a discourse of criticism can be regarded as a kind of counter-discourse to the dominant image of #MeToo as an exclusively positive and genuinely necessary movement. Nilsson and Lundgren (2020: 16) go on to say that this view structures the understanding of #MeToo quite differently from the other discourses, as it enables narratives of women who come forward with false testimonies, of media that publish unverified accusations, and of men who are misunderstood and falsely accused.

Despite the fact that false allegations are extremely rare (see Kelly, 2010; Lisak et al., 2010), some of the men also brought up the problem of fake accusations (see also Kessler et al., 2021). Hypothetical examples include women who might have been drunk and then had sex with men and regretted it the next day, and then, to salvage their pride, they end up saying they have been raped. While not saying that some men might not feel vulnerable and afraid of false accusations, we need to be alert to and critical of conversations around false accusations because they are often rooted in rape culture and may be brought up in order to dismiss the reality of rape and sexual harassment (Acquaviva et al., 2021).

Has the #MeToo debate made men feel stigmatized? And if so, has this also affected 'good' men? Men who already have progressive attitudes to gender equality and who have always adopted a sober, thoughtful and sensitive approach towards the opposite sex? Do they now overthink the way they flirt with and approach women? One of the otherwise unconcerned men who said that he was generally not afraid of violating a woman's boundaries because he was good at establishing consent described his fear as follows:

> I have thought about how you could end up in a situation where you had sex with a woman who might be in a relationship and then chooses to report it as a rape... I think I will always be able to control myself and read a woman's signals and I also have faith in the rule of law... but there is still something scary about the thought that something might happen later that is outside my control.

Talking about consent is difficult and involves complex human emotions. Unfortunately, one can often detect feelings of irritation, resistance and the tendency to make the negotiation of consent sound ridiculous because it breaks the romantic flow. Several of the men pointed out that the assertion that a stronger focus on consent will kill flirting and romance was wrong. They stressed that consent is not about signing contracts, among other things, because consent should always be revocable, but it is about paying attention and being emotionally present.

Nevertheless, in the wake of the Consent Act a new Danish iConsent app was invented with the purpose of giving advice about sex and the opportunity to document consent to intercourse. One can use it to send and receive requests for consent to sex. The company behind the app explained that they hoped it can help to create greater clarity about when it is okay to have sex with each other. Nevertheless, the app was accused on several fronts of ridiculing the new law on consent. Furthermore, the Danish Women's Society accused the app of being potentially dangerous because it gives the impression of protection but does not take into account the situation where a person rescinds consent but is unable to grab their phone and withdraw the consent.

7.4 Does Sexual Harassment Have a Statute of Limitations?

A controversial issue is how to look at situations where men are caught up by accusations related to their past (Pollack, 2019). Should there be a statute of limitations for offensive behaviour, and how serious and systematic should the harassment and offensive actions have been in order to accuse a person many years later? The study did show that some of the men had a defensive approach towards #MeToo as regards the impact of the court of public opinion. They argued that, depending on the severity of the case, public forgiveness should also be possible for men accused of sexual harassment and that being held accountable should require criminal prosecution and not only public acknowledgement and reckoning.

It was pointed out that a key aspect of how to judge is whether the abuse was related to exploitation of hierarchical relationships. For example, had the person being accused had the opportunity to silence criticism of his actions? Some of the men highlighted that it was unfair to face legal repercussions for something that took place in another time with different cultural norms where such things might have been acceptable.

It is horrendous that you can show up 10–15 years later and demand justice... the evidence is impossible to gather properly... it is hard for the accused to say that that was not what happened.

In terms of the incidents where powerful politicians had resigned, it was pointed out that in the absence of a trial it is the court of public opinion that decides whether one should step down. However, research indicates that these types of claims regarding lack of 'due process' seem problematic, given how sexual offences have been treated in the legal system (e.g., low reporting, retraumatizing, low conviction rates, limited definitions of what counts as sexual violence, etc.) (see, e.g., Haire et al., 2019).

7.5 Naming the Perpetrator

Who decides whether it is right or wrong to publish the name of the perpetrator? There has been heated debate about whether #MeToo is an accusation against all men if the offender is not identified. Does a woman necessarily need to name the man if she knows his identity? The argument has often been that this is about fighting a general sexist culture and not individual cases, and therefore names are not relevant. Nevertheless, every time a new case of sexual harassment turns up, the question arises: who is the abuser, and is the person publicly known? Reestorff (TV2, 2020) states that many feel that there is some justice involved in bringing the name to light. If a person has made serious mistakes, they must take responsibility and pay the penalty. However, Reestorff goes on to say that many fear the debate will be derailed as soon as a name is put to the offender because it immediately becomes a more gossipy story when the offender is named, and many are led to believe it is only about the individual person.

An opposite view is that of Groes Green (TV2, 2020), who asserts that it is crucial that society put a name and a face to perpetrators. He stresses that it does not derail the debate; on the contrary, it makes it far more tangible. Groes Green carries on to say that the sexist culture does not change unless we hear about some specific cases and see with our own eyes that it has consequences for the perpetrators.

Lauritsen (2020) emphasizes that some people unfortunately allow themselves to be carried away by this argument and forget that the decision lies with the woman and that her statement does not become more or less true if it is combined with a first and last name. He points out that the requirement for women to name their offender can best be understood as an attempt to divert attention away from the fact that there is a need for confrontation with an entire culture—not just with a few maladjusted men.

> Look, for example, at all those who demand that women name the abuser, because if they do not, they put all men under indictment. As if we would suddenly think that all men unsolicitedly grab women's breasts or force them to have sex. Obviously, we do not think that way. When we hear about an unnamed rapist or bank robber, we do not suspect all men of the crime.

Lauritsen (2020) further contemplates what would happen if the women actually named their abusers; would they then be believed? No, on the contrary, the women would be required to provide evidence, and since this is inherently rare, they would instead be accused of making false accusations. Just imagine, attacking an innocent man? That is how it would sound. Moreover, the man would go free, whereas the woman who experienced the abuse would be exposed to public contempt. Some of the men described the importance of taking part in confronting the systemic issues by addressing the problematic culture instead of striving to identify the names of scapegoats. As one of the men put it:

> My first reaction when Sofie Linde came forward with her story without mentioning the name of the person who had harassed her was that it was critical … but then I discussed it with some friends and started thinking about why I felt like that … then my perspective developed and I recognized that my first reaction was a kind of diversion for not taking a stand on what she was trying to address; namely, the systemic in the spread of sexual harassment … I had walked into the trap of wanting to protect myself by looking for a scapegoat.

Some of the other men stated that in reality, publicly naming a perpetrator is nothing more than a trap. The moment a name is mentioned, a new demand arises for evidence that most victims cannot provide, because most sexual offences take place in private with no other witnesses. The presence of physical evidence (such as bruises) is also rare. Without evidence, the accusation is deemed false, or the incident is treated as a case of 'he said, she said' that can never be resolved either way. The abuser becomes the victim, and the woman who experienced the assault becomes the executioner. The participants emphasized that the requirement to name names has the effect of leading to an isolated focus on those named. When the woman states the name, the problem becomes attached to specific individuals and the rest are let off. The bad apples may be removed, but new ones will turn up and the culture can continue as before. Without change and without improvement.

7.6 Summary

#MeToo can be seen as a starting point of a new era which might change how dating and flirting works. Some of the men interviewed said that they had examined their own values and attitudes in order to better understand their behaviour and how it affects women. Others expressed the view that they already had attitudes and beliefs that were anti-sexist. Nevertheless, they had all changed their view about how women are treated in society.

The conversation about sexual harassment is now all over society. It does not seem possible to go back to the world before #MeToo. Men can longer act with impunity. Generally, #MeToo may have provoked some level of reconsidering of patriarchal forms of flirting, dating, and interaction (Flood, 2019). What is new about the conversation is that it is no longer about what women can do to avoid being victims of sexual harassment—rather it is about how men need to change their behaviour. That society has reached a tipping point also means that we now criticize the behaviour of men. Moreover, for the first time there seem to be actual consequences for bad behaviour for a group of men. The justice system has changed course and time will tell whether this also means that it is no longer possible to minimize or make excuses for sexual harassment. Furthermore, it remains open whether men want to stand up and speak up. The next chapter looks at the forces that might speed up or delay men's ability to become active bystanders.

References

Acquaviva, B. L., O'Neal, E. N., & Clevenger, S. L. (2021). Sexual assault awareness in the #MeToo era: Student perceptions of victim believability and cases in the media. *American Journal of Criminal Justice, 46*(1), 6–32.

Bartlett, A., Clarke, K., & Cover, R. (2019). *Flirting in the era of #MeToo: Negotiating intimacy*. Springer.

Cossins, A. (2020). Modernisation of the substantive law of consent. In *Closing the justice gap for adult and child sexual assault* (pp. 277–337). Palgrave Macmillan.

Coy, M., Kelly, L., Elvines, F., Garner, M., & Kanyeredzi, A. (2013). *Sex without consent, I suppose that is rape: How young people in England understand sexual consent*. Office of the Children's Commissioner.

Essig, T. (2018). Examples of straight men grappling with the #MeToo movement. *Contemporary Psychoanalysis, 54*(4), 677–687.

Flood, M. (2019). Men and #Metoo: Mapping men's responses to anti-violence advocacy. In *#MeToo and the politics of social change* (pp. 285–300). Palgrave Macmillan.

Gavey, N. (2005). *Just sex? The cultural scaffolding of rape*. Routledge.

Haire, B., Newman, C. E., & Fileborn, B. (2019). Shitty media men. In *#MeToo and the politics of social change* (pp. 201–216). Palgrave Macmillan.

Holmström, C., Plantin, L., & Elmerstig, E. (2020). Complexities of sexual consent: Young people's reasoning in a Swedish context. *Psychology & Sexuality, 11*(4), 342–357.

Information. (2018, February 17). Velkommen til grænseland [Welcome to Borderland].

Kelly, L. (2010). The (in)credible words of women: False allegations in European rape research. *Violence Against Women, 16*(12), 1345–1355.

Kessler, A. M., Kennair, L. E. O., Grøntvedt, T. V., Bjørkheim, I., Drejer, I., & Bendixen, M. (2021). Perception of workplace social-sexual behavior as sexual harassment post #MeToo in Scandinavia. *Scandinavian Journal of Psychology, 62*, 1–12

Larcombe, W., Fileborn, B., Powell, A., Hanley, N., & Henry, N. (2016). 'I think it's rape and I think he would be found not guilty.' Focus group perceptions of (un)reasonable belief in consent in rape law. *Social & Legal Studies, 25*(5), 611–629.

Lauritsen, P. (2020, October 3). Det var præcis her, vi svigtede sidste gang, #MeToo gik gennem landet [This is exactly where we failed the last time #MeToo went through the country]. *Politiken.*

Lisak, D., Gardinier, L., Nicksa, S. C., & Cote, A. M. (2010). False allegations of sexual assault: An analysis of ten years of reported cases. *Violence Against Women, 16*(12), 1318–1334.

Masters, N. T., Casey, E., Wells, E. A., & Morrison, D. M. (2013). Sexual scripts among young heterosexually active men and women: Continuity and change. *Journal of Sex Research, 50*(5), 409–420.

Muehlenhard, C. L., Humphreys, T. P., Jozkowski, K. N., & Peterson, Z. D. (2016). The complexities of sexual consent among college students: A conceptual and empirical review. *The Journal of Sex Research, 53*(4–5), 457–487.

Nilsson, B., & Lundgren, A. S. (2020). The #MeToo Movement: Men and Masculinity in Swedish News Media. *The Journal of Men's Studies, 29*(1), 8–25.

Pollack, E. (2019). Sweden and the #MeToo movement. *Interactions: Studies in Communication & Culture, 10*(3), 185–200.

Roien, L. A., Simovska, V., & Graugaard, C. (2018). *Seksualitet, skole og samfund: kritiske perspektiver på seksualundervisning* [Sexuality, school and society: Critical perspectives on sex education]. Hans Reitzels Forlag.

TV2. (2020, October 11). *Hvad sker der, når en krænker navngives? Den seneste uges tumult giver svaret, siger ekspert* [What happens when an offender is named? The tumult of the past week provides the answer, says expert].

8

Will Men Take a Stand?

Men can play a powerful role in combating sexual harassment. Though this smacks of sexism, we must acknowledge that men can be heard saying something that women often cannot be heard saying (Reinicke, 2012). This chapter includes a discussion on how to make it less socially acceptable for men to harass women sexually. It discusses men's beliefs and practices in connection with speaking up in opposition towards sexual harassment.

How do perpetrators understand the silence of peers? What messages are sent to victims of sexual harassment when the perpetrator's peers do not confront him? Men often interpret other men's silence as approval. Therefore, we need men who have the courage and strength to stand up and speak up, and to take a stand together with women and not against them. It is crucial to encourage men to use their moral integrity and speak out because silence can become a form of consent and complicity. However, it is not easy for men to find their anti-patriarchal voice and to convince men to speak up when they witness other men's harassment (McMahon & Dick, 2011). Masculinity is not only implicated directly in men's perpetration of sexual violence but also in their widespread inaction or complicity in the face of sexual violence (Flood, 2019). When men engage in acts of sexual harassment, do nothing when they witness other men doing so or joke about it, they are subscribing to traditional ideologies of masculinity, and in so doing, condoning and enabling the actions of the perpetrators. Therefore, the majority of men are not used to conversations around ideas of entitlement and the right to abuse others, making it awkward for them to confront one another about their harassing behaviour.

Another reason why men should change is that the same system that produces men who abuse women also produces men who abuse other men, and most male victims of violence and sexual harassment are, in fact, victims of other men's violence. We rarely make that connection. Instead, we think about it as two separate issues. When we consider the wall of silence in male culture regarding sexual harassment, men's violence against women and rape, we should not underestimate what we are up against. There are risks involved in attempts to reshape masculinity. There are pressures and constraints on men within peer cultures (Ruxton, 2002). The resistance to change often has to do with the fact that many men think that *redefining* masculinity means *rejecting* masculinity. Some men may be afraid of ending up in a 'no man's land' if they distance themselves too much from the dominant masculine social norms (Flood, 2011).

Among the ongoing challenges is how to create compelling opportunities for men and boys to 'open up' without falling back on gendered stereotypes. Even though men and boys want to talk about sexuality and intimate life, many literally do not have the vocabulary to do so and have difficulty in finding authentic opportunities where they do not feel ashamed, embarrassed or judged by other men.

Psychotherapy is another stigmatized issue, with some men fearing that counselling will 'feminize' them. Kilmartin (2005) redefines and expands the traditional masculine virtues so that they can be used in therapeutic work, and recommends therapists to try to convince men that the therapeutic process is an expansion of positive masculine qualities rather than a feminization process. Redefining the meaning of some of the traditional male virtues may enable critical aspects of traditional masculinity to be addressed without men having to feel unnecessarily feminized. Included in the expansion of positive masculinity is the idea that *courage* is masculine. It is courageous to take a psychological risk by expressing your feelings, asking for what you want and talking about masculinity in the face of the cultural pressure to deny your feelings, get what you want through domination and uncritically accept the culturally dominant definition of masculinity. Despite the good intentions of Kilmartin and others, however, one could argue that the most important aspect is to allow men to be themselves and to teach them that there is nothing wrong with being a feminine man.

There are also men's anti-rape websites that attempt to construct alternative masculinities, which Kilmartin argues in favour of. One example is the social marketing campaign 'My strength is not for hurting', which seeks to engage young men to stand up and speak out against sexual violence. The campaign redefines and expands characteristics of traditional masculinity, such as strength, bravery and power, in order to separate 'real men' from rapists. The slogans in the campaign begin with the 'My strength is not for hurting' line and continue with phrases such as 'so when she said NO, I said OK'. Thus, one can say that the campaign speaks to an understanding that opposing date rape becomes a test of masculinity (Masters, 2010). However, despite their good intentions, these campaigns have also been criticized for reifying hegemonic masculinity. Salter (2016: 11) emphasizes that one potential understanding of the campaign is that the loss of one traditional criterion of 'real' masculinity—dominance and control in intimate relationships—will allow for another, namely (hetero) sexual success. Another point of criticism might be, as I have mentioned earlier, that it is problematic to try to categorically separate 'good' men from 'bad' men, as 'good' men too might risk committing sexual assault.

8.1 The Bystander Approach

#MeToo invites men to be pro-social bystanders who take action to prevent sexual harassment occurring in the first place. A question often asked is how men can play a positive role in changing some of the norms in male culture that support sexist and heterosexist abuse. It seems important to educate and empower men to take steps against sexual harassment. Ruxton (2020) posits that men can play an important role in challenging other men over their sexism, misogyny, and violence by calling it out, supporting victims or bearing witness.

Jackson Katz is the co-founder of Mentors in Violence Prevention (MVP), one of the longest-running and most influential gender violence prevention programmes in North America, and the first major programme of its kind in sports culture and the military. MVP introduced the 'bystander approach' to the sexual assault and relationship abuse fields. As an educational tool in the ongoing struggle to prevent sexism and misogyny and promote gender equality, the bystander approach highlights the role of people with privilege who are able to take a stand and take a risk to help vulnerable people. The idea of the bystander approach is that we have to overcome the traditional perpetrator–victim binary. The bystander approach marks a shift from relying solely on women to protect themselves to the idea that bystanders, both men and women, have a role to play in preventing sexual violence. The bystander approach is not aimed at strangers in the street; instead, it is about known peer culture groups. MVP strategy training consists of a range of classic exercises that highlight the power of gender norms to shape behaviours. The training sessions are about creating a space for dialogue that allows people to hear and express a range of viewpoints that can improve their understanding and increase the likelihood that they will be willing to act as empowered bystanders in their peer cultures.

Katz (2006, 2018) has advocated the bystander approach to gender violence and bullying prevention. Instead of focusing on women as victims and men as perpetrators of harassment, abuse or violence, the bystander approach concentrates on the role of peers in schools, groups, teams, workplaces and other social units. Katz gives special attention to the peer culture dynamics, in particular the male peer culture that helps to normalize sexism and misogyny while silencing other men in the face of abuse. The bystander approach stresses the crucial importance of appealing to people not as potential perpetrators or passive spectators, but as active bystanders and potential leaders who have a positive role to play in challenging and changing the sexist cultural norms that too often lead to gender violence and sexual harassment.

It seems crucial that bystander interventions must be acceptable to the population receiving the intervention. However, previous studies of bystanders have revealed that women and girls continue to be the *willing majority* volunteering to participate in bystander-based violence prevention training. Engaging men and boys in gender-based violence prevention efforts remains an important yet challenging goal (Coker, 2018).

8.2 Why Do Men Not Challenge Other Men's Sexist Attitudes?

One of the key questions in my study is: what facilitates or hinders men's ability to translate their strengthened individual knowledge into action? McMahon and Dick (2011) state that even men with pro-feminist attitudes and above average knowledge about violence against women express anxiety about acting as bystanders. Many forces act upon a member to remain in a group. Even though many men are uncomfortable with other men's attitudes and behaviour, they rarely express this publicly. The main reason for men's reluctance to intervene is often anxiety about rejection from the group (Katz, 2006, 2018).

One may question the empirical evidence of the effectiveness of the bystander prevention strategy. McMahon and Dick (2011) interviewed men who participated in a workshop designed to prevent intimate partner violence and which used the bystander approach. The majority of the participants indicated that the most useful part of the training was not necessarily the information that was transferred, but rather, the opportunity to talk with other men about these issues and to feel supported in their efforts. They expressed anxiety about intervening as a bystander; they worried about making a situation worse; they doubted their own efficacy in being able to intervene; and they were concerned about the possibility of failure.

Looking at the social norms surrounding masculinity, it seems clear that engaging other men is a hard task that will demand creative approaches. The question is how to intervene in a realistic and safe way. Hegemonic masculinity and dominant social norms may prohibit men's involvement in bystander behaviour on a number of levels. Sexual harassment may still be regarded as a women's issue, creating discomfort and anxiety when confronting other men with their behaviour. Men are inclined to look at the cost–benefit analysis before taking action. It is not easy to stop laughing at sexist jokes and start challenging inappropriate comments about women and girls. Breaking the informal code of silence might amount to committing social suicide (Katz, 2006; McMahon & Dick, 2011).

The dichotomy between actual and perceived norms is crucial. Men often underestimate the extent to which other men are uncomfortable with sexist behaviour towards women. This misunderstanding is likely to keep men from intervening against the inappropriate behaviour of other men (Berkowitz, 2002). If men's uneasiness with how they are taught to act as men could be revealed as normative, men might be more willing to be themselves and express discomfort with the behaviour of other men (Fabiano et al., 2003).

8.3 Talking to Male Friends About #MeToo

A sign that a campaign or movement is contributing to social change is when people discuss it or the issues it raises among their peers (Flood, 2019). A lot of young men have respectful relationships with each other, but not necessarily very close ones. For boys, friendships are often based on different rules than for girls, so transferring girls' standards for intimacy and attachment to boys is problematic (Pollack, 1998; Reinicke, 2012, 2013). In many ways, traditional forms of masculinity dictate that men should hold back when it comes to talking about vulnerabilities and feelings. Boys are socialized from an early age to hide and repress important aspects of their emotional lives. Many boys do not necessarily develop the language they need to talk about their vulnerabilities, insecurities and emotions. Bay-Hansen and Henning (2018) point out that men often lack a nuanced language to talk about their emotional lives and sexuality. One of the men described how, in his circle of friends, they are cautious when it comes to asking about personal topics.

> You don't start by asking 'How are you, really?' That's not how we do things, even if there is also a consensus that if something is wrong, then you say so... but it is not the custom to ask about personal and sensitive issues without being given permission or invited to do so... you really have to use a more indirect approach if you want to discuss sensitive topics.

Several of the men had a diverse group of friends, so how they talked to their different male friends about #MeToo and inappropriate sexual behaviour varied. Some of the men recognized that #MeToo had started a process of self-reflection and that they had had honest and serious discussions with their male friends about how it must be being a woman in a male-dominated society.

> We had some evenings where we ate some good food and drank some wine, and here we discussed the MeToo subject ... we agreed that we had all violated some boundaries with women in the past ... we all felt that we had done something which we regretted... we talked about how the way we treated women was way out of line, as it was often the case that if you wanted to take a girl home, you had to convince her instead of waiting for the time when you were both interested in that.

While some men were finding their voice and were willing to have honest conversations about #MeToo with their male friends, the majority of them chose not to talk about it. Though they admitted that recent stories about sexual harassment had made them think about their own behaviour around women, they did not necessarily speak with their friends about it. One of the men stated that when he met with his male friends, it was mostly to relax, have a good time and joke around. He did note, however, that among his male friends there was general agreement that the #MeToo movement was part of a positive trend, but that he and his friends did not elaborate on why they believed this. He explained that it would be unusual to dwell on these issues, and there was no need to explore them further, as first and foremost they just wanted to act like they usually did when together.

> We are not used to talking about inappropriate sexual behaviour, and it's simply too complicated... why should we talk about it when it's not our fight?

It was emphasized that it was wrong to claim that men were unable to talk about difficult emotions and the more controversial aspects of men's lives. However, several men made it clear that the unspoken codes of masculinity prescribed some limits on how openly one could discuss one's emotional life without it being perceived as crossing a line and interpreted as reflections that should have been left unspoken. The lack of honest recognition might also be due to many men feeling insecure about what other men might do with their intimate information (Reinicke, 2004, 2012).

8.4 The Challenge of Having to Intervene When Other Men Sexually Harass Someone

If we are to eradicate sexual harassment, we also need to get better at intervening more actively when we witness sexual harassment (Flood, 2018; Katz, 2006). Intervening as an active bystander signals to the offender that the behaviour is undesirable and may help someone stay safe. Men are often silent about the sexual harassment that other men perpetrate and that is as much the problem as the sexual harassment. There are many reasons why men rarely challenge each other's sexist attitudes and behaviour, but much of it comes down to hesitation about challenging what Kimmel (2008) has described as a 'guy code'. The guy code refers to the code of rules and regulations by which many men are encouraged to live their lives. The development of the guy code often starts in primary school and becomes 'bros before hoes'. The guy code includes a sense of entitlement, an imperative to remain silent about one's feelings and others' actions and a sense of responsibility to other men to protect each other from being held accountable for misbehaviour. Kimmel goes on to describe the guy code as a straightjacket, because masculinity is coerced and policed by other guys (Kimmel, 2008: 51). Flood (2019) states that masculinity plays an important part in men's widespread inaction to stop other men's perpetration of sexual harassment. Men who challenge other men's sexist attitudes or behaviour risk facing criticism and possibly ridicule amid doubts about their strength and masculine credentials, thereby losing their standing with their male peers (Katz, 2018).

Several of the men stated that it was important for men to learn how to object to other men's behaviour when, for instance, they witness inappropriate comments from other men about how women look and when they loudly talk about what sexual purpose they would like to use them for. They stated that if someone's boundaries were violated or if it was clear that someone was uncomfortable in a situation, one had to step in. Yet, despite the stronger focus on inappropriate sexual behaviour in the wake of #MeToo, several men stated that it could still be difficult to confront other men and make them aware that their behaviour was crossing the line. Besides being afraid of physical repercussions if they intervened in an incident, for example, during a night out on the town, they were especially afraid of the negative impact it might have on their relationships with friends or acquaintances. Their status within the peer culture might be affected. This is in line with Heilman et al. (2017), who posit that when breaking the cultural rules of the 'man box', a man takes on an extra risk of social isolation, exclusion and self-doubt. Not surprisingly, a number of the men indicated that it was not easy to challenge the attitudes and behaviour around them. They all admitted that they had let other men's sexist comments go unchallenged. Several of the men agreed that it took some getting used to. One of the men described it as follows:

> In a previous job, I saw a male colleague slapping the bottom of a female colleague. The woman stiffened up and her face turned red. I told him that that had been a weird thing to do, and he just answered 'Hey, take it easy.' In that situation there are two choices: you can continue and say 'No, I am not the one who needs to take it easy, you are – that was clearly

wrong,' or you could withdraw and say 'I just don't think it was OK,' but avoid pushing the issue… I chose to drop it, and one of the reasons why I stopped pointing out his wrong behaviour was actually that I was afraid of breaking some unwritten rule by insisting that he had done something wrong. It suddenly felt like it was taking it a step too far to have to correct him and maintain the focus on how he had treated that woman.

As indicated above, the reason why men do nothing is more related to social fear than physical fear. McMahon and Dick (2011) have stressed that it is crucial to remember that even though men are in a powerful position to disrupt disrespectful and harmful behaviour, they too are shaped by social norms. Therefore, it might be intimidating and threatening for men to confront other men who hold similar privilege. Another of the men stated that he sometimes objected to his friends if they were homophobic or sexist, but it could be difficult if the offensive speech was phrased in a way that did not make it clear whether it was a joke or serious.

> I can object to my friends if they are homophobic and say 'Hey, that's not funny, what you just said,'… but sometimes it's hard if the homophobic comment was said jokingly, then I just don't have the energy to have that discussion.

He further emphasized that if his friends were made aware of their sexual harassment, they often tried to explain that they were just trying to be fun and charming, which mostly made their behaviour culturally acceptable. Men making sexist or homophobic statements often claim that it should be obvious to the recipient that they were 'just kidding'.

It is part of the widespread 'boys will be boys' culture to set up gender relations in a grossly sexist and irresponsible manner and then claim that there is nothing serious behind it. After all, it is 'just joking around', and we are of course 'decent guys'. The 'boys will be boys' phenomenon is hard to oppose, because the gender-discriminating messages seep out in a very inconsequential manner that puts even the most critical recipient of such statements in a dilemma (Reinicke, 2002, 2004). One of the men explained it as follows:

> The toxic thing about the 'boys will be boys' culture is the name itself... because then you tend to think 'well, if people get away with it, they get away with it'... there is a lack of negative consequences, because the term itself, 'boys will be boys', indicates that it needs to be immature, irresponsible and boyish.

Some of the men also recognized that men had a clear role when it came to fighting against sexual harassment. Some of the men did seek to challenge gender inequality for reasons of moral or ethical conviction. They perceived that gender equality is right in principle—and part of a wider social justice project. They spoke about men having a responsibility to engage in the matter because so many women around the world were pointing out that inappropriate sexual behaviour was a systemic issue. One of the more pro-feminist men, who stated that he had gone through a significant amount of personal development since the first #MeToo wave in 2017, described how, when he met with old upper-secondary school friends and tried to correct their sexist language, challenging them to think about what they were saying, he was met with comments such as 'What the hell man, have you become a feminist?' followed by comments such as 'Haha, come on, I was just playing around.'

> People should be able to think about and discuss what acceptable behaviour is... but if I am being realistic, then I doubt that I would dare do it, I mean, I wouldn't have the courage to do so. Maybe this is because you want to get along with your colleagues and friends. Even though you should man up, it is difficult to break group dynamics.

This indicates that men's relationship with the ideals and practices of manhood is complex. They gain certain benefits from adhering to gender norms. To break with the unspoken norms is neither linear nor straightforward. When they obey the rules, they feel some security in their identity and they have less fear of being disliked (Heilman et al., 2017).

> I have to admit that I avoid these discussions with some people in my group of friends. We have exchanged opinions on the topic, and of course they can also see that some men are seriously crossing the line, but they

can't see that everyday sexism is harmful and they think there is too much focus on sexual harassment... that it's about going off on a tangent.

Another of the men noted how his circle of friends had 'tested each other' in terms of their feelings on the subject, and then they just avoided talking about it when together. A third man also highlighted how difficult it was to interfere and correct the behaviour of other men. However, he emphasized that due to #MeToo, men were thinking more about their role in maintaining gender inequality—but it was still difficult to intervene against other men. This was particularly the case if you also felt that you yourself had some behaviour that needed to be worked on.

> It is a barrier having to be willing to turn a light-hearted moment into something serious, and personally I tend to avoid conflict... I think that women are more willing to make things serious because they are also the ones who have personal experience of harassment... but we men have to work on that too.

This statement is interesting and points to men's privileged identities. It shows how women have more to gain from fighting sexual harassment and how men have far less to lose from doing nothing. Several of the men had groups of friends that they appreciated even if their world views were different—they just had a good time together a few times a year. One man who had grown up in the countryside but who now lived in Copenhagen and was a university student stated that he saw how different the conversations about #MeToo were in the big city compared to his home region.

> They don't take it particularly seriously... it's a whole other jargon... they can't see how it has anything to do with them and they do not think there needs to be more fairness... they haven't seriously considered the big societal issues and identity-related questions... they therefore often make fun of #MeToo... and if I make an issue out of the subject, I am simply told that I've been living in Copenhagen for too long... and then they say 'Cheers!'

He went on to say that he had no illusions about being able to convert them. At the same time, he admitted that he also enjoyed 'spending time with the boys' and doing man stuff which he also felt was relatively harmless, because in the end, most of the participants were able to distance themselves from the rough, vulgar and sexist statements that were often expressed.

One of the men described how he tended to hold himself back from intervening when out partying because there was also the risk of making it seem like women were unable to take care of themselves. He added, however, that this obviously did not apply if it was perfectly clear that a woman was uncomfortable with a situation. Another pointed out that he was afraid of being misunderstood if he intervened.

> There is the fear of being misunderstood. For example, if you were in a bar and tried to tell another man that he was behaving inappropriately, you could be told that you were just trying to make a pass on the woman you were trying to protect.

This fear is about being perceived as a 'virtue-signaler'—a man who calls out other men's morals in an effort to win points with women (PettyJohn et al., 2019: 6). However, some of the men described how they had intervened in situations in nightlife settings where it had been a matter of maintaining ordinary decency and respect.

8.5 Speaking Publicly About #MeToo and Feminism

Flood (2018), inspired by Funk (2006), described how men's relationship to violence prevention work can be understood as a continuum, from overt hostility or resistance at one end to active support at the other. Two of the stages in this continuum of men's engagement are men who are interested but not engaged, and men who are interested but hesitant. These considerations are highly relevant to the attitudes, considerations and practices of the men interviewed.

The men showed different levels of readiness or capacity to make changes. The vast majority indicated that it is important that men are taking public advocacy roles and speaking out about sexual harassment. They emphasize that it was important to look critically at the existing norms and values sustaining sexual harassment—otherwise we cannot change them. However, at the same time most of the men admitted that they were not eager to go public and speak either about their own experiences or the issue in general. The reason why they were either scared or reluctant to step forward and speak out about sexual harassment in public is that they were not sure how to do it in the right way and that they felt it would be a cultural transgression. One of the men said that he once had participated in debate on a social media platform regarding a gender issue. However, a considerable number of the men indicated that they had the conversations in private and that this was a way of taking responsibility for change.

> I am very hesitant about telling the public about my viewpoints… I would rather do it in a more personal setting… It's not because I feel unwelcome… there is no lack of inclusion in the debate… but I think that many men are insecure about participating partly because they are afraid of being wrong but also because even if they haven't done anything wrong themselves, it will still quickly end up being about themselves.

Breaking with traditional constructs of masculinity is not something men can do easily on their own. There were several who mentioned that they were still at the stage of listening, thinking and understanding. However, they did discuss the topic with friends, both male and female. They also emphasized that there was a need for men who could publicly take up the struggle so that other men might follow suit. It was also pointed out that men who went out and defended women in public could easily be perceived as a mix between a kind of traitor to their gender and someone who lets women walk all over him. It remains difficult for men to take a stand on behalf of feminism without risking appearing as a puritan 'saintly fringe'.

8.6 How to Walk into 'New Man's Land'?

In view of the difficulties of getting men to react to other men's harassment, we have to consider how we can provide tools for men to stop sexual harassment and how to convince the peer group not to accept it. Without confronting men's sense of entitlement, we will never be able to convince them that sexual harassment is not fair and just. But how do we overcome the obstacles and make gender visible for men? It seems crucial to help men understand the structure of patriarchy. Men and boys often lack a vocabulary to discuss sexuality and intimate life in a non-misogynist way. How do we facilitate self-reflection and discussion?

Flood (2018) declares that one way to inspire men's support for gender equality is to personalize women's disadvantage. Prevention and intervention work that addresses violence against women has undergone a fundamental shift over the past 15 years in highlighting the need for men and boys to become engaged in these efforts (Fabiano et al., 2003; PettyJohn et al., 2019). Ted Bunch, the co-founder of A Call to Men, has said that men need to become aware of sexual harassment and transform this awareness into action. He urges men to think critically about the cultural messages they receive about masculinity, women and girls, and how many of those messages do not value women and girls, and seek to dominate and control others. In continuation of that, Thompson (1994: 348) states that 'the key to changing the behavior of harassers is enlightenment'.

No doubt, there is a lot to overcome if we are going to start talking appropriately about sexism, sexual harassment and assault. Flood (2018) makes the point that a persistent challenge is how to simultaneously invite and involve men on the one hand and avoid colluding or reinforcing male privilege on the other. Flood goes on to say that men do have an interest in the patriarchal status quo and in various forms of unjust privilege. Nevertheless, men also have an interest in a non-patriarchal future.

8.7 Educational Initiatives

There is no doubt that the education system is one of the most effective entry points for challenging discriminatory attitudes regarding gender equality and violence against women. Research has shown that pupils' knowledge and/or competencies in this area indicate that teaching is insufficient when it comes to issues such as reproduction, sex, sexuality and sexual health, as well as norms and diversity in relation to gender, bodies and sexuality (Roien et al., 2018). Sex education is a compulsory subject in Denmark, although the amount of time that should be allocated to it is not stipulated. The Law on Public Primary and Lower Secondary Education provides that 'family skills, health education and sex education' are to be integrated as part of the school curriculum from the first year of primary school to the final year of lower secondary school (students aged 6–17 years). The academic objectives set by the Ministry of Education for this refer to the students being able to discuss, at different ages, topics such as 'gender roles and diversity' and 'sexuality and sexual diversity' and to 'evaluate norms about body, gender and sexuality' (Ministry of Education, 2018). One of the men emphasized how the sex education he received in primary school did not focus on preventing sexual assault.

> I would have preferred that the sex education in my primary school could have been more about consent and setting boundaries instead of focusing so much on contraception and reproduction … it is of course important to learn how to put on a condom, but it could have been more about emotions and about getting to know oneself better and, e.g., learn that it is ok to wait to have sex.

Sex education in Denmark does not always cover topics such as relationships, sexual autonomy or consent, often focusing solely on biology, sexual and reproductive health, contraception and preventing sexually transmitted diseases. It is crucial that sex education should not be limited to biology but should include behaviour and relationships (Als Research, 2019; Roien et al., 2018).

8.8 Engaging Boys

It is vital to engage boys in processes of critical reflection and to provide men with safe and supportive spaces for this. If society is to influence the socialization process that contributes to creating sexually abusive attitudes in men, then it is important to focus on how the normalization of stereotypical gender roles is already taking place at early school age. To improve primary prevention, sex education in schools could be upgraded, and the subject be given higher priority, with professionals recruited to teach subjects such as consent and personal boundaries. Boys pick up the messages about masculinity early on and social pressures about what it means to be a 'real man' are strong and influence the lives of most boys from a very young age (The Men's Project & Flood, 2018).

Ideas about sexual harassment as a legitimate expression of masculinity must be challenged—especially the norms that justify sexual harassment. Nevertheless, Connell (1996: 226) states that the tactics of engagement presuppose willing students, but the broad gender privilege of men gives boys an interest in the current gender order. This may make them hesitate to participate in educational work that must call that interest into question.

It seems obvious that if we can get boys to embrace and promote a healthy, respectful manhood, we will have a better chance of preventing violence and discrimination against women, sexual assault and sexual harassment. Gender cultural influence starts early and often has great significance for both opportunities and limitations in boys' lives. The creation of gender roles is a continuous process throughout life which involves negotiations with oneself and the environment. How to make it more explicit in order to address issues of gender and masculinity in schools? If cultural transmission of traditional gender attitudes is to be curbed, there is a need for teaching in primary and lower secondary schools, which in a refined way problematizes the question of gender norms in society. An increasing number of education and training programmes worldwide confirm that it is possible to change boys' attitudes in a more gender-equal direction (Carmody & Ovenden, 2013; Carmody et al., 2014; Isdal et al., 2003; Kindler, 1993). Teaching about gender in school can be a tool to enable boys to reflect on unjust and inappropriate masculinity practices in their own lives. This in turn can lead to boys developing empathy for other people's experience of discrimination in a more nuanced way.

While it is not the case that men in college or beyond cannot also learn about consent and gender socialization, it may still be easier to change gender socialization for boys because society has the opportunity of doing so continually through teaching in schools. There is a diversity of masculinities and femininities in the classroom. Connell (2000) has pointed out that even though the school is not the most important actor in the creation of masculinity, schools are still active players in the formation of masculinities. Schools can be an obvious place to talk and teach about masculinity. However, teaching about masculinity is difficult to run in practice. Issues like flirting, personal boundaries, norms and transgressions are sensitive topics that can be difficult to teach. To ensure a safe space in these kinds of courses, it is a good idea to agree with the students exactly how to work and talk together.

Of course, teaching does not take place in a social vacuum, and there are widespread risks associated with working with the subject, as boys often find it 'dangerous' to speak in too nuanced a manner about gender. The classroom is not the safest place for students to open up for sensitive, honest discussions about gender and sexuality (Connell, 1996; Foster et al., 2001; Salisbury & Jackson, 1996). Regarding the willingness of adolescent boys to interrogate masculinities in schools, Martino (2001: 92) has stated that such critical work can only take place if the students feel comfortable and respected in the classroom. Efforts should therefore be made to create a safe atmosphere in the classroom and to strengthen teachers' competencies in articulating often controversial masculinity topics (Elliott, 2018). One method of raising awareness and helping to explore ideas of what is right and wrong on sensitive issues like flirting, sex and personal boundaries is to use dilemma cards. Dilemma cards are a pedagogical tool that offers real moral dilemmas and scenarios about which students can state their opinions while listening to their peers' ideas. The pedagogical 'trick' of using dilemma cards is that the cards determine what is to be discussed. This makes it easier to start the dialogue and more legitimate for students to participate in the exchange of experiences and attitudes.

8.9 It Is Not Just 'the Bad Boys' Who Sexually Harass

A constructive initiative for the future would be to define appropriate 'rules of the game' for interaction between the sexes and to develop an active vocabulary for how to behave at work, in nightlife venues and in public more generally. However, Wøldike (2018) states that alcohol, a party atmosphere, the expectations of friends and communities, as well as gendered social norms about how women and men should behave in relation to flirting, lust and sex, make the interaction complex. Therefore, sex and intimacy are not an easy business. It cannot be solved with a round of 'yes or no' training or 'consent teaching' as a quick fix for dissonance and mistakes in intimate life negotiations, transgressive behaviour and sexual abuse.

Sexual harassment is often spoken of in the context of sexual harassment at work. However, the #MeToo movement might have the potential to change the way in which men (and women) act in their private lives. The podcast of the Danish daily, *Information*, called '*Grænseland – samtaler med mænd om sex*' ('Borderland – Conversations with men about sex') talks about the difficult aspects of sex and creates a space to talk about cultural boundaries, norms, sex and responsibility. What is missing is a language to talk about how sex can at times be difficult—in essence, it may be an activity that pushes boundaries and perhaps the world is not divided into 'good guys' who always do the right thing and 'bad boys' who always do the wrong thing, and boundaries can be fluid and hard to identify. It is not just a few bad apples who violate others.

What are the limits in terms of what men and boys can get away with when interacting with girls and women? There are grey areas where the man and woman have different perceptions of what took place. There are situations where the man does not believe that he has violated the woman's boundaries but where the woman still feels that she has been exposed to something against her will. There may be situations where the man's interpretation was: 'Your mouth says no, but your eyes say yes', and society often follows up with 'interpretations' of how it is the woman's own fault due to how she dresses. Encompassed in the rape culture is that most boys are raised to question a woman's 'No' and to allow themselves to think that the girl or woman is incapable of deciding what she wants and who she will have sex with.

The *Grænseland* podcast is an excellent tool to get men to reflect on their own sexual practices and perceptions of masculinity, and it has also been used for educational purposes in upper secondary schools. In the podcast series, heterosexual men speak about their experiences with flirting, sex, boundaries and responsibility. They talk about the times they went too far and the times they did not go far enough because they were too shy and did not dare to start flirting or having a conversation. They talk about the difficult aspects of sex. They talk about the importance of creating a language about flirting and sex, awkward situations, vulnerability, the fear of rejecting and being rejected, and being considerate of others—and how boundaries can be fluid and difficult to identify, both in yourself and others, especially when you are young. They also talk about situations where they have violated the sexual boundaries of others and the subsequent thoughts they had on the matter. They speak of being a conqueror who is expected to take the initiative without being someone who violates other people's boundaries. How does it feel to carry that responsibility—and how does it feel when you fail to live up to it? They also talk about why things sometimes go wrong and what is needed to ensure that such situations are kept to a minimum.

The men in the podcast describe themselves as down-to-earth, sympathetic and intelligent guys that no one would expect to harass women and who, in different ways, have been raised with good values about gender and equality. They touch upon both the early teenage years, where sexual identity is created, and the late teenage years where the focus is on persistent efforts to have sex and the subsequent hunger for recognition. They reflect on how they ended up in that situation when it was not their intention. The key point to take away from the podcast is that sexual harassment is also about 'good' and 'normal' men because the 'bad men' framing risks 'othering' perpetrators of harassment. The men from the podcast tend to think that violating the sexual boundaries of others has nothing to do with them. They perceive themselves as 'the good boys'. Nevertheless, when critically addressing their own behaviour and interactions, they discover that even though they have not done anything obviously harsh, they could well have violated another person's boundaries.

8.10 An Eye Opener

It seems crucial to get men to imagine how women order their daily lives. Some education programmes use gender-reversal scenarios or 'walking in women's shoes' to inspire men's awareness and empathy (Flood, 2018). A film that can make people think more about male domination in all its forms is the provocative short film *The Suppressed Majority* by French filmmaker Eleonore Pourriat. The film, which is a laterally reversed image of a social gender portrait, depicts a matriarchal society in which men are exposed to all sorts of subtle sexism and cultural degradation from women. In short, the film observes a day in a man's life and how he is exposed to multifarious forms of sexual harassment as he moves around the city he lives in. During the day he is exposed to horny glances and flattering sexist comments about his appearance, and is 'obviously' also asked whether or not he likes compliments. He is even met with loud, aggressive sexual catcalls from a homeless woman on a bench while he is calmly standing with his bike at a traffic light.

She wants to have sex with him and accuses him of making her horny because he is 'all over with that ass'. Afterwards, he encounters a bunch of gang girls who, after urinating demonstratively in the streets, call him a wanker and eventually assault him. He later reports it to the police and is questioned at the police station by a female officer, who doubts his explanation due to the fact that something like that cannot happen in 'full daylight and without witnesses'. While interrogating him, the female officer harasses one of her male colleagues by saying that he must learn to serve the coffee as she wishes and adds that he 'looks good' in his jeans. When the man's girlfriend picks him up at the police station in the evening, she expresses concern about the events, but ends up implying that it was his own fault, due to his provocative clothing. The film ends with him in a parking lot screaming that he can no longer cope with the feminist society, to which his girlfriend replies that he should quit his 'masculinist bullshit'.

The film is extremely interesting and thought-provoking, because all the gender roles are reversed, and the laterally reversed gaze challenges the viewer on many of the deep-rooted gender-cultural practices that we rarely problematize or think about deeply and that we have such a hard time opposing. We also meet women jogging around bare-chested in public and a man whose wife has forced him to remove his moustache and sideburns and made him cover his hair with a scarf. In the film, it is women who, on the symbolic and actual level, are representatives of authority, rationality and knowledge.

8.11 Summary

Men's active participation is a precondition for effecting radical change in the way we tackle sexual harassment. To some degree, the #MeToo movement has been characterized by solidarity from some men. #MeToo also provoked a critique directed towards those men who had indirectly condoned abuse by being passive and by not reacting when witnessing sexual harassment (Nilsson & Lundgren, 2020). However, how can solidarity be combined with action, how can one move from attitude to action and how can one address boys and men strategically? It is no easy task for men to develop a critical attitude towards gender and equality or to make them agents of equality in their own struggle. There are many risks and pitfalls involved in this, as men and boys often see it as 'dangerous' to talk in too open and nuanced a way about gender. The disincentives for bystander action are plentiful, as speaking out, for instance, entails taking a real personal risk of losing a friend. Furthermore, it can be hard to create a deep understanding among men about how reconstructing ideals of masculinities can benefit men. Even though we see a shift in the representation of masculinity in men's lives we must not underestimate that large numbers of men continue to endorse the norms of male sexual entitlement and sexism that structure men's sexual harassment and coercion of women (Flood, 2019).

#Metoo raised many complex feelings for men. A critical challenge was how to bring men on board with the process of change, and how to avoid reactions of disbelief, shame and resistance (Män, 2018). However, what should men learn? It is important that men are confronted with their cultural perceptions about the legitimacy of being able to abuse women. Men must learn that they are responsible for the practice of sexual harassment and men's urge to ignore and trivialize it must be challenged. At the same time, men need to be able to choose something other than the harassing behaviour.

Katz (2018) has said that we need to create an atmosphere in which men feel comfortable talking honestly about various aspects of 'guy culture', positive as well as negative. It is vital to offer men safe spaces to reflect on the feelings that the #MeToo testimonies brought to the surface, and to give men some support in reaching out and connecting with other men. Further, it seems crucial to encourage men to discard the harmful ideologies of traditional masculinity. No doubt, men can be part of the necessary change if they dare turn their new awareness into action. However, it is not easy to foster non-harassing men who feel an obligation to intervene when witnessing sexual harassment. Nevertheless, a way to confront men's sense of entitlement is by encouraging men to read some of the narratives from the Everyday Sexism Project or other feminist platforms. Here men can pick up knowledge about how women take steps to prevent sexual harassment. Reading about women's experiences is one way for men to study what it means for women to suffer in ways men do not. Bates (2014) uses this phrase to describe how her little brother gained new knowledge in the wake of the Everyday Sexism Project: 'my bravely-exploring-new-ideas-he's-never-been-exposed-to-before little brother'. The narratives on the Everyday Sexism Project could be interpreted as a long story about how women feel jeopardized on a daily basis. Men can learn how street harassment restricts women's mobility and geographical freedom (Thompson, 1994: 313). Further, they can learn about how women do not like to be treated under any circumstances, and how women suffer from 'cheer up, sweetheart' comments and from only being recognized as something decorative.

As demonstrated earlier in the book, we must not forget that when men are acting out in a sexist way and harassing women, it is often a way for them to prove their masculinity to one another. Some men lack awareness of the harassing nature of their behaviour and they simply cannot understand that any sexual harassment has ever taken place (see, e.g., Bargh et al., 1995). By exposing the magnitude of the problem, to the surprise of most men, the Everyday Sexism Project helps men find out what is going on. Men normally need much more convincing than women of 'the reality of women's oppression because they have not experienced it directly, and they take longer to move from cognitive awareness of gender inequalities to emotional identification' (Flood, 2018: 332). Here is an example from the English debate where a man describes what he has learned from reading Laura Bates' tweets:

> Reading your tweets has really opened my eyes. I knew that sexism existed, but not to that extent. It's like there's a world in which women are constantly threatened, and I've suddenly discovered that not only does that world exist but it's the same world *I* live in. (Bates, 2014: 312)

Additionally, they may pick up knowledge about how women internalize sexism to a degree that they do not question it or see it as a social problem. Instead, they just order their daily life according to the threat and this, in some situations, might imply that their coping mechanisms make them blind. Men can also educate themselves by listening to podcast like *Grænseland* where men talk about whether, when and how they have sex. Further, they can have conversations about the joys and frustrations of their sexual relationships, how to navigate their sexual relationships and hookups, and the difficult line between consent and coercion. However, it is not easy to challenge values entrenched in society and to switch from being an active participant in a sexist culture to becoming part of its dismantling.

References

Als research. (2019). *Evaluation of family skills, health education and sex education.*

Bargh, J. A., Raymond, P., Pryor, J. B., & Strack, F. (1995). Attractiveness of the underling: An automatic power → sex association and its consequences for sexual harassment and aggression. *Journal of Personality and Social Psychology, 68*(5), 768–781.

Bates, L. (2014). *Everyday sexism.* Simon & Schuster.

Bay-Hansen, J., & Henning, A.-M. (2018). *Hvad alle bør vide om mænd – pik, potens og parforhold* [What everyone should know about men—Cock, potency and relationships]. København: Lindhardt og Ringhof.

Berkowitz, A. D. (2002). Fostering men's responsibility for preventing sexual assault. In P. A. Schewe, *Preventing violence in relationships: Interventions across the life span* (pp. 163–196). American Psychological Association.

Carmody, M., & Ovenden, G. (2013). Putting ethical sex into practice: Sexual negotiation, gender and citizenship in the lives of young women and men. *Journal of Youth Studies, 16*(6), 792–807.

Carmody, M., Salter, M., & Presterudstuen, G. H. (2014). *Less to lose and more to gain? Men and boys violence prevention research project.* University of Western Sydney.

Coker, A. L. (2018). Commentary on Katz's bystander training as leadership training. *Violence Against Women, 24*(15), 1777–1784.

Connell, R. (1996). Teaching the boys: New research on masculinity, and gender strategies for schools. *Teachers College Record, 98*(2), 206–235.

Connell, R. W. (2000). *The men and the boys.* University of California Press.

Elliott, K. (2018). Challenging toxic masculinity in schools and society. *On the Horizon, 26*, 17–22

Fabiano, P. M., Perkins, H. W., Berkowitz, A., Linkenbach, J., & Stark, C. (2003). Engaging men as social justice allies in ending violence against women: Evidence for a social norms approach. *Journal of American College Health, 52*(3), 105–112.

Flood, M. (2011). Involving men in efforts to end violence against women. *Men and Masculinities, 14*(3), 358–377.

Flood, M. (2018). *Engaging men and boys in violence prevention.* Springer.

Flood, M. (2019). Men and #Metoo: Mapping men's responses to anti-violence advocacy. In *#MeToo and the politics of social change* (pp. 285–300). Palgrave Macmillan.

Foster, V., Kimmel, M., & Skelton, C. (2001). What about the boys? An overview of the debates. In W. Martino & B. Meyenn (Eds.), *What about the boys?* (pp. 1–23). Open University Press.

Funk, R. E. (2006). *Reaching men: Strategies for preventing sexist attitudes, behaviors, and violence*. Jist life.

Heilman, B., Barker, G., & Harrison, A. (2017). *The man box: A study on being a young man in the US, UK, and Mexico*. Promundo-US and Unilever.

Isdal, P., Andreassen, S. M. N., & Thilesen, R. (2003). *Vold i skolen* [Violence in school]. Kommuneforlaget.

Katz, J. (2006). *Macho paradox: Why some men hurt women and how all men can help*. Sourcebooks, Inc.

Katz, J. (2018). Bystander training as leadership training: Notes on the origins, philosophy, and pedagogy of the mentors in violence prevention model. *Violence Against Women, 24*(15), 1755–1776.

Kilmartin, C. (2005). Depression in men: Communication, diagnosis and therapy. *Journal of Men's Health and Gender, 2*(1), 95–99.

Kimmel, M. (2008). *Guyland: The perilous world where boys become men*. Harper.

Kindler, H. (1993). *Maske(r)ade: Jungen- und Männerarbeit für die Praxis* [Mask(r)ade: Boys and men work for practice]. Neuling Verlag.

Män. (2018). *Men, masculinity and #MeToo*.

Martino, W. (2001). 'Powerful people aren't usually real kind, friendly, open people!' Boysinterrogating masculinities at school. In W. Martino & B. Meyenn (Eds.), *What about the boys?* (pp. 82–95). Open University Press.

Masters, N. T. (2010). 'My strength is not for hurting': Men's anti-rape websites and their construction of masculinity and male sexuality. *Sexualities, 13*(1), 33–46.

McMahon, S., & Dick, A. (2011). 'Being in a room with like-minded men': An exploratory study of men's participation in a bystander intervention program to prevent intimate partner violence. *The Journal of Men's Studies, 19*(1), 3–18.

Ministry of Education. (2018). *Curriculum: Health and sex education and family skills*. Denmark

Nilsson, B., & Lundgren, A. S. (2020). The #MeToo Movement: Men and Masculinity in Swedish News Media. *The Journal of Men's Studies, 29*(1), 8–25.

PettyJohn, M. E., Muzzey, F. K., Maas, M. K., & McCauley, H. L. (2019). #HowIWillChange: Engaging men and boys in the #MeToo movement. *Psychology of Men & Masculinities, 20*(4), 612–623.

Pollack, W. (1998). *Real boys: Rescuing our sons from the myths of boyhood.* Henry Holt and Company.

Reinicke, K. (2002). *Den hele mand: Manderollen i forandring* [The whole man: Masculinity in transition]. Det Schønbergske Forlag.

Reinicke, K. (2004). *Mænd i lyst og nød* [Men for better or for worse]. Det Schønbergske Forlag.

Reinicke, K. (2012). *Drenge og mænd i krise? Perspektiver og indsatsområder* [Boys and men in crisis? Perspectives and focus areas]. Hans Reitzel.

Reinicke, K. (2013). *Mænd: køn under forvandling* [Men—Gender in change]. Aarhus Universitetsforlag.

Roien, L. A., Simovska, V., & Graugaard, C. (2018). *Seksualitet, skole og samfund: kritiske perspektiver på seksualundervisning* [Sexuality, school and society: Critical perspectives on sex education]. Hans Reitzels Forlag.

Ruxton, S. (2002). *Men, masculinities and poverty in the UK*. Oxfam.

Ruxton, S. (2020). *Men and gender equality: Challenges and opportunities.* ICMEO.

Salisbury, J., & Jackson, D. (1996). *Challenging macho values: Practical ways of working with adolescent boys.* Falmer.

Salter, M. (2016). 'Real men don't hit women': Constructing masculinity in the prevention of violence against women. *Australian & New Zealand Journal of Criminology, 49*(4), 463–479.

The Men's Project & Flood, M. (2018). *The man box: A study on being a young man in Australia.* A Jesuit Social Service.

Thompson, D. M. (1994). The woman in the street: Reclaiming the public space from sexual harassment. *Yale JL & Feminism, 6*, 313.

Wøldike. (2018, February 19). Det seksuelle spil er en forhandling mellem ja og nej [The sexual game is a negotiation between yes and no]. *Information.*

9

Conclusion

The starting point of *Men after #MeToo* was that we have to look at the collective socialization of men because men's gendered attitudes and beliefs about sexual harassment are grounded in wider social norms regarding gender and sexuality. Sexual harassment is not about individual men—it is a much deeper systemic problem. Perpetrators of sexual harassment can be found in all spheres of society. It is not a problem linked to a specific and limited group of men. The #MeToo movement, which gained momentum in 2017, started out by exposing serious cases of sexual harassment and rape, and now also includes discussions about appropriate ways for men to talk to women. It is an incredibly important time we are living through, but not necessarily easy to capture 'where we are'. #MeToo showed the scale of sexual coercion worldwide, and the connection of sexual coercion to gender norms and power structures. We live in an era where online movements have made it possible for survivors and victims of violence, sexual assault and sexual harassment to speak out more than ever before.

It is no simple task to analyze the consequences of the #MeToo movement, since one inevitably runs into the classic problem of identifying temporal sequence with causality. How can one prove that any observed changes were actually caused by the movement? In an interview with the *Politiken* newspaper in autumn 2017, French historian Michelle Perrot remarked that #MeToo did not appear out of the blue but expresses suffering and humiliation that has been repressed and silenced for a very long time. In that sense, #MeToo is not addressing a new problem but has, rather, functioned as a catalyst enabling us to talk about an old problem in new ways. The problematizing of masculinity has been under way for many years, but it has magnified in response to #MeToo.

Retrospectively, it is crucial to emphasize that the consequences of the #MeToo movement vary considerably depending on time and place (Askanius & Hartley, 2019; Kunst et al., 2018). Although #MeToo was a global uprising, it has spread unevenly. This means there have been significant differences in how the messages of the movement have been received around the world. Luthar and Luthar (2008) indicate that differences in cultural values shape the varying conceptions of sexual harassment behaviour across countries. Behaviours considered the norm in one culture might be considered offensive and a violation in another culture. Therefore, this study must be interpreted with a degree of caution. Overall, it should be emphasized that this study is situated in a high-income country in the context of the Nordic policy framework known for its extensive welfare system and progressive attitudes and policies towards gender equality (Reinicke, 2020). Thus, the findings may not be generalizable to all societies.

#MeToo can be seen as a moment of rupture (Maricourt & Burrell, 2021). However, little research to date has analyzed men's responses to #MeToo. The purpose of this study has been to examine men's reactions to #MeToo, in the face of the shifting landscape created by the #Metoo movement. Looking at men's reactions to #MeToo on social media, the study by Pettyjohn et al. (2019) demonstrated that some men took the hashtag #HowIWillChange seriously and said that they would commit themselves to actively engaging in dismantling rape culture, while others were indignantly resistant to social change. Still others demonstrated hostile resistance to social change along with criticism of male supporters of #HowIWillChange. The #MeToo-inspired advertising campaign from Gillette, 'The Best Men Can Be', is also an example of how a good many men react with resistance and hostility towards the notion of social change. The campaign tried to promote a new kind of positive masculinity. Nevertheless, many men viewed the campaign as controversial and accused it of promoting a problematic image of men and masculinity. Therefore, regardless of the popularity of the #MeToo movement, there remains significant resistance from men to acknowledging the pervasiveness of sexual violence and the existence of rape culture (Loney-Howes, 2020).

The study has shown we lack clear definitions of what counts as acceptable behaviour and what counts as sexual harassment. It is hard to gauge how much gender relations have changed. #MeToo has become critical mass education. Nevertheless, we can question whether we really are calling out or whether we have just begun to articulate the nature of the harm of sexual harassment. In retrospect, it is amazing that gender was the most debated issue in the world for several consecutive months in 2017/2018. Never before has a gender issue been mainstreamed, debated and kept on the media agenda for such a long time, and the movement has exposed problems that were hitherto implicit and kept out of sight.

The #MeToo movement has given us insight into a systemic culture of harassment and laid the foundations for a new and hopefully constructive kind of empathy. That is historic, and I believe it will have a significant impact on men's understanding of what constitutes abuse towards women. I also believe that it will create the necessary momentum to push other equality issues higher up the political agenda. However, we should not underestimate what we are up against. #MeToo has revealed how powerful the forces of feminism really are, but the opposition to the movement has also underlined how stubbornly rooted men's privileges are and how much remains to be done (Reinicke, 2018).

We have seen initiatives and actions taken by different countries to deal with and prevent sexual harassment in the wake of the #MeToo movement. It has been shown that the first wave of #MeToo in Denmark was characterized by few calls for men to take responsibility, and the legitimacy of #MeToo was often questioned. There is no doubt that #MeToo in 2020 in Denmark helped to create a language for sexual assault. Societal conditions have changed as regards how we discuss gender and equality in society. For example, it has become easier to use legislation as a means of political regulation when it comes to gender equality issues, which was reflected in the adoption of the new law of consent on rape. With regard to sexual harassment, we are no longer just talking about individuals; we are also focusing on the culture that makes the harassment possible. Likewise, it seems that there is no longer a statute of limitations on sexual harassment claims, and since the second wave of #MeToo public figures in Denmark have started to suffer professional repercussions due to allegations of sexual misconduct.

Although there is still an ongoing discursive argument over the meaning of sexual harassment, it seems clear that #MeToo has contributed significantly to a shift in public awareness of sexual harassment in Denmark. A 2021 survey (Djøef, 2021) showed that three out of four Danes believe that it is positive to have an increased focus on avoiding sexually transgressive behaviour. Furthermore, the study demonstrated that more people now reflect upon their own behaviour. Another 2021 survey (Lederne, 2021) also showed that 38 percent of female employees and 33 percent of male employees believe that the second wave of #MeToo has made it easier to stand up if you experience sexism and sexual harassment in your workplace.

The book has tried to highlight that even though society has started to address the issue of sexual harassment by criticizing men's harassing behaviour, and despite #MeToo undoubtedly being a fateful moment for many men (Nilsson & Lundgren, 2020), we still do not know to what extent large numbers of men continue to endorse the norms of male sexual entitlement and sexism which structure men's sexual harassment and coercion of women. Has significant change really happened? In this context, men's 'in principle attitudes' are crucial. As Flood (2019: 292) indicates, 're-evaluating one's behavior is one thing, but actually changing it is another'. He goes on to say that although men say they have changed their behaviour in romantic relationships in the wake of the movement, we do not know how such men have changed their behaviour; the changes they have in mind may be trivial or inappropriate.

One of the key issues raised in this book was that there are gaps in our knowledge about which men engage in sexual harassment and in which situations. Nevertheless, it seems clear that sexual harassment cannot be reduced to a small group of men with mental disorders and a derailed perfidious sexuality that the rest of society can be disgusted by and distance ourselves from. It is a much deeper and more systemic social problem. Sexual harassment is not primarily a question of acts committed by pathological individuals but rather a product of the normative definition of manhood (Messner, 1997; Katz, 2018). The problem with those who engage in sexual harassment is not first and foremost psychological; the majority of men who commit sexual harassment are not necessarily deviant and do not fit any profile of mentally ill men.

It seems vital to put greater emphasis on the 'every man' perspective, which says that sexual harassers are not much different from other men, than on the 'peculiar man' perspective, which says sexual harassers are characterized by huge differences and have psychological inadequacies. Obviously, we shall hold men accountable and at the same time not blame all men. We will get nowhere by oversimplifying and making monsters of men. The majority of men are perfectly able to control their sexual desires. Nevertheless, Ruspini (2011) state that we must be careful not to prioritize differences between men over commonalities of and among men.

There is growing attention on the role men can play in combating violence and sexual harassment against women. However, will #MeToo change men's existential foundation? It is possible to claim that #MeToo means the end of unquestioned male entitlement. It has, in many ways, been important in showing that some behaviours are simply no longer acceptable. The bar has been raised for what it means to be a nice guy. #MeToo has unleashed powerful forces and is an emotionally charged and powerful movement.

The #MeToo movement is not primarily about exposing people by name or shaming all men, but about showing the extent of the problem, erasing the victims' shame, and reducing the risk of sexual harassment in the future. Men should therefore not play the victim vis-à-vis the movement. Although #MeToo can be interpreted as a colossal learning experience for society as a whole, it is also important to keep a critical and impartial eye on the movement, and to monitor all aspects of it, including the fear it may unleash and its lack of appeal among certain sectors of the population.

Especially in Sweden, there has been criticism that the press has taken #MeToo's methods on board and failed to observe its proper impartial role. This criticism has arisen especially in relation to accusations against the well-known theatre director, Benny Frederiksson, which have been described as a witch-hunt and which are thought to have led to his tragic death by suicide. His death triggered debate about public shaming and the media's role in the #MeToo revolution. Pollack (2019: 6) stresses that although most of the initial #MeToo movement was dominated by broad collective actions in different societal areas, the 'outing' of names and the intense person-oriented scandal coverage in some leading media outlets also led to critique and ethical debates.

In the early phase of the #MeToo movement, the dominant focus was on taking down powerful perpetrators. However, if it is true that #MeToo is no longer aimed at taking anyone down but rather constitutes a potential learning moment for men, one might ask whether we should educate or isolate the perpetrator. Furthermore, it is interesting to discuss how much men can confess without it having consequences for their future life and career. When, in 2020, Copenhagen's Lord Mayor came out of an emergency meeting concerning allegations that he had sexually harassed several women, he said the following: 'I admit that I have been part of an unhealthy culture—now I want to be part of the solution.' He never did become so, though, because shortly afterwards, he decided to leave office due to pressure from the public.

Boys and men should not only be seen as the problem but as part of the solution. Moreover, even though gender is certainly a large part of the problem, we must take care not to demonize men. Systems of oppression are also harmful to members of the dominant group. Men are also victims of the patriarchal culture, and it is vital that we are able to talk to each other about the problem. We must not be afraid to offend men, but it is also crucial that the #MeToo movement appears inclusive. There are often personal risks involved when men are asked to be sensitive and to reflect upon their gender.

Regardless of whether the #MeToo movement has made men angry and defensive or more insightful and open to change, it certainly has had a major impact on the way men see themselves and their lives both in terms of behaviour and self-perception. Society expects and demands more of men as allegations have been exposed and sexual harassment has increasingly become more of the national conversation. Men have realized that they cannot do what they used to do, and we are witnessing a reduction in men's defensiveness. Nevertheless, it is worth reiterating that the cultural achievements in relation to #MeToo are still fragile and contradictory.

From the preceding discussion in the book, it is clear that men as allies is of huge importance for combating sexual harassment. Nevertheless, there are also dangers in involving men in gender equality work. As demonstrated extensively in the work of Flood (2011), we cannot be sure that men's involvement will be guided by a feminist agenda and done in partnership with women's groups.

Beyond changing their own abusive behaviour, #MeToo urges men to be pro-social bystanders who challenge the abusive behaviour of other men and the attitudes and behaviours which sustain this (Flood, 2019). Based on the data presented in this study, it seems reasonable to say that there are still numerous obstacles and challenges to overcome if we are to get men to advocate keenly against sexual harassment. Therefore, this study shows that we should not overemphasize the importance of men's capability in engaging other men in combating sexual harassment. It is culturally transgressive to speak up, to rise up and to act. It seems clear that the men in my study are not fully able to live up to the standard they would like to set for themselves and other men, and they are not completely able to 'walk the talk' and turn their words into action as regards being an active and pro-social bystander.

As mentioned earlier in the book, Tuerkheimer (1997) states that it is crucial to communicate the gender-specific harm to those who do not share it. From men in psychotherapy we know that #MeToo has profoundly impacted their lives (Essig, 2018; Smith et al., 2019). On a personal level and regarding the level of individual knowledge, men indicate that #MeToo has been an eye-opener and that they are changing attitudes and behaviour in romantic relationships in the wake of the #MeToo movement. Before #MeToo appeared in 2017, none of the men interviewed in my study had taken the time to think seriously about sexual harassment. This is mainly due to their upbringing, which has taught them to see sexual harassment of women as the norm and as an 'innocent' activity. They described their behaviour as completely normal and expected of men. Several men admitted that they had behaved in ways that were harassing or abusive to others and that they had tried to push girls to see how far they could go. They perceived it as something men did and something women had to put up with. Nevertheless, some of the men interviewed had gained critical insight into the impact of their upbringing, and this had helped them understand the consequences of their behaviour. They therefore stated that they had become better at reading signals and interpreting indirect communication. This is in line with Kitzinger and Frith (1999) and O'Byrne et al. (2006: 137) who state that men have and can express a sophisticated understanding of the way in which refusals are normatively performed.

Despite the fact that the cultural ideals of masculinity have changed dramatically, the men talked about the dilemmas they faced in navigating society's contradictory ideals of manhood regarding entitlement, proving one's strength, the role women play and the role of male friends. Based on the interviews, it seems obvious that it takes moral and social courage to have honest and critical conversations with other men about sexual harassment. The men interviewed were often afraid of not living up to the criteria of manhood that were passed down to them. They expressed that it was not easy to go out and state, 'I am the kind of guy who takes a stand'. Because of the unwritten rules of the 'culture of silence', they were afraid that it would backfire on them if they opposed the rigid notions of manhood too openly. However, as an example of the gradually changing cultural landscape, one of the men emphasized that it was still difficult to oppose a sexist joke among boys but that it was no longer stigmatizing for a man to reveal that, for example, he was dealing with a feminist issue in a project report.

The easy part of being a good ally in the era of #MeToo consists of listening to women, believing their stories, putting one's own house in order and educating oneself. When it comes to challenging harassment and harassment-supportive behaviour around them, many men hesitate. Nevertheless, some of the men would be ready to challenge friends and peers when witnessing inappropriate behaviour. Such new awareness took the form of concrete action, as the men tried to acknowledge their own sexism and the impact of their objectification of women. They are less willing to demonstrate their support publicly and work for wide social and cultural change. Being an active ally of the #MeToo movement can feel overwhelming. They want to help change the culture that enables sexual assault and harassment but are not sure how to do it and where to start. This also applies to those who are most supportive of the #MeToo movement. On a general level, sexual harassment is still seen as a 'women's issue' when men have to do something concrete in favour of the #MeToo movement.

So, is there anything new in all these things that we did not already know? Concerning the scope and consequences of #MeToo, one could, based on the interviews, remark that it might be the case that many of them did not realize 'deep down' what was going on. Therefore, some of the men suggested that it would be a good idea for them to perform a 'privilege check' to monitor when they exercise power without giving it a second thought.

No remarkable differences were seen in the narratives of the men interviewed regarding ethnicity. Nevertheless, further studies are needed to understand how sexual harassment informed by patriarchal norms is shaped by experiences of class and ethnicity. People from different social backgrounds tend to access different types and levels of education (Bourdieu, 1977). Because social class is found to have a major impact on individuals' behaviour and preferences, it seems likely that people from different classes might also differ in terms of sexual behaviour and interpretations of this behaviour. Younger men tend be more egalitarian and less rigid than older men and their masculinity seems more flexible and fluid. In addition, young men are more likely to challenge behaviour or comments they think are inappropriate (Fawcett Society, 2018). Therefore, it is likely that a study focusing more on older men would have shown less positive results toward #MeToo.

Despite the fact that the #MeToo movement originally began with the work of the African- American woman Tarana Burke in 2006, #MeToo has primarily been framed as a white phenomenon. Onwuachi-Willig (2018: 105) criticizes the most recent wave of the #MeToo movement for not focusing enough on the unique form of harassment and the heightened vulnerability to harassment that women of colour frequently face in society. In line with this, Larasi (2020) challenges the mainstream #MeToo discussion by saying that it is difficult to end gender injustice without addressing racial injustice. Nevertheless, the issue of race, class and sexual harassment has already been specifically addressed in American research on sexual harassment in public spaces. Here, Kearl (2010) and Fogg-Davis (2006) pointed out that women of colour are at high risk of experiencing sexual harassment and that the harassment they are exposed to is both sexist and racist.

The #MeToo movement has given us a glimpse of the extent of sexual abuse and sexism and has revealed in particular (some) powerful men's enduring abuses of power. The #MeToo revelations have given many men insight into a world of harassment they may not have known existed. Post #MeToo, men may no longer be able to get away with quite so much. Some men have become more alert and may be finding it harder to figure out what it means to be a man in an era in which the boundaries of what constitutes flirting and what constitutes abuse are up for debate. This is not necessarily a bad thing, because it may make it possible for men to reject the most rigid forms of masculinity and instead move towards more humane, peaceful and equality-oriented identities.

There is no quick fix for the problem of sexual harassment. Nevertheless, there is reason to believe that #MeToo already has been, and in the future to an even greater extent will be, the tipping point for making real and lasting change in the area of sexual harassment. There is no doubt that #MeToo broke down the historical silence about sexual harassment. However, how can society sustain the momentum behind the #MeToo movement and ensure that #MeToo does not just become a passing moment but rather an ongoing process?

It is difficult to gain an overall understanding of the extent to which men and the dominant forms of masculinity have actually changed as a result of the #MeToo movement. Since the emergence of the #MeToo movement in the autumn of 2017, we have seen a change in the societal status of sexual harassment. By focusing on the role of male perpetrators, the #MeToo movement has led to enhanced questionings of normative constructions of masculinity (Maricourt & Burrell, 2021). What previously could pass as, for example, innocent lad culture and something that women should not make a fuss about, because it was not considered a real problem, is now likely to be seen as harassment. The bringing about of such a change in perception is perhaps the most revolutionary achievement of #MeToo.

An example of how society has started to take sexual abuse more seriously was the case of abusive behaviour in the Danish Radio Girls' Choir, which has also been called the biggest #MeToo case in Denmark (Politiken, 2021). In 2021, an investigation based on interviews with 129 former choir members concluded that between 1970 and 2010 a culture of sexual misconduct was common in the Danish Broadcasting Corporation Girls' Choir, made up of teenagers and young women. In sixty-four incidents, according to the investigation, there are grounds for assuming that behaviour was exhibited, which qualifies as abusive behaviour in the form of sexual harassment, including unwanted sexual attention.

The Danish Broadcasting Corporation stated after the report came out that 'a completely unacceptable culture' had been exposed. It apologized to those who had been affected, particularly due to the complete lack of management responsibility because management had not reacted to previous information on misconduct. Following the investigation's recommendations, the Danish Broadcasting Corporation has chosen to initiate an investigation into possible liability. The 'choir case' points to how society spends resources, going back a long time to provide justice for the victims. Furthermore, it shows that society no longer hesitates to blame the culture of silence that these violations have required.

Another illustrative example of how far the #MeToo movement has come in Denmark since the second wave of #MeToo is the removal of the so-called 'massage advertisement' in *Ekstra Bladet*, a nationwide Danish newspaper in tabloid format. The 'massage advertisement' was the conventional word for an advertisement where women could sell sex. It had for many years been a controversial issue that the newspaper had profited from the sale of sex advertisements. *Ekstra Bladet* pointed out that they had listened to the criticism and that in the wake of #MeToo, time had run out for having sex advertisements in the newspaper.

The #MeToo movement has unleashed an avalanche, but how can society harness that avalanche and lead it in the right direction? In the aftermath of the movement, one can reasonably ask whether the bar has been raised, in the sense that the lowest common denominator for acceptable behaviour towards others has shifted. Is there less of a 'shut up and look pretty' culture? How can we ensure that the #MeToo movement does not just end up as a 'moment' but develops into a process? Activism researcher Silas Harrebye (Information, 2017) has the following point to make regarding the need to anchor the movement in social structures:

> If #MeToo is to evolve from being a viral campaign to a well-anchored social movement beyond the internet, it has to transform itself from online clicktivism and begin to cooperate with associations, institutions and NGOs as well as to hire well-known spokespeople and develop a kind of manifesto with demands and proposals for solutions.

Attitudes towards sexual harassment by men have, without a doubt, become less tolerant. Yet although post #MeToo the problem of sexual harassment has finally been acknowledged, the phenomenon itself can hardly be said to have disappeared. There is still, in many contexts, a need to shift perspectives so that the problem is no longer rendered invisible and socially acceptable, to counter the tendency to transfer guilt to the victim and instead to ensure that it is the perpetrators of sexual harassment who are met with a critical reception.

Behaviours to which people previously turned a blind eye are, in some respects, unacceptable today. Is it no longer OK for men to be sexually tone-deaf? Given that men now risk being censured for behaviours that were not previously considered inappropriate, some might argue that the definition of what is considered trivial has shifted, as many of the cases that have come to light are minor incidents that would not have received the same attention in the past. Are we ready for a more thoughtful, open-minded approach to power, abuse and harassment? I am convinced that #MeToo has had such a huge impact that society cannot help but learn from it.

References

Askanius, T., & Hartley, J. M. (2019). Framing gender justice: A comparative analysis of the media coverage of #Metoo in Denmark and Sweden. *Nordicom Review, 40*(2), 19–36.

Bourdieu, P. (1977). Cultural reproduction and social reproduction. In *Power and ideology in education* (pp. 487–511).

Djøef. (2021). *#MeToo har rykket befolkningens adfærd* [#MeToo has shifted the behavior of the population].

Essig, T. (2018). Examples of straight men grappling with the #MeToo movement. *Contemporary Psychoanalysis, 54*(4), 677–687.

Fawcett Society. (2018). *#Metoo one year on—What's changed?* The Fawcett Society.

Flood, M. (2011). Involving men in efforts to end violence against women. *Men and Masculinities, 14*(3), 358–377.

Flood, M. (2019). Men and #Metoo: Mapping men's responses to anti-violence advocacy. In *#MeToo and the politics of social change* (pp. 285–300). Palgrave Macmillan.

Fogg-Davis, H. G. (2006). Theorizing black lesbians within black feminism: A critique of same-race street harassment. *Politics & Gender, 2*(1), 57–76.

Information. (2017, 28. December). *#MeToo er historisk, men ikke i sig selv samfundsomvæltende* [#MeToo is historic, but not in itself socially revolutionary].

Katz, J. (2018). Bystander training as leadership training: Notes on the origins, philosophy, and pedagogy of the mentors in violence prevention model. *Violence Against Women, 24*(15), 1755–1776.

Kearl, H. (2010). *Stop street harassment: Making public places safe and welcoming for women.* ABC-CLIO.

Kitzinger, C., & Frith, H. (1999). Just say no? The use of conversation analysis in developing a feminist perspective on sexual refusal. *Discourse & Society, 10*(3), 293–316.

Kunst, J. R., Bailey, A., Prendergast, C., & Gundersen, A. (2018). Sexism, rape myths and feminist identification explain gender differences in attitudes toward the #Metoo social media campaign in two countries. *Media Psychology, 22*(5), 818–843.

Larasi, M. (2020). Black women, #MeToo and resisting plantation feminism. In *The Routledge handbook of the politics of the #MeToo movement* (pp. 230–246). Routledge.

Lederne. (2021). *Hver tredje kvinde mener, at det er blevet nemmere at stå frem om sexchikane* [Every third woman believes that it has become easier to stand up for sexual harassment].

Loney-Howes, R. (2020). *Online anti-rape activism: Exploring the politics of the personal in the age of digital media.* Emerald Publishing.

Luthar, H. K., & Luthar, V. K. (2008). Likelihood to sexually harass: A comparison among American, Indian, and Chinese students. *International Journal of Cross Cultural Management, 8*(1): 59–77.

Maricourt, C. D., & Burrell, S. R. (2021). #MeToo or# MenToo? Expressions of backlash and masculinity Politics in the #MeToo era. *The Journal of Men's Studies*, 1–21.

Messner, M. A. (1997). *Politics of masculinities: Men in movements.* Altamira Press.

Nilsson, B., & Lundgren, A. S. (2020). The #MeToo movement: Men and masculinity in Swedish news media. *The Journal of Men's Studies, 29*(1), 8–25.

O'Byrne, R., Rapley, M., & Hansen, S. (2006). 'You couldn't say "no", could you?': Young men's understandings of sexual refusal. *Feminism & Psychology, 16*(2), 133–154.

Onwuachi-Willig, A. (2018). What about #UsToo: The invisibility of race in the #MeToo movement. *Yale Law Journal Forum, 128*, 105–120.

PettyJohn, M. E., Muzzey, F. K., Maas, M. K., & McCauley, H. L. (2019). #HowIWillChange: Engaging men and boys in the #MeToo movement. *Psychology of Men & Masculinities, 20*(4), 612–623.

Politiken. (2021, November 11). *Forsker om Pigekor-sagen: Den viser et skifte i MeToo-debatten* [Researcher on the girl choir case: It shows a shift in the MeToo debate].

Pollack, E. (2019). Sweden and the #MeToo movement. *Interactions: Studies in Communication & Culture, 10*(3), 185–200.

Reinicke, K. (2018). *Mænd som krænker kvinder—refleksioner i kølvandet på #Metoo* [Men who violate women—Reflections in the wake of #MeToo]. Samfundslitteratur.

Reinicke, K. (2020). First-time fathers' attitudes towards, and experiences with, parenting courses in Denmark. *American Journal of Men's Health, 14*(5), 1–13.

Ruspini, E. (Ed.). (2011). *Men and masculinities around the world: Transforming men's practices.* Springer.

Smith, R. D., Holmberg, J., & Cornish, J. E. (2019). Psychotherapy in the #MeToo era: Ethical issues. *Psychotherapy, 56*(4), 483–490.

Tuerkheimer, D. (1997). Street harassment as sexual subordination: The phenomenology of gender-specific harm. *Wis. Women's LJ, 12*, 167–206.

References

Abbey, A. (1987). Misperceptions of friendly behavior as sexual interest: A survey of naturally occurring incidents. *Psychology of Women Quarterly, 11*(2), 173–194.

Abbey, A., & Wegner, R. (2015). Using experimental paradigms to examine alcohol's role in men's sexual aggression: Opportunities and challenges in proxy development. *Violence against Women, 21*(8), 975–996.

Abbey, A., Zawacki, T., & McAuslan, P. A. M. (2000). Alcohol's effects on sexual perception. *Journal of Studies on Alcohol, 61*(5), 688–697.

Acquaviva, B. L., O'Neal, E. N., & Clevenger, S. L. (2021). Sexual assault awareness in the #MeToo era: Student perceptions of victim believability and cases in the media. *American Journal of Criminal Justice, 46*(1), 6–32.

Als Research. (2019). *Evaluation of family skills, health education and sex education.*

Alt for Damerne (All for the Ladies). (2020). Story House Egmont A/S.

Amnesty International. (2019). *"Give us respect and justice!" Overcoming barriers to justice for women rape survivors in Denmark.*

Anderson, E. (2002). Openly gay athletes contesting hegemonic masculinity in a homophobic environment. *Gender & Society, 16*(6), 860–877.

Anderson, E. (2005). Orthodox and inclusive masculinity: Competing masculinities among heterosexual men in a feminized terrain. *Sociological Perspectives, 48*(3), 337–355.

Anderson, E. (2010). *Inclusive masculinity: The changing nature of masculinities.* Routledge.

Andreassen, R. (2006). Intersektionalitet i voldtægtsnarrativer [Intersectionality in rape narratives]. *Kvinder, Køn og Forskning, 2–3,* 93–104.

Andersen, J., & Larsen, J. E. (1998). Gender, poverty and empowerment. *Critical Social Policy, 18*(2), 241–258.

Arriaza Ibarra, K., & Berumen, R. (2019). #MeToo in Spain and France: Stopping the abuse towards ordinary women. *Interactions: Studies in Communication & Culture, 10*(3), 169–184.

Askanius, T., & Hartley, J. M. (2019). Framing gender justice: A comparative analysis of the media coverage of #Metoo in Denmark and Sweden. *Nordicom Review, 40*(2), 19–36.

Baker, P. (2001). The international men's health movement has grown to the stage that it canstart to influence international bodies. *British Medical Journal, 323,* 1014–1015.

Balkmar, D. (2012). *On men and cars: An ethnographic study of gendered, risky and dangerous relations* (Doctoral dissertation, Linköping University Electronic Press).

Balkmar, D., Iovanni, L., & Pringle, K. (2009). A reconsideration of two "welfare paradises" research and policy responses to men's violence in Denmark and Sweden. *Men and Masculinities, 12*(2), 155–174.

Bandura, A., Barbaranelli, C., Caprara, G- V., & Pastorelli, C. (1996). Mechanisms of moral disengagement in the exercise of moral agency. *Journal of Personality and Social Psychology, 71,* 364–374.

Banyard, V. L., Plante, E. G., & Moynihan, M. M. (2004). Bystander education: Bringing a broader community perspective to sexual violence prevention. *Journal of Community Psychology, 32,* 61–79. https://doi.org/10.1002/jcop.10078

Barak, A. (2005). Sexual harassment on the Internet. *Social Science Computer Review, 23*(1), 77–92.

Bargh, J. A., Raymond, P., Pryor, J. B., & Strack, F. (1995). Attractiveness of the underling: An automatic power→ sex association and its consequences for sexual harassment and aggression. *Journal of Personality and Social Psychology, 68*(5), 768–781.

Barker, G., Contreras, J. M., Heilman, B., Singh, A. K., Verma, R. K., & Nascimento, M. (2011). *Evolving men: Initial results from the international men and gender equality survey (IMAGES)*. International Center for Research on Women (ICRW) and Instituto Promundo.

Bartlett, A., Clarke, K., & Cover, R. (2019). *Flirting in the era of #MeToo: Negotiating intimacy*. Springer.

Bates, L. (2014). *Everyday sexism*. Simon & Schuster.

Bates, L. M., Hankivsky, O., & Springer, K. W. (2009). Gender and health inequities: A comment on the final report of the WHO commission on the social determinants of health. *Social Science & Medicine, 69*(7), 1002–1004.

Bay-Hansen, J., & Henning, A.-M. (2018). *Hvad alle bør vide om mænd—pik, potens og parforhold* [What everyone should know about men—Cock, potency and relationships]. Lindhardt og Ringhof.

Becker, J. C., & Swim, J. K. (2011). Seeing the unseen: Attention to daily encounters with sexism as way to reduce sexist beliefs. *Psychology of Women Quarterly, 35*(2), 227–242.

Becker, J. C., & Wright, S. C. (2011). Yet another dark side of chivalry: Benevolent sexism undermines and hostile sexism motivates collective action for social change. *Journal of Personality and Social Psychology, 101*, 62–77.

Begany, J. J., & Milburn, M. A. (2002). Psychological predictors of sexual harassment: Authoritarianism, hostile sexism, and rape myths. *Psychology of Men & Masculinity, 3*(2), 119–126.

Belknap, J., & Erez, E. (1997). Redefining sexual harassment: Confronting sexism in the 21st century. *Criminal Justice Studies, 10*(2), 143–160.

Benard, C., & Schlaffer, E. (1984). The man in the street: Why he harasses. In A. M. Jagger & P. S. Rothenberg (Eds.), *Feminist frameworks: Alternative theoretical accounts of the relations between women and men* (3rd ed., pp. 70–72). McGraw Hill.

Berdahl, J. L., Magley, V. J., & Waldo, C. R. (1996). The sexual harassment of men?: Exploring the concept with theory and data. *Psychology of Women Quarterly, 20*(4), 527–547.

Berger, J. M., Levant, R., McMillan, K. K., Kelleher, W., & Sellers, A. (2005). Impact of gender role conflict, traditional masculinity ideology, alexithymia, and age on men's attitudes toward psychological help seeking. *Psychology of Men & Masculinity, 6*(1), 73–78.

Berkowitz, A. D. (2002). Fostering men's responsibility for preventing sexual assault. In P. A. Schewe (Ed.), *Preventing violence in relationships: Interventions across the life span* (pp. 163–196). American Psychological Association.

Beynon, J. (2001). *Masculinities and culture*. McGraw-Hill Education.

Blazina, C., Cordova, M. A., Pisecco, S., & Settle, A. G. (2007). Gender role conflict scale for adolescents: Correlates with masculinity ideology. *Boyhood Studies, 1*(2), 191–204.

Bom, M., & Bjerke, N. K. (2002). *Udslag: hverdagsfeminisme i det 21.* Århundrede [Effect: everydayfeminism in the 21 century] [Kbh.]: elkjaeroghansen.

Bonde, H. (2013). *Fordi du fortjener det: fra feminisme til favorisme* [Because you earn it: From feminism to preferential treatment]. Gyldendal.

Borchorst, A., & Augustin, L. R. (2017). *Seksuel chikane på arbejdspladsen: Faglige, politiske og retlige spor* [Sexual harassment in the workplace: Professional, political and legal lead]. Aalborg Universitetsforlag.

Boyle, K., & Rathnayake, C. (2020). #HimToo and the networking of misogyny in the age of #MeToo. *Feminist Media Studies, 20*(8), 1259–1277.

Bowman, C. G. (1993). Street harassment and the informal ghettoization of women. *Harvard Law Review, 106*(3), 517–580.

Bourdieu, P. (1977). Cultural reproduction and social reproduction. In *Power and ideology in education* (pp. 487–511). Oxford University Press.

Bourdieu, P. (2001). *Masculine domination.* Stanford University Press.

Brannon, R. (1976). Looking at the male role. In J. H. Pleck & J. Sawyer (Eds.), *Men and masculinity* (pp. 795–796). Prentice-Hall.

Brooks, G. R. (2010). *Beyond the crisis of masculinity: A transtheoretical model for male-friendly therapy.* American Psychological Association.

Buchanan, N., & Mahoney, A. (2021). Development of a scale measuring online sexual harassment: Examining gender differences and the emotional impact of sexual harassment victimization online. *Legal and Criminological Psychology*, 1–19.

Budde, J. (2009). The significance of the body: The construction of masculinity among German students. *Boyhood Studies, 3*(1), 39–49.

Carmody, M., & Ovenden, G. (2013). Putting ethical sex into practice: Sexual negotiation, gender and citizenship in the lives of young women and men. *Journal of Youth Studies, 16*(6), 792–807.

Carmody, M., Salter, M., & Presterudstuen, G. H. (2014). *Less to Lose and more to gain? Men and boys violence prevention research project.* University of Western Sydney.

Cartar, L., Hicks, M., & Slane, S. (1996). Women's reactions to hypothetical male sexual touch as a function of initiator attractiveness and level of coercion. *Sex Roles, 35*(11–12), 737–750.

Charmaz, K. (2006). *Constructing grounded theory: A practical guide through qualitative analysis.* Sage.

Christensen, A.-D., & Larsen, J. E. (2007). Gender, class, and family: Men and gender equality in a Danish context. *Social Politics, 15*(1), 53–78.

Clausen, C., Lauritzen, P., & Thygesen, E. (1974). *Mænd: Det svækkede køn* [Men: The weak gender] (Kbh.): Tiderne skifter.

Cleveland, J. N., & Kerst, M. E. (1993). Sexual harassment and perceptions of power: An under-articulated relationship. *Journal of Vocational Behavior, 42*(1), 49–67.

Cochran, C. C., Frazier, P. A., & Olson, A. M. (1997). Predictors of responses to unwanted sexual attention. *Psychology of Women Quarterly, 21*(2), 207–226.

Coker, A. L. (2018). Commentary on Katz's bystander training as leadership training. *Violence Against Women, 24*(15), 1777–1784.

Connell. R. W. (1995). *Masculinities*. Polity.

Connell, R. (1996). Teaching the boys: New research on masculinity, and gender strategies for schools. *Teachers College Record, 98*(2), 206–235.

Connell, R. W. (2000). *The men and the boys*. University of California Press.

Connell, R. W. (2003). *The role of men and boys in achieving gender equality*. United Nations, Division for the Advancement of Women.

Connell, R. W. (2005). *Masculinities*. Polity.

Connell, R. W., & Messerschmidt, J. W. (2005). Hegemonic masculinity: Rethinking the concept. *Gender & Society, 19*(6), 829–859.

Cossins, A. (2019). Why her behavior is still on trial: The absence of context in the modernisation of the substantive law on consent. *UNSWLJ, 42*, 462.

Cossins, A. (2020). Modernisation of the substantive law of consent. In *Closing the justice gap for adult and child sexual assault* (pp. 277–337). Palgrave Macmillan.

Courtenay, W. H. (2000). Constructions of masculinity and their influence on men's well-being: A theory of gender and health. *Social Science & Medicine, 50*(10), 1385–1401.

Coy, M., Kelly, L., Elvines, F., Garner, M., & Kanyeredzi, A. (2013). *Sex without consent, I suppose that is rape: How young people in England understand sexual consent*. Office of the Children's Commissioner.

Dahl, K. M., Henze-Pedersen, S., Østergaard, S. V., & Østergaard, J. (2018). *Unges opfattelser af køn, krop og seksualitet* [Adolescents' perceptions of gender, body and sexuality]. VIVE—Det Nationale Forsknings- og Analysecenter for Velfærd.

Dahlerup, D. (2004). Er ligestilling opnået? Ligestillingsdebattens forskellighed i Danmark og Sverige [Has equality been reached? Differences in the gender equality debate in Denmark and Sweden]. In A. Borchost (Ed.), *Kønsmagt under forandring* [Gender power in transition] (pp. 226–246). Hans Reitzels Forlag.

Dahlerup, D. (2011). När svenska partier blev 'feminister': Om skillnader i dansk och svensk jämställdhetsdebatt [When Swedish parties became "feminists": On differences in the debate on gender equality in Denmark and Sweden]. In L. Freidenvall & M. Jansson (Eds.), *Politik och kritik: en feministisk guide till statsvetenskap* [Politics and critique: A feminist guide to political science] (pp. 193–212). Studentliteratur.

Dahlerup, D. (2018). Gender equality as a closed case: A Survey among the members of the 2015 Danish parliament. *Scandinavian Political Studies, 41*(2), 188–209.

Davis, D. E. (1994). The harm that has no name: Street harassment, embodiment, and African American women. *UCLA Women's Law Journal, 4*(2), 133–178.

De Benedictis, S., Orgad, S., & Rottenberg, C. (2019). #MeToo, popular feminism and the news: A content analysis of UK newspaper coverage. *European Journal of Cultural Studies, 22*(5–6), 718–738.

DeGue, S., DiLillo, D., & Scalora, M. (2010). Are all perpetrators alike? Comparing risk factors for sexual coercion and aggression. *Sexual Abuse, 22*(4), 402–426.

De Judicibus, M., & McCabe, M. P. (2001). Blaming the target of sexual harassment: Impact of gender role, sexist attitudes, and work role. *Sex Roles, 44*(7), 401–417.

Dempster, S. (2009). Having the balls, having it all? Sport and constructions of undergraduate laddishness. *Gender and Education, 21*(5), 481–500.

Dempster, S. (2011). I drink, therefore I'm man: Gender discourses, alcohol and the construction of British undergraduate masculinities. *Gender and Education, 23*(5), 635–653.

Digby, T. (1998). *Men doing feminism.* Routledge.

Dillon, H. M., Adair, L. E., & Brase, G. L. (2015). A threatening exchange: Gender and life history strategy predict perceptions and reasoning about sexual harassment. *Personality and Individual Differences, 72*, 195–199.

Djøef. (2021). *#MeToo har rykket befolkningens adfærd* [#MeToo has shifted the behavior of the population].

Dobash, R. E., Russell, D. P., Kate, C., & Ruth, L. (2000). *Changing violent men.* Sage.

Dziech, W. D., & Weiner, L. (1984). *The lecherous professor: Sexual harassment on campus.* Beacon Press.

EIGE. (2012). *The involvement of men in gender equality initiatives in the European Union*.
Edley, N., & Wetherell, M. (1997). Jockeying for position: The construction of masculine identities. *Discourse & Society, 8*(2), 203–217.
Edley, N., & Wetherell, M. (2001). Jekyll and Hyde: Men's constructions of feminism and feminists. *Feminism & Psychology, 11*(4), 439–457.
Edwards, K. E., & Jones, S. R. (2009). "Putting My man face on": A grounded theory of college men's gender identity development. *Journal of College Student Development, 50*(2), 210–228.
Eduards, M. (2002). *Förbjuden handling: om kvinnors organsiering och feministisk teori* [Prohibited action: On women's organization and feminist theory]. Liber ekonomi.
Eilermann, W. (2018). *Constructing #MeToo—A critical discourse analysis of the German news media's discursive construction of the #MeToo movement* (Master's Thesis, Malmö University).
Ekore, J. O. (2012). Gender differences in perception of sexual harassment among university students. *Gender and Behaviour, 10*(1), 4358–4369.
Elliott, K. (2018). Challenging toxic masculinity in schools and society. *On the Horizon, 26*(1), 17–22.
Epinion for DR. (2017). *Gramseri* [Pawing]. Epinion.
Epstein, D., Kehily, M., Mac An Ghaill, M., & Redman, P. (2001). Boys and girls come out to play: Making masculinities and femininities in school playgrounds. *Men and Masculinities, 4*(2), 158–172.
Essig, T. (2018). Examples of straight men grappling with the #MeToo movement. *Contemporary Psychoanalysis, 54*(4), 677–687.
Esping-Andersen, G. (1990). *The three worlds of welfare capitalism*. Princeton University Press.
Everyday Sexism Project.dk. *Hvad er voldtægtkultur* [What is rape culture].
Fabiano, P. M., Perkins, H. W., Berkowitz, A., Linkenbach, J., & Stark, C. (2003). Engaging men as social justice allies in ending violence against women: Evidence for a social norms approach. *Journal of American College Health, 52*(3), 105–112.
Fairchild, K. (2010). Context effects on women's perceptions of stranger harassment. *Sexuality & Culture, 14*(3), 191–216.
Fairchild, K., & Rudman, L. A. (2008). Everyday stranger harassment and women's objectification. *Social Justice Research, 21*(3), 338–357.
Farley, L. (1978). *Sexual shakedown: The sexual harassment of women on the job*. McGraw-Hill Companies.

Fawcett Society. (2018). *#Metoo one year on—What's changed?* The Fawcett Society.

Ferguson, M. A., & Ford, T. E. (2008). Disparagement humor: A theoretical and empirical review of psychoanalytic, superiority, and social identity theories. *Humor: International Journal of Humor Research, 21*(3), 677–691.

Fileborn, B. (2016). *Reclaiming the night-time economy: Unwanted sexual attention in pubs and clubs.* Springer.

Fileborn, B. (2017). Justice 2.0: Street harassment victims' use of social media and online activism as sites of informal justice. *British Journal of Criminology, 57*(6), 1482–1501.

Fileborn, B. (2019). Naming the unspeakable harm of street harassment: A survey-based examination of disclosure practices. *Violence against Women, 25*(2), 223–248.

Fileborn, B. (2020). Embodied geographies: Navigating street harassment. In *Contentious cities* (pp. 37–48). Routledge.

Fileborn, B., & Loney-Howes, R. (2019). Introduction: Mapping the emergence of #MeToo. In *#MeToo and the politics of social change* (pp. 1–18). Palgrave Macmillan.

Fileborn, B., & Phillips, N. (2019). From 'Me Too'to 'Too far'? Contesting the boundaries of sexual violence in contemporary activism. In *#MeToo and the politics of social change* (pp. 99–115). Palgrave Macmillan.

Fileborn, B., & Vera-Gray, F. (2017). "I want to be able to walk the street without fear": Transforming justice for street harassment. *Feminist Legal Studies, 25*(2), 203–227.

Fiske, S. T., & Glick, P. (1995). Ambivalence and stereotypes cause sexual harassment: A theory with implications for organizational change. *Journal of Social Issues, 51*(1), 97–115.

Fitzgerald, L. F. (1993). Sexual harassment: Violence against women in the workplace. *American Psychologist, 48*, 1070–1076.

Fitzgerald, L. F., Gelfand, M. F., & Drasgow, F. (1995). Measuring sexual harassment: Theoretical and psychometric advances. *Basic and Applied Social Psychology, 17*(4), 425–445.

Flood, M. (2008). Men, sex, and homosociality: How bonds between men shape their sexual relations with women. *Men and Masculinities, 10*(3), 339–359.

Flood, M. (2011). Involving men in efforts to end violence against women. *Men and Masculinities, 14*(3), 358–377.

Flood, M. (2014, March 28). *Feminism needs men and men needs feminism.* www. ourwatch.org.au

Flood, M. (2018). *Engaging men and boys in violence prevention*. Springer.
Flood, M. (2019). Men and #Metoo: Mapping men's responses to anti-violence advocacy. In *#MeToo and the politics of social change* (pp. 285–300). Palgrave Macmillan.
Flood, M., & Pease, B. (2006). *The factors influencing community attitudes in relation to violence against women: A critical review of the literature*. Victorian Health Promotion Foundation (VicHealth).
Flood, M., & Pease, B. (2009). Factors influencing attitudes to violence against women. *Trauma, Violence, & Abuse, 10*(2), 125–142.
Flyvbjerg, B. (2006). Five misunderstandings about case-study research. *Qualitative Inquiry, 12*(2), 219–245.
FOA. (2016). *Seksuel chikane: Rapport udarbejdet af FOA Kampagne og Analyse* [Sexual harassment: Report prepared by FOA Campaign and Analysis]. FOA.
Fogg-Davis, H. G. (2006). Theorizing black lesbians within black feminism: A critique of same-race street harassment. *Politics & Gender, 2*(1), 57–76.
Foster, V., Kimmel, M., & Skelton, C. (2001). What about the boys? An overview of the debates. In W. Martino & B. Meyenn (Eds.), *What about the boys?* (pp. 1–23). Open University Press.
Foubert, J., & Newberry, J. T. (2006). Effects of two versions of an empathy-based rape prevention program on fraternity men's survivor empathy, attitudes, and behavioral intent to commit rape or sexual assault. *Journal of College Student Development, 47*(2), 133–148.
Friborg, M. K., Hansen, J. V., Aldrich, P. T., Folker, A. P., Kjær, S., Nielsen, M. B. D., & Madsen, I. E. (2017). Workplace sexual harassment and depressive symptoms: A cross-sectional multilevel analysis comparing harassment from clients or customers to harassment from other employees amongst 7603 Danish employees from 1041 organizations. *BMC Public Health, 17*(1), 1–12.
Frosh, S., Phoenix, A., & Pattman, R. (2001). *Young masculinities: Understanding boys in contemporary society*. Macmillan International Higher Education.
Funk, R. E. (2006). *Reaching men: Strategies for preventing sexist attitudes, behaviors, and violence*. Jist life.
Gailey, J. A., & Prohaska, A. (2006). "Knocking off a fat girl": An exploration of hogging, male sexuality, and neutralizations. *Deviant Behavior, 27*(1), 31–49.

Gailey, J. A., & Prohaska, A. (2007). Bad boys in bars: Hogging and humiliation. In C. A. Santa Barbara (Ed.), *Youth violence and delinquency interventions: Monsters and myths* (pp. 81–91). Greenwood.

Gailey, J. A., & Prohaska, A. (2011). Power and gender negotiations during interviews with men about sex and sexually degrading practices. *Qualitative Research, 11*(4), 365–380.

Gardner, C. B. (1995). *Passing by: Gender and public harassment*. University of California Press.

Gavey, N. (2005). *Just sex?: The cultural scaffolding of rape*. Routledge.

Giddens, A. (1992). *The transformation of intimacy: Sexuality, love and eroticism in modern societies*. Polity Press.

Gill, R. (2011). Sexism reloaded, or, it's time to get angry again! *Feminist Media Studies, 11*(1), 61–71.

Gillette. (2019). *We believe: The best men can be | Gillette* (Short Film). Retrieved from YouTube https://www.youtube.com/watch?v=koPmuEyP3a0

Gladwell, M. (2010). Small change. *The New Yorker, 4*(2010), 42–49.

Glick, P., & Fiske, S. T. (1996). The ambivalent sexism inventory: Differentiating hostile and benevolent sexism. *Journal of Personality and Social Psychology, 70*(3), 491–512.

Glick, P., & Susan, T. F. (2011). Ambivalent sexism revisited. *Psychology of Women Quarterly, 35*(3), 530–535.

Glickman, C. (2012). *Escape the 'Act Like a Man' box*. The good men project.

Golden, J. H., Johnson, C. A., & Lopez, R. A. (2001). Sexual harassment in the workplace: Exploring the effects of attractiveness on perception of harassment. *Sex Roles, 45*(11), 767–784.

Gordon, M. T., Riger, S., Lebailey, R. K., & Heath, L. (1980). Crime, women and the quality of urban life. *Signs, 5*(3), 144–160.

Graham, K., Bernards, S., Abbey, A., Dumas, T. M., & Wells, S. (2017). When women do not want it: Young female bargoers' experiences with and responses to sexual harassment in social drinking contexts. *Violence against Women, 23*(12), 1419–1441.

Graham, K., & Homel, R. (2008). *Raising the bar: Preventing aggression in and around bars, clubs and pubs*. Willan Publishing.

Grazian, D. (2007). The girl hunt: Urban nightlife and the performance of masculinity as collective activity. *Symbolic Interaction, 30*(2), 221–243.

Greene, M. (2013). *The man box: The link between emotional suppression and male violence*. http://goodmenproject.com/featured-content/megasahd-man-box-the-link-between-emotional-suppression-and-male-violence/

Greene, M. (2018). *The little #MeToo book for men*. Think Play Partners.

Grossman, A. J. (2008). Catcalling: Creepy or a compliment. *CNN*. Retrieved April 5, 2021.

Gruber, J. E. (1992). A typology of personal and environmental sexual harassment: Research and policy implications for the 1990s. *Sex Roles, 26*(11–12), 447–464.

Guha, P. (2021). *Hear#Metoo in India: News, social media, and anti-rape and sexual harassment activism*. Rutgers University Press.

Gunnarsson, L. (2018). "Excuse me, but are you raping me now?" Discourse and experience in (the grey areas of) sexual violence. *NORA-Nordic Journal of Feminist and Gender Research, 26*(1), 4–18.

Gutek, B. A., Cohen, A. G., & Konrad, A. M. (1990). Predicting social-sexual behavior at work: A contact hypothesis. *Academy of Management Journal, 33*(3), 560–577.

Gutek, B. A., & Dunwoody, V. (1987). Understanding sex in the workplace. *Women and Work: an Annual Review, 2*, 249–269.

Haire, B., Newman, C. E., & Fileborn, B. (2019). Shitty media men. In *#MeToo and the politics of social change* (pp. 201–216). Palgrave Macmillan.

Harrison, J. (1978). Warning: The male sex role may be dangerous to your health. *Journal of Social Issues, 34*(1), 65–86.

Hearn, J. (1987). *The gender of oppression: Men, masculinity and the critique of Marxism*. Wheatsheaf.

Hearn, J. (1998). *The violences of men: How men talk about and how agencies respond to men's violence to women*. Sage.

Hearn, J. (2004). From hegemonic masculinity to the hegemony of men. *Feminist Theory, 5*(1), 49–72.

Hearn, J. (2012). A multi-faceted power analysis of men's violence to known women: From hegemonic masculinity to the hegemony of men. *The Sociological Review, 60*(4), 589–610.

Hearn, J., & Pringle, K. (2006). *European perspectives on men and masculinities*. Palgrave Macmillan.

Heilman, B., Barker, G., & Harrison, A. (2017). *The man box: A study on being a young man in the US, UK, and Mexico*. Promundo-US and Unilever.

Heiner, R. (2012). *Social problems: An introduction to critical constructionism*. Oxford University Press.

Heinskou, M. B., Marie, S. L., Friis, C., Ejbye-Ernst, P., & Liebst, L. S. (2017). *Seksuelle krænkelser i Danmark: Omfang og karakter* [Sexual abuse in Denmark: Extent and character]. Det Kriminalpræventive Råd.

Herrero, J., Rodríguez, F. J., & Torres, A. (2017). Acceptability of partner violence in 51 societies: The role of sexism and attitudes toward violence in social relationships. *Violence Against Women, 23*(3), 351–367.

Herriot, L., & Hiseler, L. E. (2015). Documentaries on the sexualization of girls: Examining slut-shaming, victim-blaming and what's being left off-screen. In *Children, sexuality and sexualization* (pp. 289–304). Palgrave Macmillan.

Hill, A. L., Miller, E., Switzer, G. E., Yu, L., Heilman, B., Levtov, R. G., Vlahovicova, K., Espelage, D. L., Barker, G., & Coulter, R. W. (2020). Harmful masculinities among younger men in three countries: Psychometric study of the man box scale. *Preventive Medicine, 139*, 106185.

Hird, M. J., & Jackson, S. (2001). Where 'angels' and 'wusses' fear to tread: Sexual coercion in adolescent dating relationships. *Journal of Sociology, 37*(1), 27–43.

Hogh, A., Conway, P. M., Clausen, T., Madsen, I. E. H., & Burr, H. (2016). Unwanted sexual attention at work and long-term sickness absence: A follow-up register-based study. *BMC Public Health, 16*(1), 1–10.

Holland, K. J., Rabelo, V. C., Gustafson, A. M., Seabrook, R. C., & Cortina, L. M. (2016). Sexual harassment against men: Examining the roles of feminist activism, sexuality, and organizational context. *Psychology of Men and Masculinity, 17*(1), 17–29.

Holm, E. (1975). *Den maskuline mystik* [The masculine mystique]. Rhodos.

Holmgren, L. E., & Hearn, J. (2009). Framing 'men in feminism': Theoretical locations, local contexts and practical passings in men's gender-conscious positionings on gender equality and feminism. *Journal of Gender Studies, 18*(4), 403–418.

Holmström, C., Plantin, L., & Elmerstig, E. (2020). Complexities of sexual consent: Young people's reasoning in a Swedish context. *Psychology & Sexuality, 11*(4), 342–357.

Holter, Ø. G. (2003). *Can men do it?* Nordisk Ministerråd.

Ilies, R., Hauserman, N., Schwochau, S., & Stibal, J. (2003). Reported incidence rates of work-related sexual harassment in the United States: Using meta-analysis to explain reported rate disparities. *Personnel Psychology, 56*(3), 607–631.

Information. (2017, December 28). #MeToo er historisk, men ikke i sig selv samfundsomvæltende [#MeToo is historic, but not in itself socially revolutionary].

Information. (2018, February 17). Velkommen til grænseland [Welcome to borderland].

Isdal, P., Andreassen Signe Marie Natvig, & Thilesen, R. (2003). *Vold i skolen* [Violence in school]. Kommuneforlaget.

Jensen, S. Q. (2007). *Fremmed, farlig og fræk: Unge mænd og etnisk/racial andenhed-mellem modstand og stilisering* [Stranger, dangerous and naughty: Young men and ethnic / racial otherness-between resistance and stylization]. Aalborg universitet.

Jordan, E. (1995). Fighting boys and fantasy play: The construction of masculinity in the early years of school. *Gender and Education, 7*(1), 69–86.

Katz, J. (2006). *Macho paradox: Why some men hurt women and how all men can help*. Sourcebooks.

Katz, J. (2018). Bystander training as leadership training: Notes on the origins, philosophy, and pedagogy of the mentors in violence prevention model. *Violence Against Women, 24*(15), 1755–1776.

Kaufman, M. (2001). *The seven Ps of men's violence, in recommendations of the E.U.* Expert Meeting on Violence against Women, Ministry of social affairs and health, Finland.

Kaufman, M. (2003). *The aim framework: Addressing and involving men and boys to promote gender equality and end gender discrimination and violence.* UNICEF.

Kaufman, M., & Kimmel, M. (2011). *The guy's guide to feminism*. Seal Press.

Kearl, H. (2010). *Stop street harassment: Making public places safe and welcoming for women*. ABC-CLIO.

Kehily, M. (2001). Bodies in school: Young men, embodiment, and heterosexual masculinities. *Men and Masculinities, 4*(2), 173–185.

Kehily, M. J., & Nayak, A. (1997). "Lads and laughter": Humour and the production of heterosexual hierarchies. *Gender and Education, 9*(1), 69–88.

Kelly, L. (1988). How women define their experiences of violence. In K. Yllö & M. Bograd (Eds.), *Feminist perspectives on wife abuse* (pp. 114–132). Sage.

Kelly, L. (1996). It's everywhere: Sexual violence as a continuum. In S. Jackson & S. Scott (Eds.), *Feminism and sexuality: A reader* (pp. 191–207). Edinburgh University Press.

Kelly, L. (2010). The (in)credible words of women: False allegations in European rape research. *Violence against Women, 16*(12), 1345–1355.

Kessler, A. M., Kennair, L. E. O., Grøntvedt, T. V., Bjørkheim, I., Drejer, I., & Bendixen, M. (2020). The effect of prototypical #MeToo features on the perception of social-sexual behavior as sexual harassment. *Sexuality & Culture, 24*(5), 1271–1291.

Kessler, A. M., Kennair, L. E. O., Grøntvedt, T. V., Bjørkheim, I., Drejer, I., & Bendixen, M. (2021). Perception of workplace social-sexual behavior as sexual harassment post #MeToo in Scandinavia. *Scandinavian Journal of Psychology, 6*, 1–12.

Kidd, D., & McIntosh, K. (2016). Social media and social movements. *Sociology Compass, 10*(9), 785–794.

Kilmartin, C. (2005). Depression in men: Communication, diagnosis and therapy. *Journal of Men's Health and Gender, 2*(1), 95–99.

Kime, P. (2014). *Incidents of rape in military much higher than previously reported*. Military Times.

Kimmel, M. (2008). *Guyland: The perilous world where boys become men*. Harper.

Kindler, H. (1993). *Maske(r)ade: Jungen- und Männerarbeit für die Praxis* [Maske(r)ade: Boys and men work for practice]. Neuling Verlag.

Kippe, E. (2004). *Kjøper «ekte mannfolk» sex?: en studie av 20 menn som kjøper seksuelle tjenester* [Do "real men" buy sex ?: A study of 20 men who buy sexual services]. Stiftelsen for nors helse-og rehabiliseringsorganisasjoner.

Kitzinger, C., & Frith, H. (1999). Just say no? The use of conversation analysis in developing a feminist perspective on sexual refusal. *Discourse & Society, 10*(3), 293–316.

Koss, M. P. (2018). Hidden rape: Sexual aggression and victimization in a national sample of students in higher education. In *Rape and society* (pp. 35–49).

Kosson, D. S., Kelly, J. C., & White, J. W. (1997). Psychopathy-related traits predict self-reported sexual aggression among college men. *Journal of Interpersonal Violence, 12*(2), 241–254.

Kronborg, A., Holmfjord, L., Rasmussen, N., & Koch, I. (2011). *Forældreansvarsloven: når der er vold i familien* [The parental responsibility act: When there is violence in the family]. Nyt Juridisk Forlag.

Kunst, J. R., Bailey, A., Prendergast, C., & Gundersen, A. (2018). Sexism, rape myths and feminist identification explain gender differences in attitudes toward the #Metoo social media campaign in two countries. *Media Psychology, 22*(5), 818–843.

Kvale, S., & Brinkmann, S. (2009). *Interviews: Learning the craft of qualitative research interviewing*. Sage.

Kvinfo. (2017, October 30). *#MeToo sætter den nostalgiske maskulinitet under pres: Interview med Christian Groes-Green* [#MeToo puts the nostalgic masculinity under pressure: Interview with Christian Groes-Green].

Køster, A. D. (2011). *Familietragedier og æresdrab—en analyse af maskulinitetsfremstillingen i mord-selvmord og mord pa en intim partner i de danske medier* [Family tragedies and honor killings—an analysis of the masculinity portrayal in murder-suicide and murder of an intimate partner in the Danish media]. Specialeafhandling. (Master thesis) Københavns Universitet.

Larasi, M. (2020). Black women, #MeToo and resisting plantation feminism. In *The Routledge handbook of the politics of the #MeToo movement* (pp. 230–246). Routledge.

Larcombe, W., Fileborn, B., Powell, A., Hanley, N., & Henry, N. (2016). 'I think it's rape and i think he would be found not guilty.' Focus group perceptions of (un)reasonable belief in consent in rape law. *Social & Legal Studies, 25*(5), 611–629.

Larkin, J. (1997). Sexual terrorism on the street: The moulding of young women into subordination. In A. M. Thomas & C. Kitzinger (Eds.), *Sexual harassment: Contemporary feminist perspectives* (pp. 115–130). Open University Press.

Lauritsen, P. (2020, October 3). Det var præcis her, vi svigtede sidste gang, #MeToo gik gennem landet [This is exactly where we failed the last time #MeToo went through the country]. *Politiken*.

Lederne. (2021). *Hver tredje kvinde mener, at det er blevet nemmere at stå frem om sexchikane* [Every third woman believes that it has become easier to stand up for sexual harassment].

Ledstrup, M. (2012). *Hvorfor er svenskerne så feministiske?* [Why are Swedes so feminist?]. Videnskab.dk.

Lee, K., Gizzarone, M., & Ashton, M. C. (2003). Personality and the likelihood to sexually harass. *Sex Roles, 49*(1–2), 59–69.

Lengnick-Hall, M. L. (1995). Sexual harassment research: A methodological critique. *Personnel Psychology, 48*(4), 841–864.

Levant, R. F. (1995). Toward the reconstruction of masculinity. In R. F. Levant & W. S. Pollack (Eds.), *A new psychology of men* (pp. 229–251). Basic Books.

Lisak, D., Gardinier, L., Nicksa, S. C., & Cote, A. M. (2010). False allegations of sexual assault: An analysis of ten years of reported cases. *Violence Against Women, 16*(12), 1318–1334.

Logan, L. S. (2015). Street harassment: Current and promising avenues for researchers and activists. *Sociology Compass, 9*(3), 196–211.

Loney-Howes, R. (2019). The politics of the personal: The evolution of anti-rape activism from second-wave feminism to #MeToo. In *#MeToo and the politics of social change* (pp. 21–35). Palgrave Macmillan.

Loney-Howes, R. (2020). *Online anti-rape activism: Exploring the politics of the personal in the age of digital media*. Emerald Publishing.

Lorentzen, J. (2000). *De tavse mænd* [The silent men]. Kvinfo webmagasin Forum.

Lövkrona, I. (2001). *Den våldsamme mannen: Mord, misshandel och sexuella övergrepp, historiska och kulturella perspektiv på kön och våld* [The violent man: Murder, assault and sexual assault, historical and cultural perspectives on gender and violence]. Nordic Academic Press.

Lucero, M. A., Allen, R. E., & Middleton, K. L. (2006). Sexual harassers: Behaviors, motives, and change over time. *Sex Roles, 55*(5–6), 331–343.

Lucero, M. A., Middleton, K. L., Finch, W. A., & Valentine, S. R. (2003). An empirical investigation of sexual harassers: Toward a perpetrator typology. *Human Relations, 56*(12), 1461–1483.

Luthar, H. K., & Luthar, V. K. (2008). Likelihood to sexually harass: A comparison among American, Indian, and Chinese students. *International Journal of Cross Cultural Management, 8*(1), 59–77.

Madan, M., & Nalla, M. K. (2016). Sexual harassment in public spaces: Examining gender differences in perceived seriousness and victimization. *International Criminal Justice Review, 26*(2), 80–97.

Madsen, S. A. (2008). Mænd i psykoterapi [Men in psychotherapy]. *Psykolognyt, 62*(19), 3–9.

Män (2018a). *Ett år #efter MeToo—En SIFO-undersökning om mäns attityder till #Metoo-opproren* [One year #after MeToo—A SIFO survey on men's attitudes to the #Metoo uprising].

Män. (2018b). *Men, masculinity and #MeToo*.

Martineau, W. H. (1972). A model of the social functions of humor. In J. H. Goldstein & P. E. McGhee (Eds.), *The psychology of humor: Theoretical perspectives and empirical issues* (pp. 101–125). Academic Press.

Mac an Ghail, M. (1994). The making of black English masculinities. In I. H. Brod & M. Kaufman (Eds.), *Theorizing masculinities* (pp. 183–199). Sage.

MacKinnon, C. A. (1979). *Sexual harassment of working women: A case of sex discrimination*. Yale Fastback Series No. 19. Yale University Press.

Malamuth, N. M. (1986). Predictors of naturalistic sexual aggression. *Journal of Personality and Social Psychology, 50*(5), 953–962.

Malamuth, N. M., & Dean, K. E. (1991). Attraction to sexual aggression. In A. Parrot & L. Bechhofer (Eds.), *Acquaintance rape: The hidden crime*. Wiley.

Maricourt, C. D., & Burrell, S. R. (2021). #MeToo or# MenToo? Expressions of backlash and masculinity Politics in the #MeToo era. *The Journal of Men's Studies*, 1–21.

Martino, W. (2001). 'Powerful people aren't usually real kind, friendly, open people!' Boysinterrogating masculinities at school. In W. Martino & B. Meyenn (Eds.), *What about the boys?* (pp. 82–95). Open University Press.

Masters, N. T. (2010). 'My strength is not for hurting': Men's anti-rape websites and their construction of masculinity and male sexuality. *Sexualities, 13*(1), 33–46.

McCann, D. (2005). *Sexual harassment at work: National and international responses.* Conditions of Work and Employment Series No. 2. International Labour Organization.

McDonald, P. (2012). Workplace sexual harassment 30 years on: A review of the literature. *International Journal of Management Reviews, 14*(1), 1–17.

McMahon, S., & Dick, A. (2011). "Being in a room with like-minded men": An exploratory study of men's participation in a bystander intervention program to prevent intimate partner violence. *The Journal of Men's Studies, 19*(1), 3–18.

Masters, N. T., Casey, E., Wells, E. A., & Morrison, D. M. (2013). Sexual scripts among young heterosexually active men and women: Continuity and change. *Journal of Sex Research, 50*(5), 409–420.

Meenagh, J. L. (2021). 'She doesn't think that happens': When heterosexual men say no to sex. *Sexualities, 24*(3), 322–340.

Mendes, K., Ringrose, J., & Keller, J. (2018). #MeToo and the promise and pitfalls of challenging rape culture through digital feminist activism. *European Journal of Women's Studies, 25*(2), 236–246.

Messner, M. A. (1997). *Politics of masculinities: Men in movements.* Altamira Press.

Messner, M. A., Greenberg, M. A., & Peretz, T. (2015). *Some men: Feminist allies in the movement to end violence against women.* Oxford University Press.

Mellon, R. C. (2013). On the motivation of quid pro quo sexual harassment in men: Relation to masculine gender role stress. *Journal of Applied Social Psychology, 43*(11), 2287–2296.

Mills, M. (2001). *Challenging violence in schools.* Open University Press.

Ministry of Education. (2018). *Curriculum: Health and sex education and family skills.* Denmark

Möller-Leimkühler, A. M. (2002). Barriers to help-seeking by men: A review of sociocultural and clinical literature with particular reference to depression. *Journal of Affective Disorders, 71*(1–3), 1–9.

Morgan, D. H. (1992). *Discovering men* (Vol. 3). Taylor & Francis.

Muehlenhard, C. L., Humphreys, T. P., Jozkowski, K. N., & Peterson, Z. D. (2016). The complexities of sexual consent among college students:

A conceptual and empirical review. *The Journal of Sex Research, 53*(4–5), 457–487.

Murphy Austin, M. J., Dardis, C. M., Wilson, M. S., Gidycz, C. A., & Berkowitz, A. D. (2016). Predictors of sexual assault–specific prosocial bystander behavior and intentions: A prospective analysis. *Violence Against Women, 22*(1), 90–111.

Naik, M. G. (2020). Mainstream media's framing of #Metoo campaign in India. *Multidisciplinary Journal of Gender Studies, 9*(1), 79–106.

Newburn, T., & Mair, G. (1996). *Working with men*. Russell House.

Nichols, K. (2018). Moving beyond ideas of laddism: Conceptualising 'mischievous masculinities' as a new way of understanding everyday sexism and gender relations. *Journal of Gender Studies, 27*(1), 73–85.

Nilsson, B., & Lundgren, A. S. (2020). The #MeToo movement: Men and masculinity in Swedish news media. *The Journal of Men's Studies, 29*(1), 8–25.

Noy, C. (2008). Sampling knowledge: The hermeneutics of snowball sampling in qualitative research. *International Journal of Social Research Methodology, 11*(4), 327–344.

O'Byrne, R., Rapley, M., & Hansen, S. (2006). 'You couldn't say "no", could you?': Young men's understandings of sexual refusal. *Feminism & Psychology, 16*(2), 133–154.

O'Donohue, W., Downs, K., & Yeater, E. A. (1998). Sexual harassment: A review of the literature. *Aggression and Violent Behavior, 3*(2), 111–128.

O'Hare, E. A., & O'Donohue, W. (1998). Sexual harassment: Identifying risk factors. *Archives of Sexual Behavior, 27*(6), 561–580.

O'Leary-Kelly, A. M., Paetzold, R. L., & Griffin, R. W. (2000). Sexual harassment as aggressive behavior: An actor-based perspective. *Academy of Management Review, 25*(2), 372–388.

Onwuachi-Willig, A. (2018). What about #UsToo: The invisibility of race in the #MeToo movement. *Yale Law Journal Forum, 128*, 105–120.

Page, T. E., & Pina, A. (2015). Moral disengagement as a self-regulatory process in sexual harassment perpetration at work: A preliminary conceptualization. *Aggression and Violent Behavior, 21*, 73–84.

Paglia, C. (1991, February 17). Perspective needed—Feminism's lie: Denying reality about sexual power and rape. *New York Newsday*.

Pascoe, C. J. (2005). 'Dude, you're a fag': Adolescent masculinity and the fag discourse. *Sexualities, 8*(3), 329–346.

Pease, B., Pringle, K., & Kimmel, M. (Eds.). (2001). *A man's world? Changing men's practices in a globalized world*. ZED Books.

Perez, C. C. (2019). *Invisible women: Exposing data bias in a world designed for men*. Random House.

Perkins, H. (2003). *The social norms approach to preventing school and college age substance abuse: A handbook for educators, counselors, and clinicians*. Jossey-Bass.

PettyJohn, M. E., Muzzey, F. K., Maas, M. K., & McCauley, H. L. (2019). #HowIWillChange: Engaging men and boys in the #MeToo movement. *Psychology of Men & Masculinities, 20*(4), 612–623.

Penelope, J. (1990). Speaking freely: Unlearning the lies of the fathers' tongues. Pergamon. Perpetrator, theory, and treatment issues. *Aggression and Violent Behavior, 14*(2), 126–138.

Perry, E. L., Kulik, C. T., & Schmidtke, J. M. (1998). Individual differences in the effectiveness of sexual harassment awareness training 1. *Journal of Applied Social Psychology, 28*(8), 698–723.

Phipps, A. (2017). (Re)theorising laddish masculinities in higher education. *Gender and Education, 29*(7), 815–830.

Phipps, A., & Young, I. (2013). *That's what she said: Women students' experiences of 'lad culture' in higher education*. National Union of Students.

Phipps, A., Ringrose, J., Renold, E., & Jackson, C. (2018). Rape culture, lad culture and everyday sexism: Researching, conceptualizing and politicizing new mediations of gender and sexual violence. *Journal of Gender Studies, 27*(1), 1–8.

Pina, A., Gannon, T. A., & Saunders, B. (2009). An overview of the literature on sexual harassment: Perpetrator, theory, and treatment issues. *Aggression and Violent Behavior, 14*(2), 126–138.

Pina, A., & Gannon, T. A. (2012). An overview of the literature on antecedents, perceptions and behavioural consequences of sexual harassment. *Journal of Sexual Aggression, 18*(2), 209–232.

Politiken. (2020, December 27). *Hun var påpasselig med ikke at blande sig: Indtil hun skrev årets mest omtalte åbne brev* [She was careful not to interfere: Until she wrote the most talked about open letter of the year].

Politiken. (2021, November 11). *Forsker om Pigekor-sagen: Den viser et skifte i MeToo-debatten* [Researcher on the girl choir case: It shows a shift in the MeToo debate].

Pollack, W. (1998). *Real boys: Rescuing our sons from the myths of boyhood*. Henry Holt and Company.

Pollack, E. (2019). Sweden and the #MeToo movement. *Interactions: Studies in Communication & Culture, 10*(3), 185–200.

Pollack, W. S. (2005). 'Masked men': New psychoanalytically oriented treatment models for adult and young adult men. In G. E. Good & G. R. Brooks (Eds.), *The new handbook of psychotherapy and counseling with men: A comprehensive guide to settings, problems, and treatment approaches* (rev, pp. 203–216). Jossey-Bass.

Prahl, F. (2018, February 26). *Grænsesætning er sexet* [Boundary setting is sexy]. Information.

Pryor, J. B. (1987). Sexual harassment proclivities in men. *Sex Roles, 17*(5–6), 269–290.

Pryor, J. B., & Fitzgerald, L. F. (2003). Sexual harassment research in the US. In H. Einarsen, H. Hoel, D. Zapf, & C. L. Cooper (Eds.), *Bullying and emotional abuse in the workplace* (pp. 79–100). Taylor and Francis.

Pryor, J. B., Giedd, J. L., & Williams, K. B. (1995). A social psychological model for predicting sexual harassment. *Journal of Social Issues, 51*(1), 69–84.

Pryor, J. B., LaVite, C. M., & Stoller, L. M. (1993). A social psychological analysis of sexual harassment: The person/situation interaction. *Journal of Vocational Behavior, 42*(1), 68–83.

Pryor, J. B., & Stoller, L. M. (1994). Sexual cognition processes in men high in the likelihood to sexually harass. *Personality and Social Psychology Bulletin, 20*(2), 163–169.

Quick, J. C., & McFadyen, M. (2017). Sexual harassment: Have we made any progress? *Journal of Occupational Health Psychology, 22*(3), 286–298.

Quinn, B. A. (2002). Sexual harassment and masculinity: The power and meaning of "girl watching." *Gender & Society, 16*(3), 386–402.

Reestorff, C. M. (2019). Affective politics and involuntary autoethnography: Backlashes against #MeToo. *Capacious: Journal for Emerging Affect Inquiry, 1*(4), ii–xix.

Reinicke, K. (2002). *Den hele mand: Manderollen i forandring* [The whole man: Masculinity in transition]. Det Schønbergske Forlag.

Reinicke, K. (2004). *Mænd i lyst og nød* [Men for better or for worse]. Det Schønbergske Forlag.

Reinicke, K. (2012). *Drenge og mænd i krise? Perspektiver og indsatsområder* [Boys and men in crisis? Perspectives and focus areas]. Hans Reitzel.

Reinicke, K. (2013). *Mænd: køn under forvandling* [Men: Gender in change]. Aarhus Universitetsforlag.

Reinicke, K. (2016). *De unge fædre* [The young fathers]. Aarhus Universitetsforlag, 156 sider.

Reinicke, K. (2018). *Mænd som krænker kvinder—refleksioner i kølvandet på #Metoo* [Men who violate women—Reflections in the wake of #MeToo]. Samfundslitteratur.

Reinicke, K. (2020). First-time fathers' attitudes towards, and experiences with, parenting courses in Denmark. *American Journal of Men's Health, 14*(5), 1–13.

Reinicke, K., Søgaard, I. S., & Mentzler, S. (2019). Masculinity challenges for men with severe hemophilia. *American Journal of Men's Health, 13*(4), 1–11.

Renold, E. (2004). 'Other' boys: Negotiating non-hegemonic masculinities in the primary school. *Gender and Education, 16*(2), 247–265.

Roien, L. A., Simovska, V., & Graugaard, C. (2018). *Seksualitet, skole og samfund: kritiske perspektiver på seksualundervisning* [Sexuality, school and society: Critical perspectives on sex education]. Hans Reitzels Forlag.

Romito, P. (2008). *A deafening silence: Hidden violence against women and children*. Policy Press.

Ronen, S. (2010). Grinding on the dance floor: Gendered scripts and sexualized dancing at college parties. *Gender & Society, 24*(3), 355–377.

Ronkainen, S. (2001). Gendered violence and genderless gender—A Finnish perspective. *Kvinder, Køn & Forskning, 2*, 45–57.

Rosenbeck, V. (2017). *Kom nu ind i #MeToo-kampen, mænd* [Now get into the #MeToo fight, men]. Altinget.

Rothgerber, H., Kaufling, K., Incorvati, C., Andrew, C. B., & Farmer, A. (2021). Is a reasonable woman different from a reasonable person? Gender differences in perceived sexual harassment. *Sex Roles, 84*(3), 208–220.

Rotundo, M., Nguyen, D. H., & Sackett, P. R. (2001). A meta-analytic review of gender differences in perceptions of sexual harassment. *Journal of Applied Psychology, 86*(5), 914–922.

Ruspini, E. (Ed.). (2011). *Men and masculinities around the world: Transforming men's practices*. Springer.

Ruxton, S. (2002). *Men, masculinities and poverty in the UK*. Oxfam.

Ruxton, S. (2020). *Men and gender equality: Challenges and opportunities*. ICMEO.

Salisbury, J., & Jackson, D. (1996). *Challenging macho values: Practical ways of working with adolescent boys*. Falmer.

Salter, M. (2016). 'Real men don't hit women': Constructing masculinity in the prevention of violence against women. *Australian & New Zealand Journal of Criminology, 49*(4), 463–479.

Salter, M. (2019). Online justice in the circuit of capital: #MeToo, marketization and the deformation of sexual ethics. In *#MeToo and the politics of social change* (pp. 317–334). Palgrave Macmillan.

Schneider, K. T., & Carpenter, N. J. (2019). Sharing #MeToo on Twitter: Incidents, coping responses, and social reactions. *Equality, Diversity and Inclusion: An International Journal*, 87–100.

Schwartz, M. D., & DeKeseredy. W. S. (1997). *Sexual assault on the college campus: The role of male peer support*. Sage.

Serisier, T. (2020). Speaking out, public judgments, and narrative politics. In *Me Too, feminist theory, and surviving sexual violence in the academy* (pp. 167–180). Lexington Books.

Shirky, C. (2008). *Here comes everybody: The power of organizing without organizations*. Penguin.

Skelton, C. (2001). *Schooling the boys: Masculinities and primary education*. Open University Press.

Smith, R. D., Holmberg, J., & Cornish, J. E. (2019). Psychotherapy in the #MeToo era: Ethical issues. *Psychotherapy, 56*(4), 483–490.

Smith, M. D. (1988). Women's fear of violent crime: An exploratory test of a feminist hypothesis. *Journal of Family Violence, 3*(1), 29–38.

Smith, O. (2018). *Rape trials in England and Wales: Observing justice and rethinking rape myths*. Springer.

Spitzberg, B. H. (1999). An analysis of empirical estimates of sexual aggression victimization and perpetration. *Violence and Victims, 14*(3), 241–260.

Stanko, E. A. (1995). Women, crime, and fear. *The Annals of the American Academy of Political and Social Science, 539*(1), 46–58.

Stockdale, M. S. (1993). The role of sexual misperceptions of women's friendliness in an emerging theory of sexual harassment. *Journal of Vocational Behavior, 42*(1), 84–101.

Stockdale, M. S., Gandolfo Berry, C., Schneider, R. W., & Cao, F. (2004). Perceptions of the sexual harassment of men. *Psychology of Men & Masculinity, 5*(2), 158–167.

Stockdale, M. S., Visio, M., & Batra, L. (1999). The sexual harassment of men: Evidence for a broader theory of sexual harassment and sex discrimination. *Psychology, Public Policy, and Law, 5*(3), 630–664.

Strauss, A., & Corbin, J. (1990). *Basics of qualitative research*. Sage.

Sue, D. W. (2010). *Microaggressions in everyday life: Race, gender, and sexual orientation*. Wiley.

Sundaresh, N., & Hemalatha, K. (2013). Theoretical orientation to sexual harassment at work place. *Journal of Business Management and Social Sciences Research, 2*(4), 74–81.

Sweeney, B. N. (2014). Masculine status, sexual performance, and the sexual stigmatization of women. *Symbolic Interaction, 37*(3), 369–390.

Søndergaard, D. M. (2000). *Tegnet pa kroppen—køn: Koder og konstruktioner blandt unge voksne i Akademia* [Drawing on the body—gender: Codes and constructions among young adults in Academia]. Museum Tusculanums Forlag.

Sørensen, N. U. (Ed.) (2000). *Pikstormerne* [The prick invaders]. Informations Forlag.

Tangri, S. S., Burt, M. R., & Johnson, L. B. (1982). Sexual harassment at work: Three explanatory models. *Journal of Social Issues, 38*(4), 33–54.

The Men's Project & Flood, M. (2018). *The man box: A study on being a young man in Australia.* A Jesuit Social Service.

Thomae, M., & Pina, A. (2015). Sexist humor and social identity: The role of sexist humor in men's in-group cohesion, sexual harassment, rape proclivity, and victim blame. *Humor, 28*(2), 187–204.

Thomas, A. M., & Kitzinger, C. (1997). *Sexual harassment: Contemporary feminist perspectives.* Open University Press.

Thompson, D. M. (1994). The woman in the street: Reclaiming the public space from sexual harassment. *Yale JL & Feminism, 6*, 313.

Thompson, Jr., E. H., & Cracco, E. J. (2008). Sexual aggression in bars: What college men can normalize. *The Journal of Men's Studies, 16*(1), 82–96.

Tinkler, J. E. (2008). "People are too quick to take offense": The effects of legal information and beliefs on definitions of sexual harassment. *Law & Social Inquiry, 33*(2), 417–445.

Tolman, D. L., Spencer, R., Rosen-Reynoso, M., & Porche, M. V. (2003). Sowing the seeds of violence in heterosexual relationships: Early adolescents narrate compulsory heterosexuality. *Journal of Social Issues, 59*(1), 159–178.

Tuerkheimer, D. (1997). Street harassment as sexual subordination: The phenomenology of gender-specific harm. *Wisconsin Women's Law Journa, 12*, 167–206.

TV2. (2020, October 11). *Hvad sker der, når en krænker navngives? Den seneste uges tumult giver svaret, siger ekspert* [What happens when an offender is named? The tumult of the past week provides the answer, says expert].

UN Women UK. (2021). *YouGov, Sexual harassment report.*

Valiente, C. (1998). Sexual harassment in the workplace: Equality policies in post-authoritarian Spain. In T. Carver & V. Mottier (Eds.), *Politics of sexuality: Identity, gender, citizenship* (pp. 169–179). Routledge.

Van der Gaag, N. (2014). *Feminism and men*. Zed Books.

Vera-Gray, F. (2016). Men's stranger intrusions: Rethinking street harassment. *Women's Studies International Forum, 58*, 9–17.

Vera-Gray, F. (2018). *The right amount of panic: How women trade freedom for safety*. Policy Press.

Vera-Gray, F., & Fileborn, B. (2018). Recognition and the harms of "Cheer Up." *The Philosophical Journal of Conflict and Violence, 2*(1), 78–95.

Vogt, D. S., Pless, A. P., King, L. A., & King, D. W. (2005). Deployment stressors, gender, and mental health outcomes among Gulf war I veterans. *Journal of Traumatic Stress, 18*(2), 115–127.

Warr, M. (1984). Fear of victimization: Why are women and the elderly more afraid? *Social Science Quarterly, 65*(3), 681–702.

Wesselmann, E. D., & Kelly, J. R. (2010). Cat-calls and culpability: Investigating the frequency and functions of stranger harassment. *Sex Roles, 63*(7–8), 451–462.

White, A., McKee, M., Richardson, N., de Visser, R., Madsen, S. A., de Sousa, B. C., Hogston, R., Zatonski, W., & Makara, P. (2011). Europe's men need their own health strategy. *BMJ, 343*.

Whitehead, S. M. (2002). *Men and masculinities, key themes and new directions*. Polity.

WHO. (2018). *Fact sheet—Men's health and well-being in the WHO European region*.

Williams, J. H., Fitzgerald, L. F., & Drasgow, F. (1999). The effects of organizational practices on sexual harassment and individual outcomes in the military. *Military Psychology, 11*, 303–328.

Willness, C. R., Steel, P., & Lee, K. (2007). A meta-analysis of the antecedents and consequences of workplace sexual harassment. *Personnel Psychology, 60*, 127–162.

Willis, P. E. (1977). *Learning to labor: How working class kids get working class jobs*. Columbia University Press.

Wøldike. (2018, February 19). Det seksuelle spil er en forhandling mellem ja og nej [The sexual game is a negotiation between yes and no]. *Information*.

Whitt, M. S. (2016). Other people's problems: Student distancing, epistemic responsibility, and injustice. *Journal of Student Philosophy Education, 35*, 427–444.

Index

A

Abusive behaviour 19, 34, 89, 117, 136, 223, 227
Advertisement 34, 153, 227
Allies 10–13, 223

B

Backlash 62, 149, 154
Bates, Laura 3, 7, 37, 43, 45, 48, 86, 118, 133, 153, 155, 211, 212
Boundaries 2, 18, 31, 42, 70, 110, 121, 125, 128, 129, 131, 137, 150, 158, 171–178, 180, 181, 195, 197, 204–209, 226
Bystander 11, 19, 149, 186, 191–194, 196, 210, 223

C

Consent law 179, 180
Crime paradox 38

D

Democracy 81
Denmark 5, 7, 15, 17, 49, 55–66, 68, 69, 71–73, 92, 117, 120, 147, 149, 156, 157, 159, 164, 167, 180, 204, 219, 220, 227
Discourse 3, 11, 14–16, 37, 43, 49, 56, 57, 61, 89–91, 98, 100, 149, 151, 157, 180

E

Education 14, 15, 56, 59, 71, 86, 108, 165, 204, 205, 209, 219, 225

Entitlement 2, 19, 108, 190, 196, 203, 210, 211, 220, 221, 224
Equality 81–83
Ethnicity 10, 33, 99, 100, 225
Everyday sexism 5, 26, 38, 200

Feminism 6, 19, 56, 84–86, 202, 219
Flirting 18, 27, 43, 63, 71, 94, 121, 129, 131, 132, 171–174, 181, 185, 206–208, 226
Flood, Michael 8, 10–13, 81, 85, 87, 90, 97, 113, 116, 124, 126, 145, 146, 148, 154, 155, 158, 185, 190, 194, 196, 197, 201, 203, 205, 209, 210, 212, 220, 223

Gender 82, 83
Gender equality 4, 5, 11, 13, 48, 55–58, 60, 61, 65, 66, 78, 81–86, 97, 100, 146, 151, 155, 156, 160, 181, 192, 199, 203, 204, 218, 220, 223
Gender neutral 17, 90, 91, 100

Health 28, 31, 57, 59, 65, 79, 86–88, 96, 204
Hegemonic masculinity 10, 79–81, 83, 95, 100, 118, 134, 178, 191, 194

Intervention 69, 193, 203

Katz, Jackson 7, 10–12, 78, 82, 89–91, 121, 192–194, 196, 197, 211, 221

Labour market 25, 30, 36, 87

Male 82
Man box 95–97, 197
Masculinity 2, 7, 9, 10, 15, 17, 55, 57–60, 62, 66, 78–80, 82–85, 87, 89, 92, 95, 97–99, 107, 113, 115–117, 119, 121, 122, 126, 127, 131, 137, 148, 152–157, 161, 162, 175, 176, 178, 189–191, 194, 196, 197, 202, 203, 205, 206, 208, 210–212, 218, 219, 224–227
Media 6, 19, 26, 34, 58–60, 62, 63, 66, 68, 72, 82, 91–93, 100, 152, 154, 157, 159, 160, 164, 180, 202, 218, 222
Men 81–85
Men's violence 11, 89, 100, 134, 145, 190
MeToo 4–7, 13–15, 17–19, 49, 55, 60–66, 68, 72, 73, 78, 91, 94, 100, 130, 137, 145–149, 151–167, 171–174, 176, 179–183, 185, 191, 195, 197, 199, 200, 207, 210, 211, 217–228

N

National conversation 17, 66, 90, 91, 223

P

Peer pressure 117, 118
Popular culture 34, 43, 93, 100
Power 82, 85
Privilege 7, 9, 18, 19, 61, 78, 83, 88, 113, 132, 148–150, 156, 157, 160, 162, 166, 192, 198, 203, 205, 219, 225
Prostitution 17, 88

R

Race 10, 33, 78, 80, 86, 95, 99, 226
Rape 2, 3, 10, 17, 33, 34, 37, 39, 42, 62, 68–71, 73, 78, 88, 91, 99, 100, 119, 120, 125, 135, 147, 152, 159, 174, 179–181, 190, 191, 217, 220
Rape culture 119, 120, 147, 148, 151, 161, 163, 181, 208, 218, 219
Resistance 13, 18, 19, 37, 58, 71, 73, 145, 148, 152, 155, 158, 162, 163, 179, 181, 190, 201, 211, 218, 219
Responsibility 5, 14, 19, 61, 65, 69, 86, 89, 91, 119, 120, 123, 124, 147, 150, 152, 153, 155, 159, 183, 196, 199, 202, 207, 208, 219, 227

S

Sexual harassment 1–19, 25–49, 60–62, 64–66, 68, 72, 73, 78, 79, 90, 91, 94–97, 99, 100, 107–119, 123, 129, 130, 133–137, 146–149, 151–155, 157–167, 172, 181–186, 189–200, 202, 203, 205, 207–212, 217–221, 223–228
Social bonding 8, 113, 114, 119, 137
Socialization 9, 17, 18, 28, 32, 77, 86, 87, 89–92, 107, 113, 205, 206, 217
Social media 6, 19, 26, 61, 63, 68, 157, 159, 202, 218
Social norms 10, 95, 97, 113, 118, 137, 162, 166, 190, 194, 198, 207, 217
Societal models 17, 37
Societal status 226

V

Violence 2, 3, 7, 10–12, 17, 25, 34, 39, 42, 57, 59, 60, 68, 69, 71, 73, 78, 79, 81, 88–92, 95–97, 99, 100, 107, 109, 111, 117, 119, 120, 133, 137, 146, 147, 151–153, 155, 156, 158, 164, 176, 183, 190–193, 201, 203–205, 217, 219, 221
Vulnerability 18, 39, 43, 86, 121–123, 131, 152, 154, 175, 208, 226

W

Women 81, 82

Y

Youth 67, 119, 128, 129

GPSR Compliance

The European Union's (EU) General Product Safety Regulation (GPSR) is a set of rules that requires consumer products to be safe and our obligations to ensure this.

If you have any concerns about our products, you can contact us on

ProductSafety@springernature.com

In case Publisher is established outside the EU, the EU authorized representative is:

Springer Nature Customer Service Center GmbH
Europaplatz 3
69115 Heidelberg, Germany

www.ingramcontent.com/pod-product-compliance
Lightning Source LLC
LaVergne TN
LVHW012009260326
834688LV00057B/294